My New Orleans

THE COOKBOOK

200 of My Favorite Recipes &
Stories from My Hometown

BY

JOHN BESH

Photography by Ditte Isager

**Andrews McMeel
Publishing, LLC**
Kansas City · Sydney · London

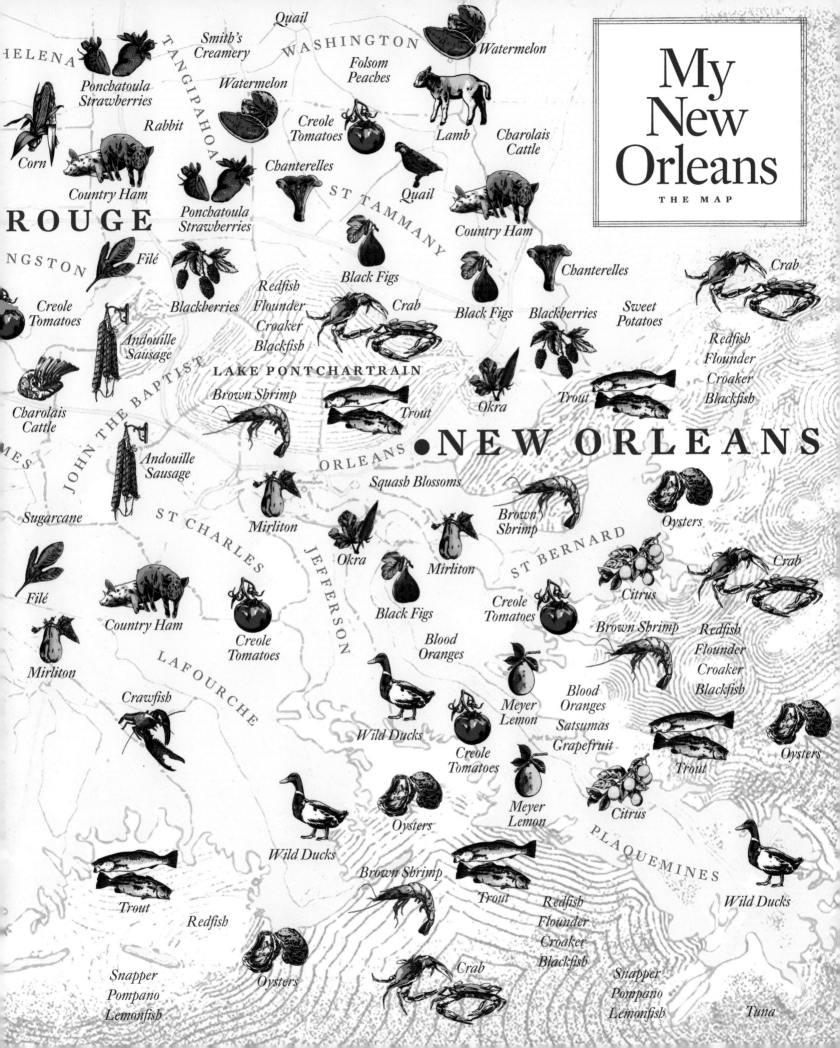

My New Orleans

THE MAP

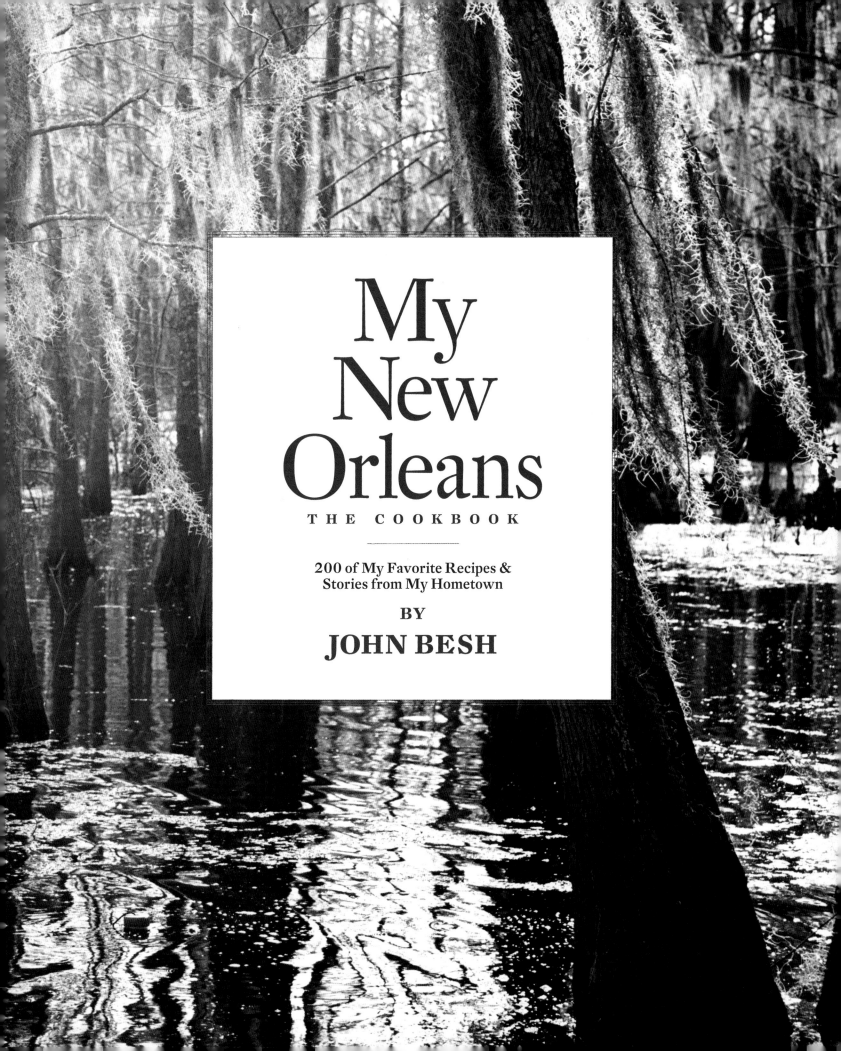

My New Orleans

THE COOKBOOK

200 of My Favorite Recipes &
Stories from My Hometown

BY

JOHN BESH

Andrews McMeel Publishing, LLC
an Andrews McMeel Universal company
1130 Walnut Street, Kansas City, Missouri 64106

www.andrewsmcmeel.com
www.chefjohnbesh.com

12 13 SDB 10 9 8 7 6 5

ISBN: 978-0-7407-8413-2

Library of Congress Control Number: 2009920846

Produced and edited by Dorothy Kalins, Dorothy Kalins Ink, LLC
Design by Don Morris Design, New York
Photographs by Ditte Isager/EdgeReps
Illustrations by Alexander Stolin

ATTENTION: SCHOOLS AND BUSINESSES
Andrews McMeel books are available at quantity discounts with bulk purchase for educational, business, or sales promotional use. For information, please e-mail the Andrews McMeel Publishing Special Sales Department: specialsales@amuniversal.com.

DEDICATION

To the people of New Orleans
and to those who hold the city close to their hearts

CONTENTS

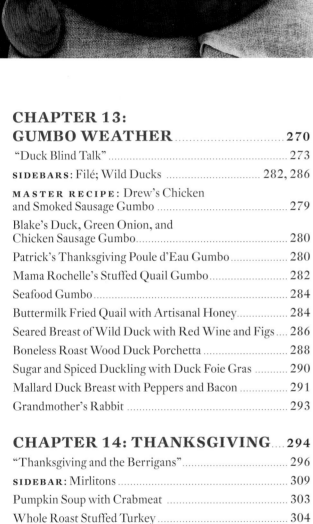

INTRODUCTION

THIS BOOK IS the story of a dreamy, starry-eyed boy brought up in the shadows of New Orleans, surrounded by cypress knees and tupelo trees, good dinners and great friends. Memories of my childhood, both good and bad, have etched themselves deep into my soul: everything that I cook and eat, see and smell, reminds me of where I come from and more or less dictates where I'm going.

It was never my intention to write yet another chef's cookbook, with yet another bunch of recipes; there are as many books about New Orleans food as there are restaurants. Still, every day, as our traditions are in danger of eroding and melting into the American Crock Pot, it seems ever more urgent to protect the classics and reinterpret them. That's what led me to launch Restaurant August, in 2001, as a world-class place that could compete with the once-great restaurants of New Orleans; Besh Steak followed in 2003, Lüke and La Provence in 2007. I wrote *My New Orleans* in the same spirit in which I launched my restaurants; it's a book dedicated to roots and rituals, to the way I cook. As each of our magical foodstuffs comes into its prime, there's cause for celebration—Crawfish and Rice, Mardi Gras, Shrimp Season, Gumbo Weather, Boucherie, and Reveillon—such is the flow of our seasons, such is the flow of the chapters in this book. I care about the ingredients and the farmers and the fishermen, the shrimpers and the oystermen I grew up with; they are the heroes who have always shaped the rich, rainbow cooking of New Orleans, and their faces enliven the pages of *My New Orleans*.

While American foodways have become alarmingly homogenized, our cooking in New Orleans is still vibrantly alive. We have no choice but to embrace our culture; it's what sets us apart from the rest of the country—and we love to consider ourselves different. We aren't the most progressive group, but we do have values. We value time and waste as much of it as we can, spending all day cooking the good stuff, the

Welcome to
My New Orleans

My favorite places are often
hiding in plain sight

Courtyards are the gems of the French Quarter; a special one, opposite, is at the Soniat House hotel on Chartres Street. The iconic St. Louis Cathedral looks over Jackson Square to the Mississippi River. It's the city's gathering place, always alive with the rhythm of jazz.

The Flavors of Home

For me, café au lait and beignets at the Café du Monde never go out of style. The Café is still a small business, run by the Fernandez family. Now only the sign is left of the mighty Jax Brewery.

gumbos and étouffées, the courtbouillons, red beans and rice, the grillades and gravies, the jambalayas, and the whole suckling pigs. New Orleans embraced its slow cooking long before that became fashionable.

Our multicultural heritage continues to inspire us. From the Creoles, the American-born descendants of the French, Spanish, and Africans who settled here, we have the worldly sophistication that elevates good cooking to a true cuisine. From the Acadian French, the Cajuns, whose ancestors were evicted in 1755 from *Acadie*, on the coast of Nova Scotia, and settled in southwestern Louisiana around Lafayette, comes robust and zesty country cooking. Germans brought us their sausages and dry-cured meats. Settlers from the Caribbean arrived with their signature spices like cayenne; from Central America, their peppers, like the famed tabasco. From Native Americans came corn and the ground sassafras called filé; Sicilians gave us their red sauces and grew our vegetables; Croatians harvest our oysters. The Isleños arrived over 200 years ago from the Canary Islands with their Spanish-inflected ways. And since the late 1970s, the thousands of Vietnamese who have resettled in East New Orleans grow and cook new ingredients that influence our cooking daily.

I WAS RAISED IN Slidell, Louisiana. It's a known fact that when you marry a New Orleans gal you will always live in New Orleans, because she'll forever want to live down the street from her family. Well, I married a New Orleans gal, and now Jenifer and I and our four boys—Brendan, Jack, Luke, and Andrew—live once again in Slidell, just a stone's throw from where we both grew up; our parents are close by. My childhood in Slidell, across Lake Pontchartrain from New Orleans, revolved around the lake. We shrimped in its waters, netted crabs from its bridges, spent hours upon hours fishing along its shores. The lake sustained us, and the lake defined us. You couldn't do a book like this without the lake.

I came up cooking in my mother's kitchen. I am proud of my degree from the Culinary Institute of America, but I didn't learn to cook there. I learned from my mom and my grandparents (three decades later, I can still conjure the aromas of food simmering in my country grand-mother's big cast-iron pots), and from the men I hunted with, who held that, if you hunt it and kill it, you (a boy like me) had better know how to clean it and cook it. Ours was a house of great food that enchanced our happy days and leavened our sad ones.

When I was about 11, my dad took me to a crab festival in Lacombe, Louisiana. Paul Prudhomme was cooking there, and to me he seemed like a rock star! I think that's when it first occurred to me

Local Pleasures

Yes, I still savor a Sazerac at the Old Absinthe House on Bourbon Street, below, before dinner at Galatoire's. And though there are many imitators, the best muffuletta sandwich in town is still made by the Tusa family at Central Grocery.

*Only in
New Orleans*

Eva Perry, above, at Tee-Eva's ("Tee" is short for "Auntie"), her famous pie shop on Magazine Street. For po'boys, it's roast beef at Domilise's, uptown; and seafood at the Parkway Bakery in Bayou St. John. Hansen's invented the snow cone in 1939. Our executive chef, Steve McHugh, right, likes the wedding cake mix with condensed milk.

that a boy who loved food could have a pretty good life being a chef. The restaurants of my childhood had a similar impact; they were hospitable—they knew their guests, they knew what they liked. I have never worked in the big, fancy New Orleans restaurants, preferring instead the mom-and-pop places, to be taught by folks like Mr. Sam Manascalco, who owned the Cast Net, and the Meyer family, at Meyer Old Europe, and chef Buster Ambrosia. Starting out, I believed that our flagship restaurants had grown complacent, sitting on reputations won a century ago, and that it was up to us—a whole new generation of cooks—to change that image. Never cooking for a classic restaurant helped me find my own style. This isn't to say I'm not perfectly happy, on some big occasion or other, to drink Sazeracs at Galatoire's, munching pommes soufflés with béarnaise, or to hang out at Commander's Palace on St. Patrick's Day. But a new generation of chefs on both coasts was reinventing America's foodways; they stimulated me with the possibilities of an exciting farm-to-table dynamic that just had not caught on here.

I GREW UP AS a conservationist before I knew what a conservationist was. In high school, we'd catch wild hogs—usually with the help of a couple of Catahoula curs, our state dog—in the marsh near home. We'd take them to a pen in the woods and feed them stale doughnuts salvaged from the Dumpster of our local Tastee doughnut shop. After my grandfather taught me the finer points of game preparation, I'd take on the butchering and cooking of those hogs myself.

Even as a kid, I had big eyes for the world's best cuisine. After serving in the marines in Kuwait and fighting in Desert Storm, and after the Culinary Institute of America, I knew I had to cook in Europe. Through family friends, I wound up with an internship in the Black Forest, learning from chef Karl-Josef Fuchs how to coax the sweetness and earthiness out of a braise of wild game and learning, too, how to create a true cuisine from farming sustainably. Karl-Josef either raised (on kitchen scraps) everything he cooked or bought locally, direct from farms in the Munster Valley. I realized then just how much I owed my grandfather, who'd taught me his ways of preserving the animals and produce he raised. This experience ignited my passion to create a sustainable restaurant.

Much of my culinary awakening, however, took place at dinner tables in France. If I looked at a menu and didn't know a dish, I'd order it and find out. Quickly I realized that French food was essentially the same food I was raised on. Sure, their trout meunière might taste a bit different because their trout was rainbow or brook and ours was white-fleshed speckled trout, but it had that same aroma I fell in love with as a boy. As a New Orleanian, you can't help feeling as if you are part French, anyway. From sauce piquante to sauce remoulade, being in France gave me a deeper understanding—and pride, too—in what it meant to be from New Orleans. When I returned home to work for my mentor, chef Chris Keragiorgiou at La Provence, across the lake in Lacombe, Louisiana, I did think that by this time I knew a little something about food. Chef Chris thought differently, however, and dispatched me to his family near Marseille, so that I could truly understand Provençal cooking. It never crossed my mind that someday I would own his treasured restaurant, La Provence, and that there I would put into practice much of what I'd learned in Europe.

BEHIND LA PROVENCE, I have my own hog farm now, where we breed Berkshire hogs, feeding them on the organic scraps from the kitchens of each of our restaurants. My smokehouse there pays homage to my grandfather's; our practices are the same as those that sustained our people for centuries. We save the blood from the hogs to make our boudin noir for Lüke; the hams are cured, aged, and lightly smoked for our estate country ham, which we use like prosciutto; we cure pork bellies in sea salt and Louisiana brown sugar and then double-smoke them over pecan wood. Pork shoulders are cooked down and made into rillettes; the livers go into the pâté served on every table at La Provence; scraps and the heart make pâté de campagne. Each pig's foot is slow-cooked, debunked, stuffed, and trussed to create Lüke's succulent little pieds de cochon. Finally we're left with the fine loins that we roast at August and the skin to render into cracklins.

Early on, my head was surely turned by Europe, but even as I rediscovered those roots in our own cuisine, it was more with reverence for our restaurant tradition than arrogance that I launched Restaurant August. But four years later, Katrina, of course, changed everything. When the

My Favorite Fried Chicken

Willie Mae, now in her mid-90s, passed the torch to her great-granddaughter Kerry Seaton, below, who's mastered the Creole classics in this homey place in the Treme neighborhood.

aftermath of that devastating storm threatened our fisheries and our farms, nothing seemed to matter to me but protecting and preserving our culinary heritage, its local ingredients, and its authentic cultural threads. The hurricane sparked something in me; I had a mission again. I don't know if I was getting soft, but the storm awoke a drive I hadn't known since combat. This tragedy allowed us to make a difference. Politics aside, our city sank in the floodwaters of Katrina. Our most vulnerable people were left by inept governments to fend for themselves. This was *my* town that was hurt; I felt the responsibility to do something. What we do is feed people. So, we fed the police department and the National Guard troops, evacuees and refugees, doctors and nurses; all who were hungry paid us with their smiles.

AFTER KATRINA, being from New Orleans became the focus of my identity. The truth is, I am from here, and I cook with our ingredients and traditions. We launched a program to breed our own white-faced cattle and Berkshire hogs, to raise chickens and gather their eggs. We became obsessed with finding ingredients with the flavor of here—not shipped in from Anywhere, U.S.A. To safeguard that flavor, we now supply some of our farmers with seed (organic when possible) for them to grow the varieties of vegetables and herbs we need; then we guarantee to buy back their produce for our restaurants. We now produce our own handcrafted butters and sauces.

Is it really so important to come from somewhere? I believe our city is a true national treasure, with one of the few native urban cultures—and cuisines—that still thrive in this country. Perhaps the idea of New Orleans hasn't always evoked so much emotion, but since Katrina, it does. Even though the hurricanes of 2008, Gustav and Ike, missed direct hits on New Orleans, they decimated the rural parishes south and west of the city, places where folks were too poor or too dispersed to evacuate. So, in the days after the storms, we went to them, setting up field kitchens and feeding thousands of folks. And, as I've come to realize how vulnerable we are to environmental chaos, I realize, again, that this is what we do: feed people. The story of our city is greater than those storms. We have been here for over 300 years, and we'll be here for another 300. Maybe it's about my children's generation, and their children's. Will they still eat red beans on Mondays? Make St. Joseph's Day altars? Will they still love the Saints? Will we ever win a Super Bowl? All I know is that I cook New Orleans food my way, revering each ingredient as it reaches the season of its ripeness. No other place on earth is like New Orleans. Welcome to the flavors of my home. Welcome to *My New Orleans*.

*Sounds of a
Summer Evening*

Lafayette Square, in the heart of downtown, comes alive on Wednesdays after work, when thousands gather for free concerts by great local musicians.

Touchstones

The building that houses our flagship, Restaurant August, left, was a tobacco warehouse since the mid-19th century; I love the glow from the dining room at dusk. *Dixie* means beer to me. Casamento's, the traditional, old-time oyster house, is open only in oyster season. Often, on the way to work, I'll stop at Dong Phuong Bakery, below, for *banh mi,* my favorite Vietnamese sandwich.

HOW I COOK

THE WAY I cook depends on the way I think about ingredients. As a kid, if I brought home a redfish, you'd better believe my mother would slow-cook it whole in a broth perfumed by onion, garlic, celery, bay leaf, allspice, Creole tomatoes, cayenne pepper, and a pinch of dried thyme. If it was an extra-special evening, crabmeat, shrimp, or oysters could end up in her courtbouillon. That's just how I cook redfish today. There's a tension in New Orleans cooking between preserving the classics and modernizing them for today's palates, between home cooking and restaurant food.

I think of the old classics as tribute food, food that honors the cooks and chefs who have made these dishes for centuries. Deconstruct a gumbo? That's not cooking. That's not love. I am not about to trivialize a recipe that has been here longer than most cities in our country. *My New Orleans* pays tribute to my favorite classics. I've developed **MASTER RECIPES** for étouffée, jambalaya, bisque, gumbo, and daube glacée and in the complete menus that will help you celebrate our holidays: Mardi Gras, St. Joseph's Day, Easter, Passover, Thanksgiving, and Reveillon. I honor these classics, but that's not to say that I can't be inventive and explore new recipes and ingredients.

Today, my cooking draws on decades of learning and experience, earned by years of working for free—or damn near it—mastering cooking techniques that I felt certain would help me years down the road. The greatest thing about being raised the way I was is that it established for me, at a remarkably early age, the relationship of the land to the table. When I approach an ingredient to cook, I will use every bit of it, from head to toe. I draw constantly on my mind's catalogue of everything I've ever tasted or cooked, so when I see a tomato at its ripest state, my mind runs through literally thousands of preparations that could work for this here tomato. Some people may look up in the sky and observe a mallard duck, but I see a slow-roasted duckling with lots of fragrant herbs, cooked down to a gravy and served over rice.

The Best Ingredients

You'll find I write more about finding the right foodstuffs than I do about using the right techniques. When you cook with farmyard eggs and organic butter and cream from a small dairy farmer who really cares about the products he sells, you will surely taste the difference in your cooking.

The Truth About Chickens

It's not just because our own chickens now run freely in a large fenced-in yard behind La Provence that I've become such a nut about never using factory-raised birds. Health, theirs and ours, is reason enough. Plus, you can hardly find a chicken these days that tastes like chicken. Look for dressed birds with orange-hued skin and yellow fat; make sure their feed was organic, and your chicken dishes will benefit. Healthy bones make more flavorful stock, too.

These are good ways to think about ingredients and to adopt freely as you cook.

Every day in our restaurants, we have family meal at four o'clock, just before the beginning of dinner service. It's amazingly easy to tell which of our cooks will be the next great chefs, just by the way they prepare family meal for their fellow cooks. This I learned from my grandmother Grace: no matter how simple the meal, she cooked and served it from the heart. When you combine these two thoughts—respecting the origins of food and serving it with love—you've got my kind of food.

Sure, I'm a restaurant chef, but I'm also a dad, and cooking for my big family is every bit as important to me. In choosing, adapting, and testing the recipes for this book, I've made sure that they work really well in the home kitchen—which is not to say they are dumbed down. The prep process in our restaurant kitchens is very different from the way I cook my food at home, and rest assured that we never confuse the two. Many of the dishes in our restaurants can take days of prep: first the readying of the base stocks, then of the sauces derived from those stocks, and so on. But there are no restaurant recipes here. To help you succeed, I've divided the recipes into easy-to-follow steps. In this chapter are the building blocks—like Roux and Basic Pan Sauces and Basic Creole Spices— that make all the difference in my cooking.

• Take the time to actually read the recipes through before you begin!

• Think of these Basic Recipes as flavor bases—direct ways to achieve the authenticity I crave. These simple stocks, pan sauces, and vinaigrettes give soul to a dish, and a sense of place. Planning ahead makes these recipes easy.

• Learn to see the peelings and shells and carcasses and bones of your ingredients as flavor boosters. Try to get in the habit of saving the carcass of a roasted chicken or turkey; just throw it into the freezer and keep it until you're ready to make a stock. Let the stock sit in the refrigerator for a day, collect the fat that's solidified on the surface, and save that to enrich a sauce. Then, freeze the stock, or turn it into a pan sauce to be frozen in small amounts. This way, you'll have the flavor bases ready, and you're well on your way to bringing complex flavors to your food, quickly.

- I believe that overcooking is the enemy of flavor and texture, so you'll discover in my recipes that I suggest adding ingredients in stages to preserve both.

- While I love and support the Louisiana ingredients specified in our recipes and encourage you to procure and experience them (Resources, page 362), I never want you not to try a recipe for want of that ingredient. Accept substitutes. For example, I love Jacob's andouille sausage, but you can sure make a great gumbo without it; you can order Creole mustard or use a sharp whole-grain mustard instead; I love Creole cream cheese and it might be fun to try some, or substitute fromage blanc or mascarpone as we do when Creole cream cheese is not at hand.

- I fear that we drown our salads in dressing. Instead, I like to toss a few handfuls of just-picked greens in a piquant vinaigrette. I use vinaigrettes, too, as sauces and marinades.

- It is far more important that you understand the spirit of a dish—and the flavor bases I've given you in this chapter—than that you follow the letter of our recipes. Yes, we do have our ways, but they are forgiving ways. Go ahead; try some that seem a touch daunting. That's how we all grow as cooks.

Roasting Vegetables

There's no easier way to intensify the flavor of root vegetables like beets, turnips, potatoes, or kohlrabi, or cauliflower and Brussels sprouts, than to toss them in olive oil and sea salt and roast them in a moderate oven until they're soft.

THOUGHTS ON ROUX

ROUX IS SO BASIC to our way of cooking that it's not even mentioned in the ingredients lists for our recipes, but anytime you find yourself beginning a dish by stirring a certain amount of flour into the same amount of of oil, you're making a roux. Roux (the word means red in French, and though roux can be blond, it's actually chocolate brown in most of my dishes) is more philosophy than recipe. The only crucial amount to remember is a ratio of one to one: one part flour (don't be tempted by other, trendier thickeners; only flour gives a roux its signature flavor) to one part oil (anything from canola oil to chicken or duck fat); the amount depends on the size of your recipe. A gumbo for ten, for example, takes one cup of each.

Folklore has it that you must brown the flour in the oil for as long as it takes to play two sides of an LP record (in the days when such things existed) or to drink two longneck beers. I no longer believe this timing thing. Here's what I do instead. First, add the oil to the pot and heat it up well. Then measure the same amount of flour and whisk it into the very hot oil; it will immediately sizzle and fizz, cooking very hard. Then, lower the flame to moderate and continue whisking the flour and oil. As long as you're whisking, your roux isn't burning; that saves you one side of a scratchy LP and maybe prevents alcoholism, too.

That way, you easily eliminate 30 minutes of slow stirring, and I think the roux is less likely to burn, because you're standing there with it, not becoming complacent. (Roux often burns because it takes so long to cook that you tend to forget about it.) Using my new and improved method, in 15 minutes I've got a roux that's milk chocolate in color and ready for the onions. I add the onions and start stirring with a wooden spoon until the onions caramelize and the roux turns a dark chocolate color. Only then do I stir in the additional vegetables; if I add them with the

onions, their water will prevent the sugars in the onions from caramelizing, and I'll never get that deep brown color.

BASIC CHICKEN STOCK

Makes 6 cups

I make my favorite chicken stock from the left-over carcasses of Sunday's herb-roasted chicken. In the same way, I hang on to the fish heads and bones and the shells of shrimp, crab, and crawfish as flavor bases for the best stocks. After making a pot of stock, I pour it into ice cube trays and freeze it. After they're frozen, I store the cubes in a freezer bag. That way, I can easily retrieve them as I need them, without having to defrost quarts of stock at a time.

¼ cup canola oil

1 onion, coarsely chopped

1 stalk celery, coarsely chopped

1 carrot, peeled and coarsely chopped

1 leek, white part, coarsely chopped

4 cloves garlic, crushed

1 pound roasted chicken bones and carcass

1 bay leaf

1 sprig fresh thyme

1 teaspoon black peppercorns

1. Heat the canola oil in a large pot over moderate heat. Cook the onions, celery, carrots, leeks, and garlic, stirring often, until they are soft but not brown, about 3 minutes.

2. Add the chicken bones and carcass, the bay leaf, thyme, peppercorns, and 3 quarts water. Increase the heat to high and bring to a boil. Immediately reduce the heat to low and gently simmer, skimming any foam that rises to the surface, until the stock has reduced by half, about 2 hours.

3. Strain through a fine sieve into a container with a cover. Allow the stock to cool, cover and refrigerate, then skim off the fat. Freeze the stock in small batches to use later.

VARIATIONS

BASIC FISH STOCK

Substitute 1 pound fish heads and bones for the chicken bones and carcass.

BASIC SHELLFISH STOCK

Substitute 1 pound shells from shrimp, blue crab, crawfish, or lobster for the chicken bones and carcass.

BASIC SHRIMP STOCK

Substitute 1 pound shrimp shells for the chicken bones and carcass.

BASIC CRAB STOCK

Substitute 1 pound crab shells for the chicken bones and carcass.

BASIC HAM HOCK STOCK

Substitute 4 smoked ham hocks for the chicken bones and carcass, saving the meat for another use.

BASIC CREOLE SPICES

Makes ½ cup

Using this spice blend is truly the easiest way to consistently achieve the flavors I grew up with. Once made, the spices will last for six months in an airtight container.

2 tablespoons celery salt

1 tablespoon sweet paprika

1 tablespoon coarse sea salt

1 tablespoon freshly ground black pepper

1 tablespoon garlic powder

1 tablespoon onion powder

2 teaspoons cayenne pepper

½ teaspoon ground allspice

1. Mix together the celery salt, paprika, salt, pepper, garlic powder, onion powder, cayenne, and allspice in a bowl. Transfer the spices to a clean container with a tight-fitting lid, cover, and store.

BASIC VEAL STOCK

Makes 7 cups

I like to use as many joints as I can in a veal or beef stock. As with chicken stock, get in the habit of saving and freezing the bones from beef or veal that you've roasted or braised, until you have enough to make a stock.

1 pound veal bones	4 cloves garlic, crushed
¼ cup canola oil	3 tablespoons tomato paste
2 onions, coarsely chopped	1 bottle red wine
1 stalk celery, coarsely chopped	1 bay leaf
1 carrot, coarsely chopped	1 sprig fresh thyme
1 leek, white part, coarsely chopped	1 teaspoon black peppercorns

What's in a Pan Sauce?

The secret to a potent pan sauce is to coax the most flavor from each morsel, not by adding richness with butter and cream, as the French do. This way, the reduction becomes a refined sauce with a silky texture.

1. Preheat the oven to 400°. Put the veal bones into a roasting pan and rub them with 2 tablespoons oil. Roast the bones until well browned, about 45 minutes.

2. Heat the remaining 2 tablespoons oil in a pot over medium-high heat. Add the onions and cook until they are almost mahogany in color, about 10 minutes.

3. Add the celery, carrots, leeks, garlic, and tomato paste and cook for 15 minutes, stirring frequently.

4. Add the browned veal bones to the pot, along with the wine, bay leaf, thyme, peppercorns and 3 quarts water, and bring to a boil. Reduce the heat to low and gently simmer, skimming any foam that rises to the surface, until the stock has reduced by half, about 2 hours.

5. Strain through a fine sieve into a container with a cover. Allow the stock to cool, then cover and refrigerate, or freeze the stock in small batches to use later.

BASIC SHELLFISH PAN SAUCE

Makes 1 cup

Great cooking takes great planning, and my basic pan sauces give you a superbly flavorful way to finish a dish at the last minute. They can be made well ahead and frozen, just as you'd do with stocks.

1 tablespoon extra-virgin olive oil	Leaves from 1 sprig fresh tarragon
1 small onion, diced	1 bay leaf
2 cloves garlic, minced	½ cup heavy cream
¼ cup minced fennel bulb	½ cup dry vermouth
1 teaspoon crushed red pepper flakes	1 cup Basic Shellfish Stock (page 13)
Leaves from 1 sprig fresh thyme	

1. Heat the oil in a small skillet over moderate heat. Add the onions, garlic, fennel, and pepper flakes. Cook the vegetables, stirring often, for 3 minutes.

2. Add the thyme, tarragon, bay leaf, cream, vermouth, and stock, increase the heat to high, and reduce the sauce by half, 10–12 minutes. Strain sauce.

VARIATIONS

BASIC CHICKEN PAN SAUCE

Substitute Chicken Stock for the Shellfish Stock.

BASIC FISH PAN SAUCE

Substitute Fish Stock for the Shellfish Stock.

BASIC OYSTER PAN SAUCE

Substitute oyster liquor for the Shellfish Stock.

BASIC CRAB PAN SAUCE

Substitute Crab Stock for the Shellfish Stock.

BASIC LOUISIANA WHITE RICE

Makes about 4 cups

This recipe will work with most long-grain rices, including Popcorn Rice. Save some of the fat skimmed from your chicken stock to perfume the rice with many wonderful flavors.

1 tablespoon chicken fat, extra-virgin olive oil, or butter	3 cups Basic Chicken Stock (page 13)
1 small onion, minced	1 bay leaf
1½ cups Louisiana long-grain white rice	1–2 pinches salt

1. Put the fat, oil, or butter and the onions into a medium saucepan and sweat the onions over moderate heat until they are translucent, about 5 minutes. Pour the rice into the pan and stir for 2 minutes. Then add the chicken stock and bring to a boil. Add the bay leaf and salt.

2. Cover the pan with a lid, reduce the heat to low, and cook for 18 minutes. Remove the pan from the heat, fluff the rice with a fork, and serve.

BASIC CORN BREAD

Makes one 9-inch round loaf

Most self-respecting Southerners wouldn't admit to adding sugar to corn bread, but it's both acceptable and good in New Orleans. Granddaddy never put sugar in his, but I find that I can omit the sugar and still have it taste right only when I use a fine-ground white organic cornmeal such as that milled by my friends at McEwen's in Wilsonville, Alabama. Make sure the skillet is so hot that the batter begins to fry when you pour it into the pan. And don't fret about the calories. Corn bread is about love—you can diet tomorrow.

3 tablespoons rendered bacon fat	1 teaspoon salt
1 cup white cornmeal, organic if possible (page 372)	1 pinch cayenne pepper
	2 eggs
1 cup all-purpose flour	1¼ cups milk
2 tablespoons sugar	2 tablespoons butter, melted
2 tablespoons baking powder	

1. Put the bacon fat into a medium (about 9-inch-diameter) cast-iron skillet. Put the skillet into the oven and preheat the oven to 425°.

2. Combine the cornmeal, flour, sugar, baking powder, salt, and cayenne in a large mixing bowl.

3. Put the eggs, milk, and melted butter into a small bowl and mix well.

4. Pour the egg mixture into the cornmeal mixture, stirring until just combined.

5. Carefully remove the hot skillet from the oven and pour the batter into the skillet. Return the skillet to the oven and bake the corn bread until it is deep golden brown, 15–20 minutes. Serve immediately.

Better Pie Dough

There is but one trick: do not overwork the dough, or it will toughen up. That's it!

BASIC PIE DOUGH

Makes one 9-inch crust

Every one of our pastry chefs comes up with his own "better" pie dough, but none has stood the test of time like this one. Here's the secret: make sure not to handle it too much. Once you've added the ice water, stop. You can roll it out in advance, then wrap it and store it in the freezer for a couple of days, if you wish. Or make the dough ahead, shape it into a disk, cover it with plastic wrap, and refrigerate it for a few hours before you need it. If you're using this basic dough for another recipe, follow the directions in step 1.

1 cup all-purpose flour, plus more for dusting the pan

1 teaspoon sugar

¼ teaspoon salt

7 tablespoons cold butter, diced, plus softened butter for greasing the pan

1. Whisk together the flour, sugar, and salt in a large bowl. Using a pastry cutter or 2 knives, cut the butter into the flour until it resembles cornmeal. Sprinkle in ice water, as needed, as many as 4 tablespoons, mixing it into the dough until it comes together into a ball. Press the dough into a round, flat disk, then wrap it in plastic wrap. Refrigerate for 30 minutes before rolling it out.

2. Liberally coat a 9–10 inch pie pan with softened butter, then dust with flour. Roll out the dough on a floured surface to a thickness of ¼ inch.

3. Wrap the dough around the rolling pin, then gently fit the dough into the pan. Trim off overhanging dough and crimp the edges.

BASIC HOMEMADE PASTA

Makes 1 pound

The flour you use for fresh pasta determines its texture. All-purpose makes softer noodles, while bread flour or semolina (milled durum wheat), makes sturdier pasta with more bite, like this one. The recipe determines which you'll choose. Cook the pasta after it's cut and serve it immediately. Or, shock it in cold water, drain it, and reserve it to use later. Fresh pasta, well wrapped, can be frozen and cooked just moments before serving.

1 pound or 2 cups semolina flour

1 tablespoon olive oil

1 pinch salt

5 eggs

1. Put the flour, olive oil, salt, and eggs into the bowl of a standing mixer fitted with a dough hook and mix the dough together on medium speed for 15 minutes.

2. Press the dough into a round, flat disk, then wrap it in plastic wrap and refrigerate for at least 30 minutes.

3. Cut the dough in half. Roll one piece of dough at a time through the widest setting of a pasta machine until the dough is very smooth. This can take as many as 10 passes. Then, continue to roll the dough, each time on a narrower setting, until you reach the second-to-thinnest setting. Cut the pasta sheet into the desired shape, either on the machine or on a lightly floured surface, depending on your recipe.

4. Cook for 3 minutes in a big pot of boiling salted water over high heat. Drain and serve with your favorite sauce.

BASIC SAUCE HOLLANDAISE

Makes 1 ½ cups

To clarify the butter, bring it to a boil in a small saucepan and reduce the heat to a simmer. As the butter simmers, its water will boil off and its solids will drop to the bottom of the pan and foam will rise to the top. Skim away the foam until the butter becomes clear and stops foaming.

½ cup white wine	Juice of ½ lemon
1 shallot, minced	4 egg yolks
1 sprig fresh thyme	1 cup hot clarified butter (between 135° and 145°)
1 teaspoon black peppercorns	
1 bay leaf	1 pinch cayenne pepper
1 tablespoon white wine vinegar	Tabasco
	Salt

1. Put the wine, shallots, thyme, peppercorns, bay leaf, and vinegar into a small saucepan and boil over medium-high heat until reduced by half. Strain the reduction into a small bowl, discarding the solids.

2. Put 2 tablespoons of the reduction into a medium heatproof mixing bowl. (Keep the remaining reduction in the refrigerator for a future batch of sauce hollandaise, if you like.) Whisk in 1 tablespoon water and the lemon juice.

3. Place the bowl over a pot of gently simmering water over moderate heat. Whisk in the egg yolks and cook them, whisking constantly, until the mixture is thick enough to heavily coat the back of a spoon, 7–10 minutes. Remove the bowl from the pot.

4. Steady the bowl (or have someone hold it) and continue whisking the eggs. Drizzle the hot clarified butter into the egg yolks in a slow, steady stream, whisking constantly. Season the sauce with cayenne, Tabasco, and salt.

5. Transfer the sauce to a warm sauceboat and serve relatively soon. It will last for 1 hour or so, but it's best to use it just after it's been made and is still hot.

VARIATION

BASIC CITRUS SAUCE HOLLANDAISE
Substitute ½ cup fresh orange juice for the white wine and add 1 teaspoon coriander seeds and a ½-inch slice fresh ginger, crushed, to the saucepan in step 1. Continue with the directions above.

BASIC AÏOLI

Makes about 3 cups

My time in Provence taught me that the proper amount of garlic to use in this garlicky mayonnaise is one clove per person. There, a festive meal called the *grand aïoli* is casually eaten on a Sunday, when friends and family gather to dip raw vegetables, eggs, escargots, shellfish, and salt cod into a generous bowl of aïoli.

6 cloves garlic	Salt
1 tablespoon fresh lemon juice	2 cups extra-virgin olive oil
2 egg yolks	

1. Put the garlic, lemon juice, 1 tablespoon ice water, and the egg yolks into the work bowl of a food processor. Process until the mixture is thick and puréed.

2. While the food processor is running, add a pinch of salt through the feed tube, then slowly drizzle in the olive oil. If the aïoli begins to look oily, add a touch more ice water. The color should be pale yellow, and the texture matte, not glossy.

BASIC SAUCE VINAIGRETTE

VINAIGRETTE, TO ME, is much more than salad dressing. I use vinaigrette as a marinade, as a glaze, and to sauce a finished dish like roast chicken or grilled fish. Sometimes, rather than dress a whole salad, I'll make a little vinaigrette then just toss some greens in it and scatter them over a dish. Basic vinaigrette is so simple that it can be made with just about anything you have in your pantry. It's just a combination of acids (normally vinegar, but it could be fruit juices like lemon, grapefruit, or passion fruit or unripened grape juice, called *verjus*) with an oil (normally a vegetable oil like olive, canola, walnut, or grapeseed).

The rule of thumb is four parts oil to one part acid. If your acid—like balsamic vinegar or aged sherry vinegar—isn't very acidic, then cut back on the oil. It all comes down to taste. If it needs salt, add some; if it's a little tart, add more oil or a pinch or two of sugar. If it needs more spice, add a touch of pepper or mustard. The personality of each vinaigrette will come through according to its ingredients. Each oil imparts a different flavor; each vinegar adds its unique character. Combine your oil and acid in a bowl using a wire whisk.

Here are some of my favorite vinaigrettes, each with its own flavor base. The method is the same: just put all the ingredients into a bowl and whisk until well mixed. You'll notice that, after whisking, the vinaigrette will begin to separate. This doesn't bother me at all; if it bothers you, then I suggest you give it a good whisk before you use it. Or, better yet, pour the vinaigrette into a squeeze bottle and give it a good shake before you squirt.

BASIC VINAIGRETTE

Makes 1 ¼ cups

¼ cup vinegar	Freshly ground black pepper
1 cup oil	
Salt	

VARIATIONS

BASIC BALSAMIC VINAIGRETTE

Makes 1 cup

¼ cup balsamic vinegar (the older the better)	1 sprig fresh basil, minced
¾ cup extra-virgin olive oil	Salt
1 clove garlic, minced	Freshly ground black pepper

BASIC LEMON VINAIGRETTE

Makes 1 ¼ cups

3 tablespoons rice wine vinegar	1 small pinch crushed red pepper flakes
3 tablespoons fresh lemon juice (use Meyer lemons if you can find them)	¾ cup extra-virgin olive oil
2 teaspoons fresh lemon zest	1 dash Meyer lemon–infused olive oil
1 shallot, minced	Salt
	Freshly ground black pepper

BASIC WALNUT OIL VINAIGRETTE

Makes 1 ¼ cups

¼ cup sherry vinegar
   (preferably aged)

2 pinches sugar

½ cup walnut oil

½ cup canola oil

Salt

Freshly ground
black pepper

BASIC CHAMPAGNE VINAIGRETTE

Makes 1 ¼ cups

1 dash champagne

¼ cup champagne
   vinegar

2 pinches sugar

1 cup canola oil

Salt

Freshly ground
black pepper

BASIC WILDFLOWER HONEY AND CREOLE MUSTARD VINAIGRETTE

Makes 1 ¾ cups

4 tablespoons Creole
   mustard (page 362)

¼ cup sherry vinegar

3 tablespoons wildflower
   honey

1 clove garlic, minced

1 cup canola oil

Salt

Freshly ground
black pepper

BASIC LAVENDER HONEY VINAIGRETTE

Makes 1 ¼ cups

¼ cup white wine
   vinegar

2 tablespoons
   lavender honey

1 shallot, minced

1 clove garlic, mined

1 cup extra-virgin
   olive oil

Salt

Freshly ground
black pepper

BASIC PEPPER JELLY VINAIGRETTE

Makes 2 ½ cups

½ cup pepper jelly

½ cup red wine vinegar

1 teaspoon sambal
   chile paste

1½ cups canola oil

Salt

BASIC SAUCE RAVIGOTE

Makes 1 ½ cups

Ravigoter in culinary French means to refresh, here with a dash of vinegar or lemon juice. In this book sauce ravigote is the slightly tangy dressing we use to enliven the flavor of anything from delicate crabmeat to a hearty standing rib roast of beef.

1 cup mayonnaise
   Juice of 2 lemons

¼ cup prepared
   horseradish

2 teaspoons Dijon
   mustard

1 teaspoon white wine
   vinegar

2 teaspoons chopped
   fresh chives

1–2 pinches cayenne
   pepper

1½ teaspoons salt

1 pinch freshly ground
   white pepper

1. Combine all the above ingredients in a large bowl and whisk until well combined. Transfer the sauce to a small bowl. The sauce will keep in the refrigerator for up to 2 days.

BASIC SAUCE REMOULADE

Makes 1 ½ cups

Remoulade recipes vary from cook to cook. This is the one I prefer. I toss it with shrimp, crabmeat, crawfish, lobster, lettuces, or celery root; or spice it up as a dip. Make this a day ahead, and let its flavors develop overnight in the refrigerator.

1 cup mayonnaise

¼ cup Dijon mustard

2 tablespoons prepared
   horseradish

2 tablespoons chopped
   fresh parsley

1 shallot, minced

1 clove garlic, minced

1 tablespoon white wine
   vinegar

1 teaspoon fresh lemon
   juice

1 teaspoon hot sauce

½ teaspoon sweet
   paprika

¼ teaspoon cayenne
   pepper

¼ teaspoon garlic powder

Salt

1. Combine all the above ingredients in a large bowl and stir well, then add salt. Transfer the sauce to a container with a cover and refrigerate.

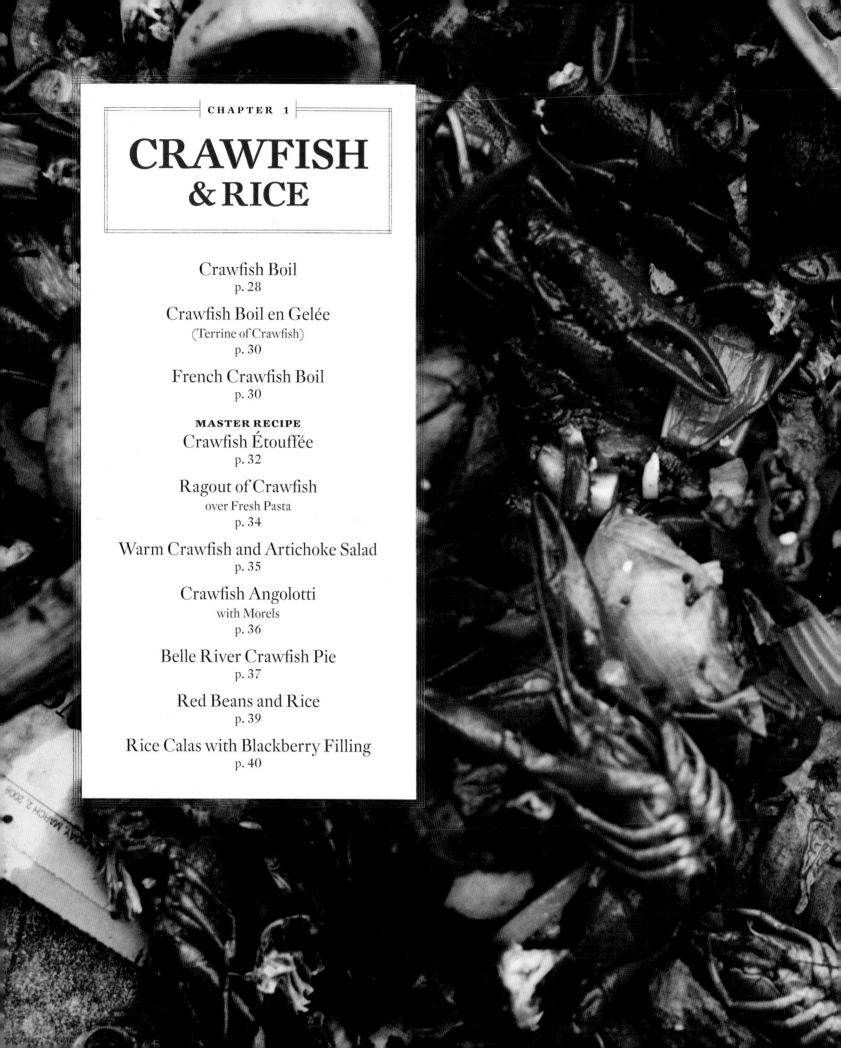

CHAPTER 1

CRAWFISH & RICE

Crawfish days: A crawfish boil, above, just emptied on a newspaper-covered table. My son Jack, right, catching crawfish in a wire mesh trap. Crawfish float in a Rice Festival parade in Crowley, Louisiana, 1965; photo: Joe L. Herring.

La Grosse Écrevisse

My Birthday and the Crawfish Boil

"Crawfish and long-grain rice cohabit in our swampy lowlands, and there's no better pairing on the plate."

It may seem odd for a boy from South Louisiana who grew up catching mudbugs in his backyard to admit that he learned about cooking crawfish abroad. Yet I look at crawfish very differently from most other chefs in New Orleans because I spent so much of my formative cooking time in Europe, where crawfish are relatively rare, held in great esteem, and generally called crayfish. French chefs would be amused, then horrified, by our practice of boiling crawfish by the pound, fearing the assault of robust spices on the delicate flavor of their beloved *écrevisses*. They consider the crawfish a luxury ingredient, quite expensive—rather like tiny lobster; instead of a potful, they'd use ten. They would gently poach them, remove the meat from

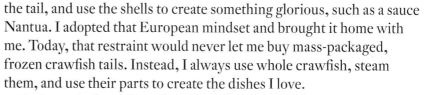

Rice and spice:
Ripening rice in the field, below, near Gross Tete, Louisiana; photo: Alexander Stolin. Foundations of the crawfish boil: cayenne, salt, and a mix of coriander, allspice, mustard seed, and black pepper.

the tail, and use the shells to create something glorious, such as a sauce Nantua. I adopted that European mindset and brought it home with me. Today, that restraint would never let me buy mass-packaged, frozen crawfish tails. Instead, I always use whole crawfish, steam them, and use their parts to create the dishes I love.

And yet. And yet. In my heart I'm still the 12-year-old who, waist deep in a cypress swamp, discovered crawfishing for the first time. My birthday, in mid-May, comes toward the end of the wild crawfish season, before the heat forces the crawfish to bed down in the mud for the rest of the summer (hence their nickname, mudbugs). Crawfishing remains my favorite birthday adventure.

Moving carefully among the tupelo gum trees so as to not spook the crawfish, we—a group of friends and someone's father—would set our traps, basically a dozen cane poles with folding nets. It is so easy to get lost in the shallow slough that we would try to stick our poles in the mud in some kind of pattern, about ten feet apart, so that we could hope to find them again. We would spend the day with pails tied around our waists collecting those critters, overeager to check our traps, which could yield just one or two or maybe a dozen mudbugs. We'd empty the nets into our pails, then into a potato sack trailing in the water. Nearly every one of our crawfish excursions would have a serious brush with danger—like a run-in with a water moccasin or an alligator. In later years there'd be six-packs of Dixie.

When we figured we had enough—about five pounds per person— we'd go home and make a crawfish boil, using things that Mom had in the pantry, like Zatarain's boiling spices. Crawfish boils are the main social event throughout the spring, a way to socialize with family and friends. As my son Brendan says, "The best thing about being Catholic is a crawfish boil every Friday during Lent."

INGREDIENTS IN A crawfish boil vary from household to household and can become borderline extravagant. All begin the same way—by heating a large pot of salted water, preferably outdoors. First you add cayenne and black pepper, then coriander, mustard seeds, allspice, bay leaves, onions, celery, garlic, lemons, corn on the cob, and new potatoes. Here's where cultural differences set in: most people add sausage. I love smoked hot sausages, whole artichokes, button mushrooms, sometimes carrots. Some folks throw in turkey necks, whole chickens, hot dogs, eggs, Brussels sprouts,

Mudbugs: Carrying our basket, top, which holds about 20 pounds or a half sack of crawfish. Live crawfish, above. Left, crawfish racing at a festival in Breaux Bridge, Louisiana, 1972.

Living together:
Waterfowl feed on rice (and crawfish) fields near Gross Tete, above; photo: Alexander Stolin.

To peel a crawfish:
Opposite, gently remove the tail from the body by twisiting and pulling. Then remove a section or two of shell, pinch the tail, and the meat will release neatly.

even tamales. To each his own. When it's done, you measure the success of a boil by the pile of discarded crawfish shells in front of each participant. Leftover crawfish is prized: peeled and frozen for an étouffée with rice, or a stew or a bisque, or stuffed into pastry for a crawfish pie, or tossed in vinaigrette with the crawfish boil artichoke hearts. And let's not forget that the best potato salad is made from crawfish boil potatoes.

From winter to early summer, crawfish both wild and commercially cultivated are harvested from swampy fields, so it's a cult crop every bit as anticipated as the beginning of LSU football or the first split of duck season. Even close to New Orleans, crawfish inhabit the lowlands, which is to say nearly everywhere. It's easy to spot the places with the best wild crawfish populations; just look where the most pickup trucks are parked along the highways.

Come summer, as the crawfish burrow into the swampy lowland, long-grain rice begins to flourish. It is glorious to gaze out over miles and miles of those once-watery fields as they begin to look like vast Western prairies, with tall rice stalks rippling like wheat in the breeze. Nothing breaks up the view—except for the inevitable oil drilling platform or gas pipeline, that is. When the rice is harvested in the late summer or early fall, a second crop of rice often emerges. Since this second crop is relatively low yield, it's usually left in the field to feed wintering waterfowl as well as the next generation of crawfish. Now, that's what I consider a magical circle of life.

I'd be lying if I said crawfishing is an easy thing to do; it takes all day to collect enough mudbugs to eat. Truth is, you expend so much energy finding them, catching them, cooking them, and you still have the quasi-arduous task of peeling them. Here's where my French training kicks in. We peel every little critter ourselves, and consequently we don't waste a bit: every shell is used for stock, every morsel of tail meat is handled frugally and respectfully. In this way I pay homage to the child in me and still excite the cook in me.

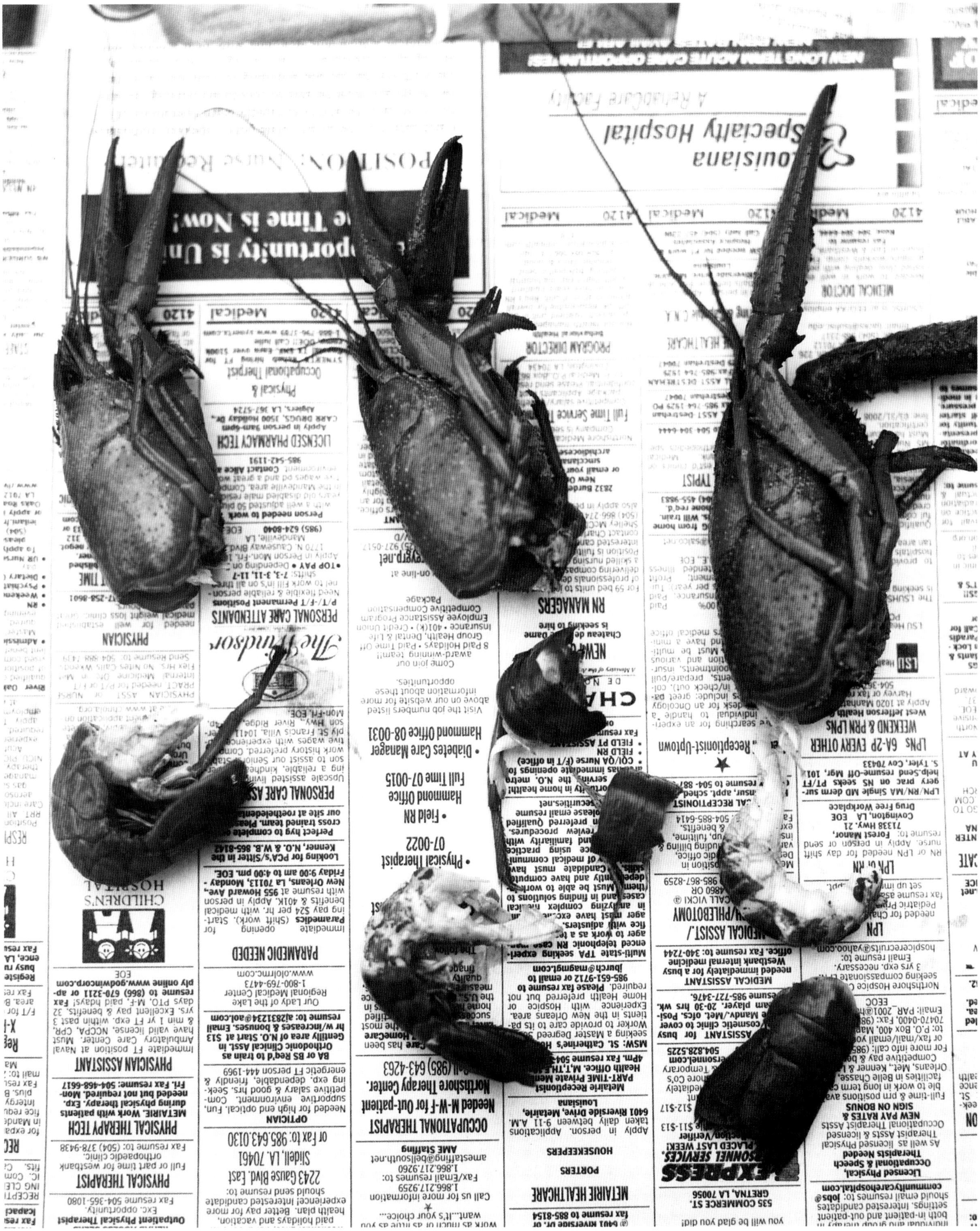

Crawfish

The red swamp crawfish (*Procambarus clarkii*) and the white river crawfish (*Procambarus zonangulus*) are the two species raised in the swampy lowlands of Louisiana and the south-central Atchafalaya Basin, accounting for close to 90 percent of the nation's crop. A typical harvest can be 82 million pounds of the succulent crustaceans, most of them farmed. The term *crawfish* was coined back in 1817 by Thomas Say, the first American zoologist to study them, and it stuck in the South even after the English renamed them crayfish and the French, *écrevisses*.

Up to the mid-1900s, crawfish eaters relied on wild harvests, but rice farmers, who flooded their fields after the harvest to attract waterfowl, noticed that the leftover rice plants attracted and sustained a crawfish population. Flooding became deliberate as commercial farming took off, and today over half of the crawfish produced from December to June is rotated with rice growing. We call them mudbugs because of their habit of burrowing in muddy swamps, which helps them reproduce.

The delicious substance we call crawfish fat is really an organ—the hepatopancreas—that stores energy; it's located in the center of the carapace. There's a reason crawfish resemble little lobsters: millions of years ago, these saltwater creatures sought food and shelter at the mouths of rivers. As they gradually adapted to freshwater, they traveled farther upriver and into ponds and swamps, somehow shrinking in size along the way.

CRAWFISH BOIL

Serves 8

A boil is a real event, so make this meal when you have ample time and lots of friends to share it with. Traditionally, participants peel leftover uneaten crawfish so that the hosts can save the tails for many other delicious crawfish dishes, like étouffées, salads, and pies. You can do the boil inside on the stove or outdoors on a grill or on a propane-fueled burner.

While it's typical to measure five pounds of crawfish per guest, it's also easy to assume that, with so many other ingredients, this recipe will easily satisfy eight people. There are excellent sources for ordering crawfish delivered by air freight (page 362). Most purveyors send them already boiled, and if that's how you receive them, follow the recipe but add the boiled crawfish as you turn off the heat and let the pot sit for 15–20 minutes.

2 cups kosher salt	3 pounds smoked sausage, cut into 4-inch lengths
1 package Zatarain's Crab Boil spices	20 small red bliss potatoes
5 lemons, halved	8 ears corn, shucked and halved
3 tablespoons cayenne pepper	8 whole artichokes, untrimmed
5 whole heads garlic, halved crosswise	20 pounds whole crawfish, rinsed with fresh water
5 small onions, halved	1 pound button mushrooms
3 stalks celery, cut into large pieces	
3 green bell peppers, seeded and diced	
¼ cup canola oil	

1. Fill a very large pot with 10 gallons water, leaving plenty of room for all the other ingredients. Bring water to a boil with the kosher salt, boiling spices, lemons, cayenne, garlic, onions, celery, bell peppers, and oil. Reduce heat and allow to simmer for 10 minutes.

2. Now add the smoked sausage, potatoes, corn, and artichokes and continue to simmer for 15 minutes.

Secrets of the boil:
What makes it yours are the ingredients you add. Drew Mire, left, and I pour out corn on the cob, artichokes, small potatoes, whole onions, and garlic heads that melt in your mouth.

3. Next add the crawfish and mushrooms and allow the pot to simmer for another 10 minutes. Turn off the heat and let the crawfish sit for 15–20 minutes before straining everything from the boiling liquid.

4. A large colander will make it easier to fish out all the good bits (crawfish, vegetables) from the pot and dump them onto a picnic table well covered with newspaper (preferably the *Times-Picayune*). Then strain the last juicy bits from the pot (a two-person job) and feast while drinking an Abita Amber beer.

CRAWFISH BOIL EN GELÉE (TERRINE OF CRAWFISH)

Serves 6

Shellfish in aspic—mainly shrimp—chilled in molds used to be a special lunch dish in New Orleans. My idea was to create a jellied crawfish mold flavored with the bold spices of the crawfish boil that, with a salad, could be an elegant first course. Use what molds you have on hand: ramekins, flex pans, even Dixie cups. You can easily substitute other shellfish using the same amount. Save the vegetables from a crawfish boil, if you have them, to use in the aspic.

2 envelopes unflavored gelatin	½ cup andouille sausage, diced small
1 quart Basic Shellfish Stock (page 13)	1 cup cooked corn kernels
1 shallot, minced	½ cup chopped fresh chives
1 or 2 cloves garlic, minced	Salt
1 cup boiled and peeled crawfish tails (page 362)	Freshly ground black pepper
1 russet potato, peeled, boiled, and diced small	¼ cup Basic Lemon Vinaigrette (page 18)
	1 cup small arugula leaves

1. Sprinkle the gelatin over 1 cup of chilled Shellfish Stock in a large bowl, stir well, and set aside for 3–5 minutes to let soften and swell.

2. Bring the remaining 3 cups Shellfish Stock to a boil in a medium saucepan over moderate heat, stirring periodically and skimming off the impurities that float to the surface. Add the shallots and the garlic to the stock and simmer for 5 minutes. Then add the stock to the bowl of gelatin.

3. Stir for a few minutes, then add the crawfish, potatoes, sausages, corn, and chives to the bowl of gelatin. Season well with salt and pepper.

4. Pour the mixture into 6 individual, 3-inch-diameter ramekins or molds and chill for several hours, until set.

5. To unmold, quickly dip each ramekin into a bowl of hot water to loosen the aspic. Run a paring knife around the edges, turn the ramekin over, and unmold each aspic onto a plate. Then drizzle each aspic with a teaspoon of Lemon Vinaigrette. Use the remaining vinaigrette to dress the arugula, and scatter the leaves over the tops of the aspic.

FRENCH CRAWFISH BOIL

Serves 2

This is a refined but simple approach that the French take to the whole crawfish they call *écrevisses*; the little sauce you'll make is so delicious you'll want to eat it with a spoon.

1 pound whole crawfish (page 362)	Leaves from 1 sprig fresh tarragon, minced
Salt	1 pinch crushed red pepper flakes
2 tablespoons olive oil	
¼ cup armagnac	1 small fresh black truffle, minced
1 cup Basic Shellfish Pan Sauce (page 14)	

1. Bring a large pot of heavily salted water to a boil. Add the crawfish and let sit for 30 seconds. Drain.

2. Heat a large skillet over high heat, add the crawfish and oil, and toss together, cooking the crawfish for 3 minutes, stirring often. Then reduce the heat to moderate and cook for 2 minutes more.

3. Slide the skillet off the heat, add the armagnac, and shake the skillet to loosen the pan juices. Then light the armagnac with a match.

4. Return the skillet to moderate heat and cook for several minutes. While the armagnac flames, add the Shellfish Pan Sauce, then the tarragon, pepper flakes, and minced truffle. Simmer for 5 minutes, season, and serve in bowls.

CRAWFISH ÉTOUFFÉE

Serves 6

Étouffée means smothered, and this dish is smothered both with a lid and with its holy trinity of vegetables: onion, celery, and bell pepper. The leading role in this savory crawfish stew is taken by the crawfish shells used for making the stock, which, when toasted, give the dish great depth of flavor. Contrary to what's traditionally done, I like to add the crawfish meat at the very end so that it does not become tough.

The velvety texture of the étouffée comes from browning the flour in oil in the early stages; this makes our roux, the quintessential base of this classic dish. And although you'll find some so-called progressive recipes that use other starches and thickeners, the flour-based roux is the only way to get the true flavor of étouffée. Please see my Thoughts on Roux, on page 12. Shrimp étouffée and crab étouffée are excellent variations on this classic. Proceed with the Master Recipe, substituting crab and shrimp for the crawfish.

---

3 tablespoons canola oil

3 tablespoons flour

1 small onion, diced

1 stalk celery, diced

Half a red bell pepper, diced

2 cloves garlic, minced

Leaves from 2 sprigs fresh thyme

¼ teaspoon cayenne pepper

1 teaspoon smoked paprika

1 small tomato, peeled, seeded, and diced

1 quart Basic Shellfish Stock (page 13)

3 tablespoons butter

1 pound peeled crawfish tails (page 362)

2 green onions, chopped

2 dashes Worcestershire

2 dashes Tabasco

Salt

Freshly ground black pepper

3 cups cooked Basic Louisiana White Rice (page 15)

1. Heat the oil in a large saucepan over medium-high heat. Whisk the flour into the very hot oil. It will immediately begin to sizzle and fizz. Keep whisking and reduce the heat to moderate. Continue whisking until the roux takes on a gorgeous dark brown color, about 15 minutes. Add the onions, reduce the heat, and cook until the onions caramelize. If you add all the vegetables at the same time, the water that results will boil the onions and their sugars won't caramelize.

2. When the onions have turned the roux shiny and dark, add the celery, bell peppers, garlic, thyme, cayenne, and paprika. Cook for 5 minutes.

Now add the tomatoes and the Shellfish Stock and increase the heat to high.

3. Once the sauce has come to a boil, reduce the heat to moderate and let simmer 5–7 minutes, stirring often. Be careful not to let it burn or stick to the bottom of the pan.

4. Reduce the heat to low and stir in the butter. Add the crawfish tails and green onions. Season with Worcestershire, Tabasco, salt, and black pepper. Once the crawfish tails have heated through, remove the saucepan from the heat.

5. Serve in individual bowls over rice.

Building an étouffée: Rice makes the dish, above; tails in the pot, right. Opposite, nothing's wasted: heads and shells go into the stock.

RAGOUT OF CRAWFISH OVER FRESH PASTA

Serves 6

A smart cook is always thinking several steps ahead. If you decide to make fresh pasta, make more than you need and freeze the rest. Every time you have a chicken carcass or enough shells from crab or lobster, make a stock and freeze that, too. That way, simple stews like this one can come together easily.

¼ cup olive oil

¼ pound fresh morel mushrooms

1 recipe Basic Homemade Pasta (page 16) or 1 pound dried linguine or fettuccine

1 cup Basic Shellfish Pan Sauce (page 14)

3 tablespoons butter

½ cup cherry tomatoes, quartered

½ cup fresh fava beans, shelled and peeled

1 pound peeled crawfish tails (page 362)

   Salt

   Freshly ground black pepper

1 cup shaved Parmesan cheese

6 sprigs fresh chervil

Crawfishing: Rewards of the expedition in a bowl, above. Emptying a wire-mesh crawfish trap in the shallow waters of one of our many bayous, right, in the 1970s.

1. Heat the olive oil in a shallow saucepan over moderate heat. Add the morels and sauté them until soft. Transfer the mushrooms to a plate and set them aside.

2. Using the setting for either linguine or fettuccine on your pasta machine, cut the fresh pasta, then cook for 3 minutes in a large pot of boiling salted water, or cook the dry pasta until tender. Drain, return to the pot, and keep warm.

3. Heat the Shellfish Pan Sauce in a shallow saucepan (you can use the same pan you used to sauté the morels) over medium-low heat. Just before serving, whisk in the butter a bit at a time. Add the tomatoes, fava beans, crawfish, and sautéed morels. Cook for 2 minutes, and season with salt and pepper.

4. Divide the pasta into bowls, ladle on the crawfish stew, and garnish with the shavings of Parmesan and chervil sprigs.

WARM CRAWFISH AND ARTICHOKE SALAD

Serves 6

This salad offers a wonderful way to use leftovers from yesterday's crawfish boil—the crawfish tails, the artichokes, plus any vegetables that look good.

1 shallot, minced	1 pound boiled and peeled crawfish tails (page 362)
1 clove garlic, thinly sliced	Leaves from 1 sprig fresh tarragon, minced
A generous ¼ cup olive oil	Salt
3 tablespoons rice wine vinegar	Freshly ground black pepper
1 small tomato, peeled, seeded, and diced	4 cups baby dandelion leaves or other greens, washed and patted dry
1 pinch crushed red pepper flakes	1 tablespoon minced fresh chives, or a few chive blossoms
1 pinch saffron threads	
4 large artichokes from a crawfish boil, cleaned and quartered, or fresh artichokes, prepared as explained at right	

1. Cook the shallots and garlic in the olive oil in a large skillet over moderate heat until they are soft. Add the vinegar, tomatoes, pepper flakes, and saffron to the skillet and cook for another couple of minutes.

2. Add the artichokes and cook for another couple of minutes. Add the crawfish and tarragon to the skillet and remove from the heat. Stir carefully, making sure the crawfish are warmed through but not overcooked.

3. Season with salt and pepper. Using a slotted spoon, serve the crawfish and artichokes on 6 plates.

4. Toss the greens in a mixing bowl with a couple of tablespoons of the sauce left in the skillet. Scatter a handful of greens over each plate, then sprinkle the chives or chive blossoms on top.

FOR THE ARTICHOKES

2 tablespoons salt	2 cloves garlic, crushed
1 lemon, halved	1 tablespoon olive oil
1 teaspoon crushed red pepper flakes	4 large artichokes

1. Bring 2 quarts water to a boil in a large pot, then add the salt, lemon halves, pepper flakes, garlic, and oil.

2. Meanwhile, prepare the artichokes by slicing off and discarding the top 2 inches of each artichoke. With your fingers, peel off the large outer leaves (exposing the tender pale green leaves). Peel the stem with a vegetable peeler or a paring knife and trim the end.

3. Put the trimmed artichokes into the spicy boiling water and let them simmer for 25 minutes or until the stem end is tender when probed with a sharp knife. Remove the artichokes from the water, then cool them in a bowl of ice water for a minute or so, until they're cool enough to handle.

4. Drain, then slice each artichoke in half lengthwise and carve out the fuzzy choke with a spoon. Then slice each half lengthwise again into quarters and proceed with the recipe.

CRAWFISH AGNOLOTTI WITH MORELS

Serves 6

While I was cooking in Germany, we'd often cross the border to Italy, and there I fell in love with the idea of stuffed pasta. Consequently, we've always had a stuffed pasta on the menu at August. When crawfish are in season, I'll combine them with morels for the stuffing; in shrimp season I'll use them with chanterelles; or I'll make the stuffing with crabmeat, porcinis, and fresh corn. This recipe takes some concentration, but the results are well worth it.

FOR THE FILLING

- 1 tablespoon extra-virgin olive oil
- 1 shallot, minced
- 2 garlic cloves, minced
- 1 cup peeled and deveined fresh crawfish tails (page 362)
- 2 cups mascarpone cheese
- 2 tablespoons fresh tarragon leaves
- Salt

FOR THE PASTA

- Flour
- ¼ recipe Basic Homemade Pasta (page 16)
- ¼ cup melted butter

FOR THE SAUCE

- ¼ cup finely chopped bacon
- 1 shallot, minced
- 1 clove garlic, minced
- 1 cup cleaned fresh morels or other wild mushrooms, halved lengthwise
- ¼ cup shelled peas
- ¾ cup Basic Shellfish Pan Sauce (page 14)
- ½ cup peeled and deveined crawfish tails (page 362)
- 2 small tomatoes, peeled, seeded, and diced
- ½ teaspoon crushed red pepper flakes
- 2 tablespoons cold butter, diced

1. For the filling, heat the oil in a medium skillet over moderate heat. Add the shallots and garlic and cook until soft and aromatic, about 5 minutes. Remove from the heat and stir in the crawfish. Transfer to a food processor, along with the mascarpone, tarragon, and a pinch of salt. Pulse until the mixture is smooth. Scoop the purée into a pastry bag fitted with a large or medium round tip and refrigerate.

2. For the pasta, on a well-floured surface, cut the pasta dough in half and flatten both pieces. Roll each piece through the smooth cylinders of a pasta machine, decreasing the setting by one notch at a time, until you've reached the narrowest setting. You should have two 24-inch-long by 4-inch-wide sheets of pasta.

3. Lay a sheet of pasta in front of you on a well-floured surface with the long side parallel to the edge. Pipe half the crawfish filling onto the pasta in one long line, about 1 inch from the edge of the long side closest to you. With a pastry brush dipped in water, moisten the pasta on the other side of the filling (to help it seal). Then, carefully roll the dough over and around the filling one and a half times. Repeat with the second sheet of pasta and remaining filling. Freeze any leftover dough.

4. Using your two index fingers spread 1½ inches apart, make indentations along each roll of pasta, starting at one end and continuing all the way down to the other. You have now formed little pillows in the dough. Crimp the little pillows where you've indented them by pinching them closed at every crimp, carefully sealing the dough so that they don't burst open while cooking. Using a small pastry or pasta wheel, cut between pillows at each crimp. Now you've made little individual agnolotti of crawfish-stuffed pasta.

5. For the sauce, cook the bacon in a medium skillet over moderate heat for about 2 minutes. Add the shallots and garlic and cook, stirring a few times, for another 2 minutes. Add the morels or wild mushrooms, the peas, and the Shellfish Pan Sauce and cook for another 2 minutes. Stir in the crawfish, tomatoes, red pepper flakes, and butter. Cook until the butter melts, about 1 minute.

6. While the sauce is cooking, bring a large pot of salted water to a boil over medium-high heat. Working in batches, carefully add the agnolotti to the gently boiling water and cook them for 2 minutes. Use a large slotted spoon to transfer the cooked agnolotti to a large platter, and drizzle with a little melted butter to keep them from sticking to one another. Just before serving, spoon the sauce over the pasta.

BELLE RIVER CRAWFISH PIE

Serves 6

Some folks think the best crawfish in the state comes from the fresh waters of the Belle River, which runs through Assumption Parish in south-central Louisiana. Both the dough and the filling for this pie may be made up to a couple of days in advance and kept in the refrigerator until you're ready to use them. You may prefer to use a nine-inch prepared pie shell instead of the individual shells; just know that when you slice the big pie it'll be slightly runny.

5 tablespoons butter	1 bay leaf
4 tablespoons flour, plus more for dusting	½ cup Basic Shellfish Stock (page 13)
1 onion, diced	½ cup heavy cream
½ green bell pepper, seeded and diced	1 pound peeled crawfish tails (page 362)
1 stalk celery, diced	2 dashes Tabasco
1¼ teaspoons salt	2 dashes Worcestershire
¼ teaspoon cayenne pepper	1 recipe Basic Pie Dough (page 16) or one 9-inch prepared pie shell
½ teaspoon freshly ground black pepper	
1 medium tomato, seeded and chopped	

1. Preheat the oven to 325°. Make a roux by melting 4 tablespoons of the butter in a large skillet over moderate heat. Stir in the flour until it is incorporated. Cook, stirring frequently with a wooden spoon, until the roux is lightly browned, about 10 minutes. Then add the onions and cook for a few minutes more until the roux becomes golden brown.

2. Add the bell pepper, celery, salt, cayenne, black pepper, tomatoes, and bay leaf. Reduce heat to medium-low and let simmer for 10 minutes more.

3. Stirring constantly, slowly add the Shellfish Stock and cream to the skillet. Raise the heat to moderate and simmer the sauce until it has reduced by half. Remove the skillet from the heat and add the crawfish,

Tabasco, and Worcestershire and stir to combine. Set the filling aside; discard the bay leaf.

4. Liberally coat each of 6 individual 3- to 4-inch tart pans with the remaining 1 tablespoon butter, then dust with flour.

5. Roll the dough out on a floured surface to a thickness of ¼ inch. Cut into 6 individual circles, each a bit larger than the tart pan. Gently fit the dough circles into the prepared tart pans.

6. Place the tart pans (or the 9-inch shell) on a cookie sheet and fill with the crawfish mixture. Bake for 25 minutes or until the pie shells are golden brown.

In our backyard: Jack and his uncle Patrick Berrigan in a pirogue, a dugout canoe, on Maple Slough, right out our back door.

RED BEANS AND RICE

Serves 6

Time is the key to making successful red beans: they need to cook slowly and well. Using flavorful fat is another secret. Just as my grandmother did, I keep the fat from every batch of bacon I make, and I save the fat that solidifies on the surface of chilled chicken soup and roast chicken drippings, too. Just a little bit adds big flavor.

2 onions, diced	½ teaspoon cayenne pepper
1 green bell pepper, seeded and diced	3 green onions, chopped
1 stalk celery, diced	Salt
2 tablespoons rendered bacon fat	Freshly ground black pepper
1 pound dried red kidney beans	Tabasco
2 smoked ham hocks	3 cups cooked Basic Louisiana White Rice (page 15)
3 bay leaves	

1. Sweat the onions, bell peppers, and celery in the rendered bacon fat in a heavy soup pot over medium-high heat.

2. Once the onions become translucent, add the kidney beans, ham hocks, bay leaves, and cayenne, then add water to cover by 2 inches.

3. Increase the heat and bring the water to a boil. Cover the pot, reduce the heat to low, and allow the beans to slowly simmer for 2 hours. Periodically stir the beans to make sure that they don't scorch on the bottom of the pot, adding water if necessary, always keeping the beans covered by an inch or more of water.

4. Continue cooking the beans until they are creamy and beginning to fall apart when they're stirred.

5. Remove the ham hock meat from the bones, roughly chop it, and add it back to the pot of beans.

6. Stir in the green onions and season with salt, black pepper and Tabasco. Serve with white rice.

Rice is nice: Rice farmers in Abbeville, Louisiana, below, part of a series by the photographer Russell Lee for the Farm Security Administration, 1938. Some of our favorite grains, bottom, clockwise from top left, Konriko Wild Pecan Aromatic, Konriko Brown Rice, Creole Rose Popcorn Rice, Ellis Stansel Gourmet Rice, and Panola Popcorn Rice.

RICE CALAS WITH BLACKBERRY FILLING

Serves 6

"Calas tout chaud"—hot, crispy rice balls—were once classic street food in New Orleans, hawked daily in the marketplace. Somehow, these little delicacies fell off our culinary map, and only in the past decade have they been restored to our menus. My variation is very simple. You do need a bit of planning to make the filling in advance, but feel free to use your favorite prepared jam instead, or even omit filling the calas altogether.

FOR THE FILLING

- 4 cups fresh blackberries
- 1 teaspoon fresh lemon juice
- 7 tablespoons sugar
- 2 tablespoons powdered pectin

FOR THE CALAS

- 2 cups flour
- 1 tablespoon cinnamon
- 1 dash grated nutmeg
- 2 tablespoons baking powder
- 2 cups cooked long-grain white rice
- 4 eggs
- 2 cups sugar
- ¾ cup milk
- 4–6 cups vegetable oil for frying

1. For the filling, stew the blackberries with the lemon juice in a heavy-bottomed pot over low heat for 20 minutes until they become very soft. Purée berries in a blender, then pass them through a fine-mesh sieve to remove the seeds. Return the strained berries to the pot over moderate heat and add the sugar and pectin. Slowly bring the mixture to a boil, whisking constantly. After it boils, remove the filling from the heat and allow to cool completely.

2. For the calas, put the flour, cinnamon, nutmeg, and baking powder into the work bowl of a food processor and pulse a few times. Add the rice, eggs, and 1 cup of the sugar and process until smooth. Add the milk and process until fully incorporated into the dough. Using a rubber spatula, transfer the dough to a bowl or cover with plastic wrap and refrigerate for about an hour.

3. Heat the vegetable oil to 350° in a large heavy skillet. A candy thermometer is helpful here.

4. Form the dough into 1-inch round balls and very carefully drop them into the hot oil, a few at a time. Fry until brown and cooked through. Use tongs to remove the calas from the oil, and drain them on paper towels.

5. To fill the warm calas, fit a plain, ¼-inch metal tip into a pastry bag. Then fill the pastry bag with the blackberry filling and inject it into the calas. Fill all the calas with the blackberry filling, then roll them while still warm in the remaining 1 cup of sugar.

Harvest time: Pitching bundles of rice into the thresher in Crowley, Louisiana; photo: Russell Lee, 1938.

CHAPTER 2

MARDI GRAS

"Rich or poor, black or white, we each have our own version of Carnival. My Mardi Gras is all about families."

The closer you get to the Quarter, the racier the celebration becomes, and it's the Quarter's excesses that get the press. But most families, like mine, would head to the neighborhoods—Uptown, across Canal Street into the gracious Garden District and the parade route along St. Charles. We'd arrive early and stake out a place with a couple of ladders we'd brought, and ice chests full of drinks, Cokes—we call everything Cokes—and Big Shots (cheap and bright, the colors of New Orleans, pineapple, strawberry, and root beer). We'd bring our own red beans and rice, quintessential Mardi Gras food. Friends nearby would have a grill; someone would start a jambalaya pot. There are many

Panorama: The Mardi Gras scene on Canal Street, 1910, above; photo: A. L. Barnett. A favorite house in the heart of the Garden District, left. Below, beads still adorn lampposts in the Quarter for months after Mardi Gras.

Rue D' Orléans

Orleans

BUS

Mardi Gras routes, but the Beshes and the Kreigers and the Reillys and the Gendusas determined their place by whoever had a friend close by where we could use the bathrooms.

There were no street vendors, and anyway, nobody had the money. We just made our food at home, and we'd eat all day. Mardi Gras started early. The idea was to head out at sunrise, go by McKenzie's for doughnuts and King cake, and make it to the parade route before Zulu started to roll, at eight o'clock. On the Uptown route—from Magazine on Napoleon to St. Charles, around Lee Circle down to Canal Street—the prize for a kid was to get there in time to see the Zulu king and catch one of the painted coconuts they'd throw from their floats. Getting a Zulu coconut was a big deal. Spears, too, if you could catch them, real colorful ones, made from bamboo.

THEN WOULD COME Rex, which was the parade to see: Rex is the aristocracy, elaborate, serious. For the Rex krewe, Mardi Gras is religion. Rex threw doubloons, but you'd never pick one up off the ground; people would stomp on them to claim them. They'd throw pretty beads, too, glass or ceramic. After Rex would come the truck parade—20 to 30 floats pulled by 18-wheelers. These were the people's floats, organized by groups like the Masons and the Elks. They'd throw trashier stuff, but lots of it, and as a kid you'd collect garbage bags full and you could really rack up.

Though the celebration has medieval roots, which are still honored in places dominated by the Roman Catholic Church, in New Orleans for most people Mardi Gras is no longer a religious holiday. Our season of Mardi Gras begins on Twelfth Night or Kings' Day, a holy feast day that originally celebrated the three wise men's—the three Kings'—paying homage to the infant Jesus. Today, Kings' Day is most commonly associated with the first

day a King cake can be eaten. And believe me, we will have a King cake in the house every day from Twelfth Night until Mardi Gras.

The King cake is one of the few foods we buy, but you'll find my recipe on page 58. Once called a galette royale or galette des rois, the cake had a miniature *santon*, a replica of a Catholic saint, inserted into the unbaked pastry. Over time the saint was also represented by a fava bean or *fève* (and eventually a little pink plastic baby). The lucky soul who discovers it in his piece is obligated to present the cake at the next year's Mardi Gras. King cake is usually a braided, round Danish pastry, decorated with sugary icing in the vivid colors of Mardi Gras: purple for justice, green for prosperity, and gold for honor. People gravitate to their favorite neighborhood bakery. I was raised on McKenzie's King cake, so I opt for the traditional flavor, while others prefer theirs stuffed with Creole cream cheese, apple, or other fruit.

It's true that there is a Mardi Gras taking place in every household and in every neighborhood of New Orleans on Fat Tuesday, but I don't know anybody who takes it more seriously than Timmy Reily, one of the nicest people you'll ever meet. Timmy is the most dedicated reveler of the Mardi Gras season I've ever come across. As part of the

Dancing in the streets:
Zulu parade in the 1970s, opposite. King cake from Randazzo's Camellia City Bakery, below left. Above, Chief of the Black Eagles from the New Orleans Mardi Gras Indian Tribe, 1978.

city's high society, he was born into those circles that one associates with the finer Mardi Gras krewes, a tradition that dates back generations. But what makes Tim so special is that he does Mardi Gras for love, for the enjoyment of the entire community, helping to make it the most spectacular, free, and entertaining event for everyone. For Timmy, preparations for the following year begin the day after Mardi Gras. As a lieutenant of the Rex krewe, he organizes efforts to clean up the city, works with designers on the next year's floats, plans the repairs to this float or that, and obsesses over a million details to ensure that everything will be shipshape for the next season. Timmy's year, Timmy's life, begins and ends with Mardi Gras.

I FIRST MET TIMMY when I was cooking at the Windsor Court. The Reilys are a legendary family in this town: Reily Foods makes Luzianne coffee and tea, and I'm the biggest fan of its Blue Plate mayonnaise. We became close friends just before I opened August. In the months before Mardi Gras, planning for the elaborate ceremonies is traditionally done over dainty tea sandwiches. But that's not Tim's style. Mardi Gras season at Timmy's house features a casual brunch, where friends and family gather to cook and savor slow-cooked grillades of veal served over creamy stone-ground grits, warm buttermilk biscuits with Steen's cane syrup, and crispy beignets drifting white powdered sugar. It wouldn't be brunch at the Reilys' without a sip or two of brandy milk punch. It was Timmy Reily, and those closest to him, who saw to it that Mardi Gras continued just months after Katrina wrecked our city. Why? Because he understood that Mardi Gras is not just a party. It's that crucial glue that keeps our city bonded. It is the one thing we can all agree on: that there's no place we'd rather be than down on the streets watching the Zulu parade swing on by, waiting for the surprise of the black Mardi Gras Indians to dazzle us with their fantastic costumes, hearing the drums beating so loud, with the smell of fresh-baked French bread, rich coffee, sausages browning in the pot, red beans perfumed with bay leaves simmering away, spicy seafood beginning to boil. We munch on fried chicken and fried crawfish and meat pies and revel in the spirit of Mardi Gras that brings us all together, with food and music that we all love so dearly or we wouldn't be here. We eat our jambalaya with children on our shoulders as we dance to the beat of a city bursting with music. This is New Orleans, and it's good to be alive!

Pageantry: Banquet of the Carnival kings, 1912; photo: John N. Teunisson. Opposite, Timmy Reily, properly masked, as a lieutenant of Rex krewe.

GRANDMOTHER WALTERS'S BISCUITS

Makes about 1 dozen

I believe the secret to my grandmother Grace's biscuits is that she would talk to them, saying, "Rise, Mr. Biscuit, rise!" And they would. Her buttermilk biscuits were quite similar to these, made with whole milk, but sometimes she'd substitute buttermilk and use baking soda instead of baking powder.

I find that biscuits made with European-style high-fat butter have less water and therefore taste and look a lot better. After you have made the dough, carefully pat it down with your hands and fold it over two or three times; it's the layers that make biscuits so flaky. Let the dough rest for half an hour or so, roll it out to the thickness you like, then cut it into circles and bake it.

2 cups all-purpose flour, plus more for dusting	1 teaspoon salt
2 tablespoons baking powder	5 tablespoons cold butter, preferably European style, diced
2 teaspoons sugar	1 cup whole milk

1. Preheat the oven to 425°. Sift the flour, baking powder, sugar, and salt into a mixing bowl. Using a fork or a pastry cutter, cut the butter into the flour until it resembles cornmeal. Add the milk, stirring until the dough just comes together to form a ball.

2. Turn the dough out onto a well-floured surface. Gently pat the dough down with your hands and fold it over on itself. Pat the dough down and fold it over once or twice more. Loosely cover the dough with a clean kitchen towel and let it rest for a half hour or so.

3. Being careful not to overwork the dough, roll it out until it is ¾ to 1 inch thick. Cut dough into biscuits using whatever cutter you like. Grandmother used an inverted juice glass, which was really an old preserves jar. For more biscuits, use a smaller glass.

4. Place the biscuits on a cookie sheet and bake until uniformly golden brown, 10–14 minutes.

A light hand with the dough makes all the difference. Fold the dough over several times to add flaky texture. I like to cut my biscuits with a water glass, left.

BEIGNETS

Makes 30

Like many delicious treats, this preparation takes a bit of time and planning. You can speed up the process of proofing the dough if you leave the dough covered at room temperature for an hour or so, instead of letting it rest in the refrigerator overnight.

1 cup lukewarm milk, about 110°	½ teaspoon salt
½ cup granulated sugar	½ teaspoon vanilla extract
1 package dry yeast	4–6 cups canola oil
4 cups all-purpose flour	1 cup powdered sugar
½ cup melted butter	

1. Pour the warm milk into a large bowl. Mix 1 tablespoon of the granulated sugar, the yeast, and a heaping tablespoon of the flour into the milk, mixing with a whisk, until both the sugar and the yeast have dissolved.

2. Once bubbles have developed on the surface of the milk and it begins to foam, whisk in the butter, salt, and vanilla. Add the remaining flour and sugar, folding them into the wet ingredients with a large rubber spatula. Knead the dough by hand in the bowl for about 5 minutes, then cover the bowl with plastic wrap and refrigerate the dough for 6–8 hours.

3. Remove the dough from the refrigerator and roll out on a floured surface to a thickness of ¼ inch. Cut into 2-inch squares, cover loosely with plastic wrap, and allow the beignets rise for about an hour.

4. Heat the oil in a large deep skillet over high heat until it reaches 350°. Use a candy thermometer to check temperature. Fry the beignets in small batches in the hot oil, turning them every 30 seconds or so with tongs, until golden brown all over. Use tongs to remove beignets from the oil and drain on paper towels. Put the powdered sugar into a fine-mesh strainer and dust the warm beignets generously with the sugar.

Sugar baby: Timmy's daughter Katy Rubion greets a just-fried beignet. Opposite, Mardi Gras brunch table, ready for the celebration.

Grits

What I look for in grits is minimal processing because the mixture of textures—some bigger grains and some cornmeal powder—gives good grits an extra creaminess. Most commercial brands grind the corn kernels quickly and crudely, a method that completely loses the corn's texture; the heat it generates causes the grain to oxidize, robbing it of its nutrients. For those reasons alone, nothing beats the old stone-ground cornmeal, because it allows an inconsistent grain size and retains all sorts of goodness.

I favor the grits milled by Frank McEwen, south of Birmingham, Alabama, who transforms organic yellow, white, and blue corn into grains of the most flavorful grits, cornmeal, and polenta around. Frank feeds the corn kernels (from an organic farm in Illinois) into his old-fashioned stone burr gristmill, where they are slowly ground between two granite stones. He then flows the corn through a sifter to separate it from the husks, which he sells as cow feed, and the finely ground cornmeal, for corn bread. He grinds about 4,000 pounds of grits a month. "The stone-ground kind takes longer to cook, at least 30 minutes, maybe more," he says. "The longer they cook, the better they are." Because they still contain the nutritious germ, they need to be refrigerated or frozen. Frank's grits are a living thing.

JALAPEÑO CHEESE GRITS

Serves 6–8

These cheesy grits are the perfect base for veal grillades or almost anything else.

1 cup stone-ground white corn grits (page 362)	2 tablespoons mascarpone or cream cheese
1 jalapeño pepper	¼ cup grated Edam cheese
3 tablespoons butter	Salt

1. Heat 4 cups of water in a large heavy-bottomed pot over high heat until it comes to a boil. Slowly pour in the grits while whisking constantly. Reduce the heat to low, cover, and cook, stirring occasionally with a wooden spoon, for about 20 minutes.

2. While the grits are cooking, pan-roast the jalapeño pepper in a small skillet over high heat until the skin is brown and blistered. Cut the pepper in half lengthwise and remove the skin and the seeds from the pepper and discard. Mince the flesh and add it to the pot of grits.

3. Remove the pot from the heat and fold in the butter, mascarpone, and Edam cheese. Season with salt.

SLOW-COOKED VEAL GRILLADES

Serves 6–8

Grillades is a Creole version of pot roast; the meat is sliced or pounded thin, then slow-cooked in a pungent sauce. If veal shoulder isn't available, substitute boneless, sliced Boston butts of pork. Sure, you can use a leaner cut of veal (and if you do, you'll want to cut the cooking time down by half). But I encourage you to find those cheaper cuts of meat that have much more flavor than either the loin or the leg.

4 pounds boneless veal shoulder, sliced into thin cutlets

Salt

Freshly ground black pepper

2 cups flour

2 teaspoons Basic Creole Spices (page 13)

¼ cup rendered bacon fat

1 large onion, diced

1 stalk celery, diced

½ bell pepper, diced

2 cloves garlic, minced

2 cups canned whole plum tomatoes, drained, seeded, and diced

2 cups Basic Veal Stock (page 14)

Leaves from 1 sprig fresh thyme

1 teaspoon crushed red pepper flakes

1 bay leaf

1 tablespoon Worcestershire

Tabasco

2 green onions, chopped

1. Season the veal cutlets with salt and pepper. Whisk the flour together with the Creole Spices in a medium bowl. Dredge the cutlets in the seasoned flour and shake off excess. Reserve a tablespoon of seasoned flour.

2. Melt the bacon fat in a large skillet over high heat. Fry the cutlets, several at a time, until golden brown on both sides. Take care not to overcrowd the skillet. Remove cutlets from skillet and continue to cook in batches until all the veal has been browned. Set the veal aside while you continue making the sauce.

3. Reduce the heat to medium-high, add the onions to the same skillet, and cook, stirring with a wooden spoon, until they are a deep mahogany color, about 20 minutes. Add the celery, bell pepper, and garlic, reduce the heat to moderate, and continue cooking, stirring often, for about 5 minutes. Sprinkle the 1 tablespoon of reserved seasoned flour into the skillet and stir to mix it into the vegetables.

4. Increase heat to high, stir in the tomatoes and Veal Stock, and cook until it comes to a boil. Reduce the heat to moderate and stir the thyme, pepper flakes, bay leaf, and Worcestershire into the vegetables. Add the veal cutlets, cover, and simmer until the veal is fork tender, about 45 minutes.

5. Season with salt, pepper, and Tabasco, then add the green onions. Serve over creamy Jalapeño Cheese Grits.

GREEN ONION SAUSAGE AND SHRIMP GRAVY

Serves 6–8

In South Louisiana, any sauce is called gravy. This dish would be our equivalent of biscuits and sausage gravy, except we've got all this seafood down here that finds its way into nearly everything. Serve this gravy over biscuits with oeufs au plat, and you've really got something. As a chef, I make this a bit more complicated than it needs to be: I start with the shrimp in the pan, then remove them so they don't overcook, and then I add them back once it's all come together.

1 tablespoon rendered bacon fat	½ green bell pepper, seeded and diced
1 pound green onion pork sausage, removed from casings (page 362)	1 clove garlic, minced
	1 teaspoon crushed red pepper flakes
1 small onion, diced	1 pinch allspice
1 tablespoon flour	2 dashes Worcestershire
1 pound jumbo shrimp, peeled and deveined	⅓ cup diced canned tomatoes
Salt	1 cup Basic Chicken Stock (page 13)
Freshly ground black pepper	Leaves from 1 sprig fresh thyme
	1 green onion, chopped

1. Melt the bacon fat in a large heavy-bottomed pan over high heat, then add the pork sausage and cook, breaking up the meat with the back of a wooden spoon, until it is browned, 12–15 minutes. Add the onions and cook, stirring often with the spoon, until the onions are deep brown, about another 15 minutes.

2. Reduce the heat to moderate, then sprinkle the flour into the pan, stirring to mix it into the sausage and onions. Cook for about 2 minutes to remove the raw flavor from the flour.

3. Season the shrimp with salt and pepper, then add them to the pan, stirring and tossing them with a spatula. Sauté until they turn pink, about 3 minutes.

Remove the shrimp from the pan and set aside while you continue making the sauce.

4. Add the bell pepper, garlic, pepper flakes, allspice, Worcestershire, tomatoes, and Chicken Stock to the pan, stirring well. Increase heat and bring the sauce to a boil. Reduce the heat to low and cook for 15 minutes. Add the thyme, green onions, and shrimp and cook for another 5 minutes. Season with salt and pepper.

OEUFS AU PLAT

Serves 1 or 2

A simple dish like fried eggs can be so good, and because it's so simple it's important to start with the best eggs, butter, and salt you can find. Pay attention to the cooking process and you'll have the most memorable eggs ever.

2 teaspoons softened butter	2 eggs
	2 pinches salt

1. Rub a room-temperature 9-inch skillet with the butter. Place the skillet on the burner without turning it on. Crack the eggs into the skillet on opposite sides of the pan from each other.

2. Turn the heat on to medium-low and cook the eggs until the whites have coagulated and turned opaque. Season the eggs with salt and serve with Green Onion Sausage and Shrimp Gravy, if you like.

KING CAKE

Serves 10–12

As you knead the dough for this Mardi Gras cake, watch for it to begin to pull away from the sides of the mixing bowl. If that doesn't happen (because the moisture content in flour fluctuates with the humidity), add a spoonful or two more flour.

FOR THE CAKE
- 1 cup lukewarm milk, about 110°
- ½ cup granulated sugar
- 2 tablespoons dry yeast
- 3 ¾ cups all-purpose flour
- 1 cup melted butter
- 5 egg yolks, beaten
- 1 teaspoon vanilla extract
- 1 teaspoon grated fresh lemon zest
- 3 teaspoons cinnamon
- Several gratings of fresh nutmeg

FOR THE ICING
- 2 cups powdered sugar
- ¼ cup condensed milk
- 1 teaspoon fresh lemon juice
- Purple, green, and gold decorative sugars
- 1 *fève* (fava bean) or plastic baby to hide in the cake after baking

1. For the cake, pour the warm milk into a large bowl. Whisk in the granulated sugar, yeast, and a heaping tablespoon of the flour, mixing until both the sugar and the yeast have dissolved.

2. Once bubbles have developed on the surface of the milk and it begins to foam, whisk in the butter, eggs, vanilla, and lemon zest. Add the remaining flour, cinnamon, and nutmeg and fold the dry ingredients into the wet ingredients with a large rubber spatula.

3. After the dough comes together, pulling away from the sides of the bowl, shape it into a large ball. Knead the dough on a floured surface until it is smooth and elastic, about 15 minutes.

4. Put the dough back into the bowl, cover with plastic wrap, and set aside in a draft-free place to let it proof, or rise, for 1½ hours or until the dough has doubled in volume.

5. Preheat the oven to 375°. Once the dough has risen, punch it down and divide the dough into 3 equal pieces. Roll each piece of dough between your palms into a long strip, making 3 ropes of equal length. Braid the 3 ropes around one another and then form the braided loaf into a circle, pinching ends together to seal. Gently lay the braided dough on a nonstick cookie sheet and let it rise until it doubles in size, about 30 minutes.

6. Once it's doubled in size, place the cookie sheet in the oven and bake until the braid is golden brown, about 30 minutes. Remove the cake from the oven, place on a wire rack, and allow to cool for 30 minutes.

CARNIVAL-1935

Long before my time: A children's Mardi Gras parade in Slidell, 1935; photo: Charles L. Franck, The Historic New Orleans Collection. Below, Dennis Rubion serves up his father-in-law's milk punch.

7. For the icing, while the cake is cooling, whisk together the powdered sugar, condensed milk, and lemon juice in a bowl until the icing is smooth and very spreadable. If the icing is too thick, add a bit more condensed milk; if it's a touch too loose, add a little more powdered sugar.

8. Once the cake has cooled, spread the icing over the top of the cake and sprinkle with purple, green, and gold decorative sugars while the icing is still wet. Tuck the *fève* or plastic baby into underside of the cake and, using a spatula, slide the cake onto a platter.

TIMMY'S BRANDY MILK PUNCH

Serves 4

My friend Timmy Reily makes the best version of this classic New Orleans drink. He likes to use the finest brandy, but once you've added all the other ingredients the brandy doesn't matter so much. You may need to add a bit more sugar, so taste a little and sweeten as you go.

1 cup brandy	4 gratings fresh nutmeg
3 cups milk	Handful of ice cubes
3 tablespoons powdered sugar	Crushed ice in 4 glasses
1 teaspoon vanilla extract	

1. Put the brandy, milk, sugar, vanilla, nutmeg, and ice cubes into a blender and blend for 20 seconds.

2. Strain into glasses of crushed ice and serve.

Strawberry fields: Henry Amato on the North Shore with his Ponchatoula berries, above and right. Amato makes strawberry wine nearby. Clockwise from top left, squeezing blood oranges, selling Ponchatoula strawberries in the 1930s, Becnel's citrus in the orchard, and at the Orange Festival in Buras, Louisiana, 1930s. Top right, a ceramic strawberry basket.

Strawberry Shortcake on the Champs-Élysées

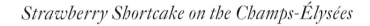

"I'm such a fan of *Iron Chef*, I used to borrow old videotapes of the original Japanese show."

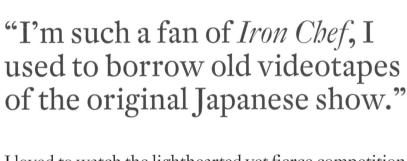

I loved to watch the lighthearted yet fierce competition. Over the years I kept up with these famed Japanese chefs and their challengers, secretly wondering what it would be like to cook my contemporary Louisiana French cuisine under such pressure. Years later, of course, the show came to America on the Food Network. American Iron Chefs were anointed, and the show became instantaneously Americanized with a sobering dose of political correctness. I remember watching the old Japanese shows in amazement as chefs would dive into a tank, retrieve a live brown sea eel, and slay it on air. I'd wonder what I'd do in this situation. The American show won't use foie gras or live any-thing—cook with lobster, and you risk being assaulted

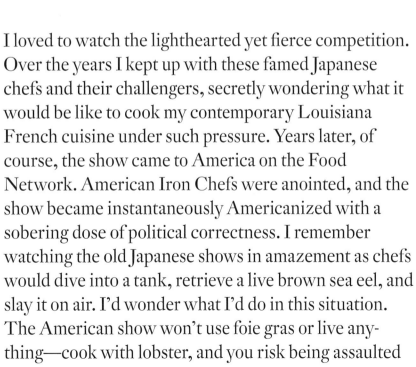

Louisiana citrus: One of our lesser-known treasures, grown by Ben Becnel, top left, with his son, Ben, in Belle Chasse, just south of New Orleans. Above, the Ponchatoula Strawberry Festival Queen cuts a huge shortcake, 1960s.

on the street outside Kitchen Stadium by shellfish protesters dressed up in lobster suits.

The American show was hosted by one of my favorite chefs in the country, Mario Batali. Eventually and out of the blue, I was asked to compete against him. Elated as I was to have been chosen, I was caught completely off guard. The filming was to happen just a couple of months after Katrina hit. Much of our staff had not yet returned; many of us had lost everything—our knives, our chefs' clothes, even our clogs. But we decided to try anyway, to compete against the best.

Against Mario, we didn't even practice. I was too naïve to be scared. I focused on one thing: this had to be good for our business. We decided to head to New York and just have fun. We came as a team needing to let off steam. It was such a great opportunity to show off my guys and give them a boost that I brought everyone I could—our chefs, Steve McHugh, Mike Gulotta, Erick Loos, and Todd Pulsinelli. I wasn't even stressed—that is, until I learned that the secret ingredient was andouille sausage. I knew that Mario and his father make their own andouille. But andouille is *our* ingredient; it's pure Louisiana. Then I knew we had to win. Mario is still a cook at heart, and just thinking about that made me uneasy. But cooking against him turned out to be exciting. We competed well and ultimately defeated Iron Chef Batali.

A YEAR OR SO later, I was invited to embark on a journey to film six episodes of a television show called *The Next Iron Chef*, where, at the end of the competition with seven other chefs, one of us would be named the new Iron Chef America. Again, I decided to compete, not just for myself but for our team, our city, and all of us who have been through so much. So, I set out to represent my people well. That show took me to New York City; to my alma mater, the CIA at Hyde Park; to Munich; and then to Paris. I've been a Francophile all my adult life, and you can imagine my exhilaration when I was told that the fifth episode of this series would take place in the residence of the American ambassador, just steps from the Champs-Élyseés, in a house built in 1855 by one of our own, the notorious New Orleans–born Baroness de Pontalba (she also commissioned the two famous old apartment buildings that border Jackson Square in the heart of the French Quarter). The competition had narrowed to three contestants, Chris Cosentino from San Francisco, Michael Symon from Cleveland, and me. We were

each given 2,000 euros and three hours' shopping time in a selected list of markets to make a three-course dinner for the U.S. ambassador to France and 19 other luminaries. And here's the twist: the menu had to be *American*.

My biggest challenge was to figure out what to serve. My America is not hot dogs and root beer floats. My American food sounds French—maybe too French, I worried. So, I set out to find inspiration. If a cook can't get inspired by the sights, sounds, and smells of a French market, he's got no hope. The French have such style. Just look at their chickens—those venerable *poulets de Bresse*—displayed in a butcher's case in full formation, their chests pushed out, proud of their breed, showing off their ribbons.

And then I came upon the strawberries. Truly, I smelled their fragrance even before I saw them. There were strawberries of every shape and size, though all much smaller than ours. Each berry came from a different region of France, each had its distinct flavor, and each was destined for a different preparation. The one thing all those French strawberries had in common is that, unlike most of our supersize, cottony American berries, all of them tasted wonderful.

WHEN YOU COME from New Orleans, it's scandalous to even *think* of eating any berry but those grown on our North Shore, in Ponchatoula, Louisiana. If America had its version of an *appellation contrôlée*, Ponchatoula strawberries would qualify. My children refuse to eat any other berry (unless they're lucky enough to be in France, that is). French strawberries have, to me, an exaggerated flavor; and as for texture, a great French berry is so soft it won't hold up to the tongue against the roof of the mouth—a good French berry should literally melt in the mouth. And then there are the wild strawberries, or *fraises des bois*, tiny, magic berries; their perfume, like nothing else I've ever smelled.

Fixated on those berries, the idea came to me: I would make strawberry shortcake for my American dinner and serve it with a sorbet of those fragrant *fraises des bois*. At the *poissonnerie*, the fish market, I decided to pay homage to my roots and make a crab BLT (the recipe's in Crab Season, on page 210), with fried Belon oysters and the crabmeat tossed in a sauce ravigote. Those proud *poulets* would become an elegant version of chicken and dumplings (the recipe for a similar dish is on page 221). That I had to work with young French cooks as souschefs didn't throw me, since I had been cooking in French kitchens for years; nor did the fact that the ovens did not function in the American ambassador's kitchen—I just cooked everything on the stovetop. I guess my dinner succeeded, for I was not eliminated that night. I lived to cook another day.

Kitchen Stadium: Under The Chairman's watchful eye, I meet Mario Batali in battle andouille sausage on *Iron Chef America*, 2006. Opposite, building strawberry shortcake on biscuits, (recipe page 79).

STRAWBERRY SHORTCAKE

Serves 8

This is the dish I created for *The Next Iron Chef* at the ambassador's residence in Paris (photo on page 67). It might look complicated, but when you take each component separately, it's as easy as making biscuits, marinating the berries, and freezing a sorbet.

FOR THE SAUCE

- 1 cup Creole cream cheese or fromage blanc
- ⅓ cup heavy cream
- Seeds from half a vanilla bean
- 3 tablespoons granulated sugar

FOR THE BISCUITS

- 2 cups all-purpose flour, plus more for dusting
- ¼ cup granulated sugar
- 2 tablespoons baking powder
- 1 pinch salt

- Grated zest of 1 lemon
- 6 tablespoons cold butter, diced
- ¾ cup whole milk

FOR THE BERRIES

- 2 pints strawberries, hulled and diced
- ¼ cup granulated sugar
- 2 tablespoons Grand Marnier
- Leaves from 1 sprig fresh mint, minced
- 2 cups Watermelon Strawberry Sorbet, or store-bought
- Powdered sugar

1. For the sauce, put the Creole cream cheese, heavy cream, vanilla bean seeds, and granulated sugar into a medium mixing bowl and whisk together until well combined. Cover and refrigerate.

2. For the biscuits, preheat the oven to 400°. Combine 2 cups of the flour, the sugar, baking powder, salt, and lemon zest in a medium mixing bowl. Using a fork or a pastry cutter, cut the butter into the flour until the texture resembles cornmeal.

3. Gradually stir in just enough milk for the dough to form a ball. Be careful not to overwork the dough, or the biscuits will be tough.

4. Roll the dough out on a lightly floured surface to a ¾-inch thickness and cut out 8 disks with a 2½-inch round biscuit or cookie cutter.

5. Place the biscuits on a baking sheet at least 1 inch apart and bake until golden brown, 12–15 minutes. Set aside to let cool.

6. For the berries, toss the berries, granulated sugar, Grand Marnier, and mint together in a medium bowl. Cover and let marinate in the refrigerator for at least 30 minutes and up to 6 hours.

7. To assemble each shortcake, spoon 1–2 tablespoons of the sauce in the center of a dessert plate. Cut a biscuit in half crosswise and set the bottom half on the sauce, cut side up. Spoon some berries over the biscuit and scoop some sorbet on top. Dust the top half of the biscuit with powdered sugar and lean it jauntily on top of the berries.

WATERMELON STRAWBERRY SORBET

Makes about 3 cups

Here's a trick to make sure the sorbet mixture has the right amount of sugar: float a clean egg in it (that's right, shell and all). If the egg sinks, add more sugar to your sorbet mixture. You want the egg to float near the surface, with a nickel-size spot of the egg exposed above the liquid. If it floats more than that, add more juice or water. Then the sorbet mixture is ready to freeze perfectly.

- 1 pint strawberries, hulled
- 1 cup diced seeded watermelon
- 1 teaspoon fresh lemon juice
- ½ cup sugar

1. Purée the strawberries, watermelon, lemon juice, and sugar together in a blender until smooth. Check that the purée has the correct amount of sugar, using the method described above. Add more sugar or juice if necessary.

2. Transfer the purée to the canister of an ice cream maker and process according to the manufacturer's instructions. Keep the sorbet in the freezer until ready to use.

WILD STRAWBERRY FLAMBÉE OVER LEMON RICOTTA–FILLED CRÊPES

Serves 6

I like to cook these crêpes on one side only, so that they don't become brittle when I stuff and roll them. This is a pretty simple recipe; just be careful with the strawberries—cook them too long and they'll fall apart. And have all your ingredients assembled before you begin.

FOR THE CRÊPES
- 1½ cups milk
- 3 eggs
- 1 pinch salt
- 3 tablespoons butter, melted
- 1½ cups all-purpose flour
- Cooking spray

FOR THE FILLING
- 2 cups ricotta cheese
- Grated zest of 1 lemon
- Grated zest of 1 orange
- 1 teaspoon vanilla extract
- ½ cup sugar

FOR THE SAUCE
- ½ cup sugar
- 3 cups wild strawberries, hulled
- ½ cup fresh orange juice
- ¼ cup Grand Marnier
- 2 tablespoons butter

1. For the crêpes, put the milk and eggs into a blender and blend them thoroughly for just a few seconds. With the blender running at low speed, add the salt, melted butter, and flour, in that order, through the feed hole in the blender lid, blending the batter until it is smooth. Refrigerate the batter, covered, for at least 30 minutes and up to 4 hours.

2. Heat a 6-inch nonstick skillet over low heat. Spray it with the cooking spray. Pour a couple of tablespoons of batter into the center of the skillet and swirl the skillet around to make 1 thin, even layer of batter. The goal is not to brown the crêpe but to cook it just enough to flip. Once the crêpe gets lacy around the edges and pulls away from the skillet, about 2 minutes, slide a nonstick spatula underneath and flip the crêpe over. Cook the second side for only about 30 seconds (or not at all). Transfer the crêpe to a large plate. Repeat the process with the remaining batter, making about 18 crêpes in all. (Once the crêpes are cooked, they can be stacked and wrapped in plastic for later use.)

3. For the filling, put the ricotta, citrus zests, vanilla, and sugar into a medium mixing bowl and stir until smooth.

4. Preheat the oven to 200°. Lay a crêpe out on a clean surface, cooked side down. Put 2 tablespoons of the filling in the center of the crêpe and smooth it out with the back of the spoon. Fold the crêpe in half, then fold it in half again into a quarter. Repeat the filling and folding process with the remaining crêpes and filling. Set the folded crêpes on a cookie sheet and keep them warm in the oven.

5. For the sauce, heat a large sauté pan over high heat until warm. Add the sugar and strawberries and cook until the sugar starts to caramelize, about 5 minutes. Add the orange juice and Grand Marnier. Using a long-handled lighter, very carefully ignite the alcohol in the pan. Stand back from the stove, as the flames may shoot up. Once the flames burn out, stir in the butter.

6. To serve, arrange 3 crêpes on each of 6 dessert plates and spoon some wild strawberry sauce over the crêpes.

SIMPLE STRAWBERRY AND CREOLE CREAM CHEESE ICE CREAM

Makes 1 quart

At the height of strawberry season, our restaurants will go through cases of strawberries each day. Every night before closing, our cooks sort the berries, removing those that are at peak ripeness, and we'll purée and freeze them. No sugar, no cooking; just purée and freeze. We do this often at home, and Jenifer uses the purées for ice cream or with champagne or in a daiquiri.

- 2 cups Creole cream cheese or fromage blanc
- 1 cup strawberry purée
- ½ cup sugar
- ¼ cup heavy cream

1. Put the Creole cream cheese, strawberry purée, sugar, and cream into a medium heavy-bottomed saucepan and heat over moderate heat, whisking constantly, until the sugar has dissolved.

2. Transfer the cream mixture to a bowl, cover, and refrigerate until the mixture is cold.

3. Pour the chilled cream mixture into the canister of an ice cream maker and process according to the manufacturer's instructions.

Cream of the crop: Heather Robertson, left, sells Ponchatoula strawberries at our Uptown Farmers Market. Top, strawberry ice cream and wild strawberries. Warren Smith, above, at Smith Creamery, in Mt. Hermon, supplies our milk, cream, and butter, all from his grass-fed cows.

Ponchatoula Strawberries

Ponchatoula, a town in Tangipahoa Parish, north of New Orleans, has been synonymous with strawberries for almost a century now, ever since buyers used to flock down here from New York and Chicago to bid for our early-ripening spring crop. So esteemed was their quality that during the 1920s nearly 30,000 acres were planted to fill the hundreds of railway cars that were whisked away every April on a special fruit train known as the Crimson Flyer.

Tangipahoa went from being the most economically impoverished parish in the state to becoming the leading supplier of strawberries in America. Conveniently situated on the Illinois Central Railroad line, Ponchatoula had a climate that produced the first batch of the year, to brighten the jaded winter palates of the wealthy (elsewhere in the country the season began in May/June), enough straw for mulching, and trees to provide essential buffering. The industry was so critical to local families that schools would shut down during the March picking season so that children could roll up their sleeves and help.

Today, the nationwide strawberry industry operates differently, and we no longer compete on that level. Our strawberries, however, are still splendid and succulent, and we have some 500 acres planted with the Strawberry Festival and Camarosa varieties, which continue to uphold the past and present glory of the Ponchatoula strawberry—just closer to home.

STRAWBERRY RAVIOLI WITH MEYER LEMONS AND PISTACHIOS

Serves 6

This is, admittedly, a restaurant dessert, but it's doable at home if you break it down into steps. First make the pasta, then the filling; then form the ravioli. Freeze the ravioli, and don't remove them from the freezer until you're ready to drop them into boiling water. You can make the sauces an hour or two before dinner, so that everything is at your fingertips when you're ready to serve. Substitute regular lemons and lemon oil if you must.

FOR THE FILLING
- 1 cup strawberries, hulled
- ½ cup sugar
- ¼ teaspoon finely minced fresh lavender flowers
- 1 cup mascarpone cheese

FOR THE RAVIOLI
- 1 pound all-purpose flour, plus more for dusting
- ¼ cup unsweetened cocoa powder
- 1 pinch salt
- 5 eggs
- 1 teaspoon olive oil

FOR THE STRAWBERRY SAUCE
- 2 cups strawberries, quartered
- 2 tablespoons sugar
- ½ cup toasted shelled pistachios

FOR THE FROTH
- 1 cup heavy cream
- 1 cup fresh orange juice
- 1 tablespoon fresh Meyer lemon juice
- ¼ cup sugar
- 1½ tablespoons Meyer lemon oil
- Small fresh mint leaves

1. For the filling, put the strawberries, sugar, and lavender flowers into a small saucepan and cook over medium-high heat for 15 minutes. Remove the pan from the heat and let the strawberries cool. Put the cooled strawberries, their syrup, and the mascarpone into a blender and purée until smooth. Transfer the filling to a pastry bag fitted with a large plain pastry tip. Keep the filling refrigerated until ready to use.

2. For the ravioli, beat the flour, cocoa powder, a pinch of salt, eggs, and olive oil together in the bowl of a standing mixer fitted with the paddle attachment on moderate speed until a dough forms. Cover the dough with plastic wrap and let it rest for 30 minutes.

3. Divide the dough into 6 pieces and shape them into 2-by-2-inch squares. Set them on a floured surface and cover them with plastic wrap.

4. Working with one piece of dough at a time, feed the dough through the smooth cylinders of a pasta machine set on the widest setting. Fold the dough into thirds and feed the narrow end through the cylinders again. Repeat this folding and feeding process 5 or 6 times more until the dough is smooth.

5. Feed the wide end of the dough through the cylinders set on the widest setting. Decrease the setting by 1 notch and feed the narrow end of the pasta through the cylinders again. Repeat, decreasing setting by 1 notch each time. On the final setting, the dough will come out in a long sheet about 1/16 inch thick. Cut the sheet of pasta in half crosswise.

6. Drape the sheet of pasta over a ravioli mold. Pipe some of the prepared filling into each pocket in the sheet of pasta. Brush the edges of the ravioli with water and lay the other sheet of pasta over the mold. Using a rolling pin, roll it over the length of the mold to crimp and seal the ravioli. Invert the ravioli mold and place the ravioli on a parchment paper–lined cookie sheet. Repeat the pasta making and filling process with the remaining pieces of dough and filling, making 36 ravioli in all. Freeze the ravioli until ready to use.

7. For the strawberry sauce, sauté the strawberries and sugar together in a large skillet over medium-high heat, stirring frequently, until the berries soften and the juices in the skillet are syrupy, 3–5 minutes. Set the skillet aside.

8. Bring a large pot of lightly salted water to a boil over high heat. Add the ravioli and cook for 3 minutes. Drain the ravioli and gently toss them with the strawberry sauce.

9. Divide the ravioli between 6 wide bowls. Spoon some of the strawberry sauce over each and scatter a few pistachios over the top.

10. For the froth, bring the cream, citrus juices, sugar, and lemon oil to a boil in a medium deep saucepan over medium-high heat. Reduce the heat to low. Using an electric hand mixer, half-submerge the beaters in the cream mixture and beat on high until a rich froth forms.

11. Spoon a small scoop of lemon froth on each bowl of ravioli and scatter mint leaves over the top.

STRAWBERRY MILLEFEUILLE

Serves 6

This elegant dessert depends on a Creole cream cheese mousse that's light and airy. The key is to measure out everything ahead and complete each step in the proper sequence. To save a little time you can make the pastry and strawberry gelée a day or two ahead.

FOR THE PASTRY

- 2¼ cups all-purpose flour, plus more for dusting
- ½ cup powdered sugar
- 12 tablespoons cold butter, diced
- Grated zest of 1 orange
- 1 egg
- Cooking spray

FOR THE GELÉE

- 3 cups strawberries, hulled
- ¾ cup granulated sugar
- ½ cup fresh orange juice
- ¼ cup Creole Shrubb orange rum liqueur or orange liqueur
- 2 envelopes unflavored gelatin

FOR THE MOUSSE

- 2 eggs
- ⅓ cup granulated sugar
- 1 envelope unflavored gelatin
- ½ cup Creole Shrubb orange rum liqueur
- ¾ cup heavy cream
- 2 tablespoons Creole cream cheese or fromage blanc, at room temperature
- 1 cup strawberries, hulled

1. For the pastry, put the flour and powdered sugar into the bowl of a standing mixer fitted with the paddle attachment and mix together on low speed. Continue to mix on medium-low speed while adding the butter, a few pieces at a time, beating until all the butter is fully combined.

2. Beat in the orange zest and egg on moderate speed until well combined and the dough is smooth, about 1 minute. Shape the dough into a squat, square block. Wrap the dough in plastic wrap and refrigerate for 1 hour.

3. Preheat the oven to 325°. Line a 9-by-9-inch baking pan with parchment paper and coat it evenly with cooking spray.

4. Roll the dough out on a lightly floured surface into a 9-inch square about ¼ inch thick and transfer to the prepared pan. Bake the pastry until it is golden brown, 12 minutes. Remove the pastry from the oven and let it cool to room temperature, then transfer it, still in the pan, to the refrigerator and let it rest for 30 minutes.

5. For the gelée, combine 2 cups of the strawberries, the granulated sugar, orange juice, and orange liqueur in a medium bowl and let macerate for 20 minutes. Transfer the strawberry mixture to a blender and purée until smooth.

6. Sprinkle the gelatin into ¼ cup cool water in a small bowl and let swell and soften. Put 2 cups of the strawberry purée into a small saucepan, saving the rest for another use (morning toast!), and heat over moderate heat until just hot. Remove the pan from the heat and whisk in the gelatin until it is completely dissolved. Let the gelée cool to room temperature.

7. Dice the remaining 1 cup of strawberries and set aside. Pour the gelée over the chilled pastry in the pan, then quickly scatter the diced strawberries evenly over the top and lightly press them into the gelée with your fingertips. Loosely wrap the pastry in plastic wrap and refrigerate for 45 minutes.

8. For the mousse, set a large heatproof bowl over a pot of simmering water over moderate heat. Whisk the eggs and granulated sugar together in the bowl, whisking constantly until the mixture is thick. Continue to beat the eggs and sugar together over the water bath, beating vigorously until they are pale yellow and have tripled in volume, about 15 minutes. Remove the bowl from the heat.

9. Sprinkle the gelatin into ¼ cup cool water in a small bowl and let swell and soften. Warm the liqueur in a small saucepan over low heat. Remove the pan from the heat and whisk in the gelatin until it is completely dissolved. Fold the rum gelatin into the whipped eggs.

10. Working quickly, beat the heavy cream in a large mixing bowl with an electric mixer on high speed until soft peaks form. Fold in the Creole cream cheese, then fold into the whipped egg-rum mixture.

11. Unwrap the pastry from the refrigerator and immediately spread the mousse evenly over the top. Return the pastry to the refrigerator, uncovered, and let it set for another 45 minutes.

12. Carefully slice the pastry with a hot knife or a square cutter, left, into 6 individual squares. Stack one layer on top of the other and serve each on a plate with fresh strawberries.

AMBROSIA

Serves 6

My grandmother wouldn't make Ambrosia this way, but then she didn't have Ben Becnel's citrus farm in Plaquemines Parish nearby. Fall is our citrus season, and ambrosia is a great way to use all our different varieties of citrus at once. If you can't get your hands on this many varieties of citrus, just use what you can find.

2	satsuma or other mandarin oranges	4	kumquats, washed, thinly sliced crosswise, and seeded
2	navel oranges	1	cup sugarcane juice or simple syrup
2	blood oranges	1	whole coconut
2	ruby red grapefruits		Small leaves from 10 sprigs fresh mint
12	red seedless grapes, halved		

1. Using a sharp knife and working with one piece of fruit at a time, remove the segments of oranges and grapefruit by first cutting off the top and bottom of each fruit. Then stand the fruit on one end and slice from top to bottom, between the white pith and the fruit. Cut around the entire orange and grapefruit, removing as much peel as possible and leaving as much of the flesh as you can.

2. Working over a bowl to catch the juices, cut out each fruit segment from between the membranes on each side. Put the segments into the bowl and squeeze whatever juice remains in the cut fruit center into the same bowl. Discard the spent centers.

3. Add the grapes and kumquats to the bowl of citrus segments and juice and gently stir in the sugarcane juice or simple syrup.

4. Crack open the coconut with a hammer and save the coconut water for another use, if you like. Pry the flesh from the shell, then discard the shell. Using a vegetable peeler, shave long ribbons of coconut and add them to the bowl of fruit. Scatter mint leaves over the salad.

Louisiana Citrus

Citrus trees have taken to our rich Louisiana soil and warm, humid climate since the days when sailors would disembark at the port of New Orleans and scatter the seeds from the fruit they had consumed on their travels to ward off scurvy. Plaquemines Parish, just outside New Orleans and our state's warmest pocket, was an ideal spot for the fruits of those journeys. During the mid-1800s, and even throughout the Civil War, our navel oranges were sent across the country by railroad.

Another juicy detail of our citrus heritage is that we were among the first states to grow the satsuma (*Citrus unshiu*), that small, sweet, seedless member of the mandarin family, grown on trees brought back from a diplomat's trip to Japan. Unlike California and Florida, we have never been able to develop a formal citrus industry, because Louisiana gets hit every 20 years or so by a killer freeze that wipes out every last tree. But we all grow citrus in our backyards; they're such blessedly generous providers that one grapefruit tree can produce as much as 500 pounds of fruit.

Plaquemines Parish supplies us with all the citrus we need, growing some 20 types of citrus, including ruby, red, and white grapefruits; our favorite Meyer lemons; sweet and sour kumquats; Valencia, navel, red navel, and blood oranges; and several types of satsuma and mandarin. No risk of scurvy in these parts.

PRESERVED MEYER LEMONS

Makes 24 preserved lemon halves

Yes, you can preserve regular lemons using this recipe—a variation of a North African process we love—but Meyer lemons are so much more fragrant. Preserved lemons can spark up roast chicken, fish, crab salad, stews, and any light meat, such as baby goat, veal, and rabbit.

12 Meyer lemons, washed	Freshly squeezed
1 cup sea salt	Meyer lemon juice

1. Trim off and discard both ends of each lemon. Cut the lemons in half crosswise and squeeze the juices into a clean, lidded glass jar large enough to accommodate the lemons snugly. Rub the spent lemon halves all over with the salt, packing the cavities with any leftover salt, and fit the lemons into the jar. If there isn't enough lemon juice in the jar to cover the lemons, add more freshly squeezed juice.

2. Tightly cover the jar with the lid and store the lemons in the refrigerator, turning the jar upside down and right side up again every few days.

3. The lemons will be ready to use when the rinds have become a deep orangey yellow and the texture has become soft and supple. This will take at least 1 month. The lemons will keep in the refrigerator for another 6 months.

4. To use the preserved lemons in cooking, first rinse the lemon under cold running water. Cut the rind away from the flesh, discarding the flesh and seeds. The supple, salty rind is now ready to use.

Good as gold: Evans Breaux III harvests citrus at Becnel's farm in Plaquemines Parish. Opposite, lemons prepared for preserving.

LOCAL GOAT CHEESE SEMIFREDDO

Serves 8

I'd invest in a candy thermometer before making this dessert. It's actually quite easy, but it does take a little focus. It's important to cook the sugar carefully so that it gets hot enough but doesn't burn. When we add hot sugar to whipped egg whites, we call it an Italian meringue.

1 cup heavy cream	1 teaspoon freshly grated lemon zest, preferably from a Meyer lemon
¾ cup sugar	
4 egg whites	
1 cup fresh goat cheese, at room temperature	1 teaspoon vanilla extract

1. Beat the heavy cream in the bowl of a standing mixer fitted with the whisk attachment on medium-high speed until soft peaks form. Transfer the whipped cream to another bowl, cover, and refrigerate.

2. Stir the sugar and ¼ cup cold water together in a small saucepan, then let the mixture boil over medium-high heat until the syrup reaches the soft-ball stage or 235° on a candy thermometer.

3. Meanwhile, put the egg whites into the clean bowl of the standing mixer fitted with the clean whisk attachment and beat on medium speed until the whites are frothy. Increase the speed to high and continue beating until the whites hold medium-stiff peaks. Continue beating on high speed and gradually pour in the hot syrup in a slow, steady stream. Beat continuously until the whites are smooth and glossy and have cooled to room temperature, about 10 minutes.

4. Mix together the goat cheese, lemon zest, and vanilla extract in a small bowl, then gently fold the mixture into the egg whites. Fold in the whipped cream.

5. Line a terrine roughly 3 inches by 3 inches by 12 inches with plastic wrap and transfer the semifreddo mixture to the terrine. Cover with another sheet of plastic wrap and put into the freezer to let chill until firm, a couple of hours.

6. Tip the semifreddo out of the mold, unwrap, and scoop or slice into 1-inch-thick slices. Serve with Chilled Blood Orange Soup, if you like.

CHILLED BLOOD ORANGE SOUP

Serves 6

Arrowroot is a good, gentle thickener for this soup; if you add a touch more arrowroot, it will become a blood orange sauce.

Freshly grated zest from 1 blood orange	½ cup sugar
	1 tablespoon arrowroot
4 cups blood orange juice (from about 15–20 blood oranges)	1 recipe Local Goat Cheese Semifreddo, optional
1 teaspoon fresh lemon juice	Leaves from 2 sprigs fresh mint

1. Put the blood orange zest and juice, the lemon juice, and the sugar into a medium heavy-bottomed saucepan and bring to a simmer over moderate heat.

2. Meanwhile, make a slurry by mixing the arrowroot with 2 tablespoons cold water in a small bowl, then drizzle it into the simmering juice, stirring constantly. Reduce the heat to medium-low and continue to simmer the juice, stirring often, for 2 minutes. Remove the pan from the heat and set aside to let the soup cool. Refrigerate the soup until completely chilled.

3. Divide the soup among 6 chilled soup bowls and serve with a large scoop of the semifreddo, if you like. Scatter mint leaves over the soup.

LOUISIANA CITRUS POTS DE CRÈME WITH LAVENDER MADELEINES

Serves 8

The best way to eat these lovely custards is to dip into them with hot madeleines fresh out of the oven. Make the pots de crème a day or two in advance; wait until they are completely cooled, then wrap them tightly and store in the refrigerator.

FOR THE POTS DE CRÈME

- 2 cups heavy cream
- 1 cup granulated sugar
- ¼ cup fresh lemon juice, preferably from Meyer lemons
- ¼ cup fresh orange juice, from satsuma oranges or tangerines
- 1 tablespoon freshly grated orange zest
- ¼ teaspoon vanilla extract
- ¼ teaspoon lemon oil
- 4 whole eggs
- 4 egg yolks

FOR THE MADELEINES

- 2 tablespoons butter, softened
- ¾ cup granulated sugar, plus more for dusting
- 3 eggs
- 1 teaspoon freshly grated lemon zest
- ½ teaspoon vanilla extract
- 1⅓ cups all-purpose flour
- 1 teaspoon dried lavender blossoms
- ½ cup clarified butter, at room temperature
- Powdered sugar for dusting

1. For the pots de crème, preheat the oven to 325°. Put the cream, granulated sugar, citrus juices, orange zest, vanilla, and lemon oil into a medium heavy-bottomed saucepan, bring to a boil over high heat, stirring often, then immediately reduce the heat to low.

2. Whisk the whole eggs and the yolks together in a large mixing bowl until well combined. Slowly pour about one-third of the hot cream mixture into the eggs, whisking constantly to keep the eggs from curdling. Gradually add the remaining hot cream, whisking constantly.

3. Strain the custard into 8 pot de crème cups or other small ramekins. Set the cups in a pan and pour enough boiling water into the pan so that it reaches halfway up the sides of the cups. Carefully transfer the pan to the oven and bake the custards until they are fully set, about 30 minutes. Remove the cups from the water bath and set them on a wire rack to let cool. Wrap the pots de crème well and refrigerate them until cold.

4. For the madeleines, preheat the oven to 450°. Grease the molds of a madeleine cake pan with some of the softened butter and dust the molds with some of the granulated sugar.

5. Beat the eggs, ¾ cup of the granulated sugar, and lemon zest together in a large mixing bowl with an electric mixer on high speed until the mixture is light and fluffy and has tripled in volume. Stir in the vanilla. Gently fold in the flour, then the lavender, then the clarified butter.

6. Fill each madeleine mold two-thirds full with the batter and bake the cakes until golden brown, 7–8 minutes. Remove the madeleines from the oven and let them rest for a minute or two before tipping them out of their molds.

7. Prepare the madeleine cake pan again with more of the softened butter and granulated sugar and repeat the filling and baking process with the remaining batter, buttering and sugaring the molds with each batch, making approximately 40 madeleines in all.

8. Serve each pot de crème with a small plate of warm madeleines dusted with powdered sugar.

CHAPTER 4

FEAST DAYS

Easter on Bayou Liberty:
Spring's in full swing, and it's warm enough to drag a table and chairs out to the lawn for a feast of slow-roasted goat. Top left, our Easter basket. Right, making chocolate Easter eggs at Fuerst and Kraemer, a classic old candy manufacturer in New Orleans; photo: Covert.

On Faith and Food

"All our holy days are rooted in one food tradition or another; sometimes we feast and sometimes we abstain."

I have friends of nearly every faith—or the major ones, at least—and it always intrigues me how great a role religion plays in what we eat. We may be what we eat, but we certainly eat what we profess to believe. Had New Orleans been founded by teetotalers, I doubt that we'd have the oldest coffee culture in the States; nor would we be the cocktail capital of the world.

The immigrants who built our city's foodways brought with them the best of their own. As a very young man, I spent a lot of time with Joe Gendusa, who was from an old Sicilian family in New Orleans. When I ate with Mr. Joe, I could put my elbows on the table and have fun. We'd eat bracciolini of veal, piles

Making Easter Eggs
Fverst & Kraemer Ltd.

of pasta, jumbo shrimp with garlic, and artichokes stuffed with crabmeat and shrimp—food I can still taste today. His family had a famous bakery that claimed to have invented the "poor boy," the po'boy sandwich. Mr. Joe's mother would chop up her holy trinity— onion, celery, and bell pepper—and sell it from the bakery. Southern Italians prize the holy trinity as a base for sauces and stews, and the Spanish, too, who call it sofrito and use it in much the same way. Years later, Mr. Joe started a company that cut, packaged, and froze one-pound blocks of the holy trinity, and I'd help him distribute it to every grocer in the city. Most of the groceries in town were owned by southern Italians who had farms either on the North Shore or south in St. Bernard Parish. As we toured those grocery stores, we'd never leave empty-handed; there'd always be a lagniappe for us to take home—you know, a little something extra. (For years, New Orleans resisted supermarket chains, but eventually the chains prevailed, nearly putting every small grocery out of business. It's a dream of mine to re-create an old New Orleans Italian grocery someday, selling artisanal foods raised by people who care.)

T HE SICILIAN COMMUNITY has had a profound impact on our city's culinary lexicon. Today, churches of Creole, German, Irish, and French origins all celebrate the patron saint of Sicily, San Giuseppe, or Saint Joseph, who reputedly saved the island from famine in the Middle Ages. On March 19, St. Joseph's Day, churches commemorate his feast day by decorating their altars with extravagant food displays. One of my favorite things is to help the ladies of our parish prepare our Saint Joseph's altar. The patron saint is honored by a mind-boggling array of Sicilian cookies, pastries, pastas, sauces, and condiments—dishes whose recipes have remained pretty much unchanged over centuries.

Though neither Jenifer nor I has Italian roots, Brendan, our oldest son, is torn between loving St. Patrick's Day, which falls just two days before his birthday, when he's allowed to break his Lenten fast, and celebrating his birthday itself, which falls on March 19, St. Joseph's Day, when he's again permitted to break his Lenten fast and gets to play Saint Joseph at the altar in our parish. There, he feasts on plates of pasta Milanese, stuffed artichokes, baked redfish, fig cake, biscotti, almond amaretti, and pignolati. His younger brother Jack, who played Jesus Christ on last year's St. Joseph's Day, proclaimed it his favorite day because, as Jesus, he got to eat all the cookies he wanted.

Most of the immigrants who settled New Orleans did have a common religion or two, and over time those cultures began to merge.

Abundance: Celebrating St. Joseph's Day in Gretna, opposite, at St. Joseph's Church, which has the largest altar in New Orleans, 2003; photo: Kerri McCaffety. The Francos' seder plate at their annual Passover dinner, above.

That could be why even the Irish families in New Orleans would eat cod cakes during the Lenten season, a practice that probably didn't come from Ireland but likely came from the Spanish or even the Italians, who arrived here some years after the Irish.

HISTORICALLY, NEW ORLEANS has had a large Jewish community, which has adopted local customs and dining traditions that wouldn't exactly fit in a kosher kitchen. One of my good friends and our resident rabbi points out that some families (who'll remain nameless) have even been known to eat crabmeat and shrimp on the High Holy Days. Over the years, our friends Alan Franco and his wife, Diane, always generously welcome our employees to their home to enjoy a seder with their family. And every year we'll have a Passover dinner at Restaurant August, where 30 or so people will gather to feast on our Red Bluff Farm baby lamb, our special Lüke matzo ball soup, handmade matzo, and charoses with apples, nuts, and . . . figs.

Another dear friend, chef Alon Shaya, came to New Orleans from Israel and had no Jewish friends. One day at our house, our friend Father Randy Roux, a Catholic priest, heard about Alon's predicament and quietly set off to visit every synagogue in the city. What a sight that must have been: Father Roux, dressed in his typical Catholic priest's garb, requesting information on joining the synagogue. The next week, he sat down with Alon and gave him all the information he needed to connect with the Jewish community in town. What a great example of "only in New Orleans."

The food traditions of both Passover and the Easter season are important as we transition from the heavier dishes of winter to lighter spring fare. The new grass greens up, young leaves appear on the trees, and our strawberries and Louisiana citrus come into season together.

I fell in love with the big, bold, and honest flavors of Greek Easter while working with Constantine Chris Kerageorgiou, a Frenchman with Greek Orthodox roots who owned La Provence, where I cooked for years. My ramped-up use of olive oil and garlic today is probably due to the influences of my gregarious late mentor, who'd have me go down to the Greek church on Bayou St. John to borrow the spits to impale a baby goat. I'd buy that goat from the Arab market, where they most

Happy days: Jenifer Besh with Andrew at our Easter lunch, below. At Red Bluff Farm in Folsom, Louisiana, our young goats and sheep frolic and range free.

Joie de vivre: My mentor, chef Chris Kerageorgiou of La Provence, with his sidekick, Gofreddo Ficaro, filming an early television show in the late 1970s.

certainly weren't French—or Greek—but did have the best local baby goats and lamb in the area. That's right; those markets would contract with farmers on the North Shore and in southern Mississippi to raise the sheep and goats that supplied both the Islamic and the Greek communities of New Orleans. Go figure.

CHEF CHRIS WOULD have me cook that goat over a small open fire— just a few pieces of charcoal at a time—and let that tender young animal roast all night. I'd continuously lubricate it with oregano, lemon juice, and olive oil, using branches of rosemary to baste with. I would make the fire off-center, so the heat would be indirect; that allowed us to place a pan underneath the carcass and catch every single tasty dripping. That's how the vegetables and the potatoes would cook—with the ambient heat of the charcoal and the warm drippings that fell from the spit. The result, some eight hours later, was tender and aromatic beyond belief.

The only problem I had with this approach was that some of the muscles, like the legs and the loins, weren't as tender as they'd have been if they'd been roasted. So, I figured out a way to slow-cook the neck and shoulders with all the aromatics that I love but then remove the meat from the neck and shoulder bones and stuff it into the deboned legs, which we then roast. That way we have medium-rare leg of lamb or goat and slow-cooked meat just falling from the bone— all in one bite.

PASTA MILANESE

Serves 10

This sauce is a classic for New Orleanians of Sicilian descent and those of us who love their food. What it has to do with Milan beats me. The recipe varies from household to household, but I've found that good-quality canned tomatoes can be brought back to life by adding a little extra spice and a pinch or two of sugar.

- ¼ cup extra-virgin olive oil
- 1 bulb fennel, diced
- 2 onions, diced
- 2 cloves garlic, minced
- 4 anchovy filets
- 3 12-ounce cans diced tomatoes
- 1 tablespoon sugar
- ¼ cup tomato paste
- 1 teaspoon fennel seeds, toasted and ground

  Leaves from 4 large sprigs fresh basil, chopped

- Leaves from 2 large sprigs fresh oregano, chopped
- 1 teaspoon crushed red pepper flakes
- 1 tablespoon Basic Creole Spices (page 13)
- 1 teaspoon freshly ground black pepper

  Salt
- 2 pounds Basic Homemade Pasta (page 16) or dried fettuccine
- 1 recipe Mudrica, optional

1. Heat a large saucepan over moderate heat. Add the olive oil, then the fresh fennel and onions, and cook, stirring occasionally, until browned and caramelized, 10–15 minutes. Add the garlic and cook very briefly, then stir in the anchovies. Add the diced tomatoes, sugar, tomato paste, ground fennel, basil, oregano, pepper flakes, Creole Spices, and black pepper to the pan. Simmer the sauce for 1 hour, stirring occasionally.

2. Bring a large pot of salted water to a boil over high heat. Add the pasta and cook until just tender. Drain the pasta. Serve the pasta in a serving dish with the tomato sauce ladled on top. Sprinkle the Mudrica over the sauce, if you like.

MUDRICA (ST. JOSEPH'S SAWDUST)

Makes 1 cup

In addition to elaborate altars celebrating St. Joseph's Day at church, many families pay tribute to the Sicilian carpenter saint by sprinkling this flavorful bread crumb "sawdust" over pasta.

- ½ cup white bread crumbs from day-old bread
- ¼ cup extra-virgin olive oil
- 3 tablespoons freshly grated Parmesan cheese
- 2 tablespoons pine nuts, toasted

- 2 tablespoons dried currants
- 1 teaspoon crushed red pepper flakes
- ¼ teaspoon ground cinnamon
- 1 pinch chopped fresh oregano leaves
- 1 pinch salt

1. Put all the ingredients into the work bowl of a food processor and pulse 4 or 5 times or until the mixture is well combined. Serve over pasta.

Making pasta: Executive chef Steve McHugh, left, runs ever thinning sheets of fresh pasta dough through the pasta machine, then cuts it into fettucine and drys it on a pole, above. The finished pasta milanese, left, is dusted with mudrica—bread crumbs, pine nuts, currants, olive oil, and Parmesan, far left.

STUFFED ARTICHOKES WITH CRABMEAT AND SHRIMP

Makes 6

The artichoke is a symbol of abundance and a staple of St. Joseph's Day feasts. Simmer the artichokes slowly so that they'll cook evenly; they're ready as soon as the base is tender. You may poach them a day ahead, then stuff and bake them just before serving.

6 large artichokes
Salt

FOR THE STUFFING
1¼ cups extra-virgin olive oil
3 cloves garlic, thinly sliced
1 teaspoon crushed red pepper flakes
2 cups dried bread crumbs
1 cup freshly grated Parmesan cheese
Leaves from 1 sprig fresh basil, chopped
Leaves from 1 sprig fresh thyme
1 pound medium shrimp, peeled and chopped
Freshly ground black pepper
1 pound jumbo lump crabmeat, picked over
¼ cup Basic Sauce Ravigote (page 19)
1 green onion, chopped

1. Cut the stems off the artichokes and snap off the small leaves at the bottom. Cut off the top quarter of each artichoke with a sharp knife. Use scissors to trim off the pointy tips of the remaining leaves.

2. Simmer the artichokes in a large pot of lightly salted water, covered, over moderate heat until the bases are tender, 20–30 minutes. Transfer them to paper towels and let them drain upside down until cool.

3. Meanwhile, make the artichoke stuffing by heating 1 cup of the oil in a large skillet over moderate heat until warm. Add the garlic and cook until soft. Stir in the pepper flakes and the bread crumbs and remove the skillet from the heat. Stir in the Parmesan cheese, basil, and thyme and set aside.

4. Heat the remaining ¼ cup oil in another large skillet over medium-high heat until hot. Season the

shrimp with salt and pepper and sauté for 2 minutes. Add the crabmeat, Sauce Ravigote, and green onions and sauté for 1 minute. Remove the skillet from the heat and stir in 3 tablespoons of the bread crumb mixture. Season the stuffing with salt and pepper.

5. Preheat the oven to 350°. Gently pry open each artichoke leaf and pack a spoonful of the stuffing between the leaves. Set the stuffed artichokes in a roasting pan or baking dish and pack their tops with the remaining bread crumb mixture.

6. Tightly cover the pan with aluminum foil and bake the stuffed artichokes for 35 minutes. Remove the foil and continue baking the artichokes until the stuffing is golden brown, 10–15 minutes more.

ST. JOSEPH'S FIG COOKIES

Makes about 2 dozen

These cookies are wonderful made in advance. As a matter of fact, the ladies of our parish start their preparation long before St. Joseph's Day. A simple way to do that is to make the cookie dough ahead, and freeze it or keep it wrapped in the refrigerator. Make the filling ahead, too, and do the assembling and icing when you have time.

FOR THE FILLING

- 3 tablespoons sherry
- 2 teaspoons fresh orange juice
- 1 cup dried figs, stems removed
- ¼ cup raisins
- ¼ cup shelled walnuts, chopped
- ¼ cup honey
- 1 dash ground cinnamon
- 1 teaspoon freshly grated lemon zest

FOR THE DOUGH

1¼ cups all-purpose flour

- ¼ cup granulated sugar
- ¾ teaspoon baking powder
- ¼ teaspoon salt
- 4 tablespoons cold butter, diced
- 1 egg, beaten
- 3 tablespoons milk

FOR THE ICING

1½ cups powdered sugar, sifted

- 3 tablespoons milk
- ¼ teaspoon vanilla extract

   Colored sprinkles

1. For the filling, bring the sherry and the orange juice just to a boil in a small saucepan. Meanwhile, put the figs, raisins, walnuts, honey, cinnamon, and lemon zest into the work bowl of a food processor and pulse until the nuts are very finely chopped.

2. Pour the sherry mixture through the feed tube of the food processor and continue processing the fig mixture to a finely chopped paste.

3. Using a rubber spatula, scrape the filling into a pastry bag fitted with a medium round tip, or, instead of using a pastry bag, put the filling into a bowl, cover, and set aside.

4. For the dough, sift together the flour, granulated sugar, baking powder, and salt into a large mixing bowl. Using a pastry cutter or 2 knives, cut the butter into the flour until it resembles cornmeal. Stir in the eggs and milk, mixing until the dough is well combined.

5. Divide the dough in half. Roll each piece through the smooth cylinders of a pasta machine, decreasing the setting, one notch at a time, until each sheet is about ⅛ inch thick and about 4 inches wide. Cut each sheet in half lengthwise so that you have 4 long, narrow strips of dough. Or, instead of a pasta machine, use a rolling pin to roll the dough out on a lightly floured surface into 2 long strips ⅛ inch thick and about 4 inches wide. Cut the strips in half lengthwise.

6. To fill the dough, use the pastry bag or a spoon to pipe or spoon a quarter of the filling down the middle of each strip of dough. Using a pastry brush, moisten the dough with water on either side of the filling. Roll the dough over the filling, completely enclosing the filling, then gently press on the seam to seal the dough.

7. Preheat the oven to 350°. Place the pastry logs seam side down and slice them on the bias into cookies about an inch long. Place the cookies at least ½ inch apart on nonstick cookie sheets and bake until pale golden brown, 15–20 minutes. Set the cookies on a rack to let cool.

8. For the icing, whisk together the powdered sugar, milk, and vanilla in a wide bowl.

9. Dip the top of each cookie into the icing, then scatter sprinkles over the tops.

CAULIFLOWER AND CRAWFISH SOUP

Serves 6–8

Depending on the size of both the cauliflower and the potato, you may need to add more stock; the consistency will become obvious after you purée the soup. You don't need to add more cream; just add a touch more stock.

¼ cup extra-virgin olive oil	4 cups Basic Chicken Stock (page 13)
Half a head of cauliflower, cored and chopped	2 cups heavy cream
1 onion, chopped	1 pinch crushed red pepper flakes
1 leek, white part, chopped	1 sprig fresh thyme
1 bay leaf	Salt
1 medium Yukon Gold potato, peeled and diced	Freshly ground white pepper
1 clove garlic, minced	2 tablespoons butter
	½ pound crawfish tail meat (page 362)
	1 tablespoon chopped fresh chives

1. Heat the olive oil in a large heavy-bottomed pot over moderate heat. Add the cauliflower, onions, leeks, bay leaf, potatoes, and garlic and cook, stirring with a wooden spoon, until the cauliflower softens slightly and the onions are translucent, about 20 minutes.

2. Add Chicken Stock, cream, pepper flakes, and thyme to the pot. Increase the heat to high, bring the soup to a boil, then reduce heat to medium-low and gently simmer until the potatoes are fully cooked, 15–20 minutes. Remove bay leaf and thyme sprig.

3. Purée the soup in a blender and strain through a fine sieve. Season with salt and pepper. Return to the pot, cover, and keep warm.

4. Melt the butter in a small skillet over medium-high heat, add the crawfish tails, and sauté for a minute. Season with salt and pepper. Ladle the soup into bowls, add crawfish tails, and sprinkle with chives.

Glory days: Missy Mantilla, near right, with her daughter Isabella in Easter bonnet at our table set with the first tulips of spring, right. Cauliflower and crawfish soup, below.

DAUBE OF RABBIT WITH WHITE ASPARAGUS AND CHAMPAGNE VINAIGRETTE

Serves 8–10

This rabbit terrine is another variation of the Beef Daube Glacée (page 344), and as you can imagine, just about any braised meat would work well here. Make sure you've seasoned the rabbit fairly aggressively, as chilled terrines require more salt. At August, we shape our daube into a cylinder using plastic wrap, but the terrine mold, as suggested here, is easy to use at home.

3 tablespoons extra-virgin olive oil	1 pinch crushed red pepper flakes
1 dressed young rabbit, quartered	2 quarts Basic Chicken Stock (page 13)
Salt	4 envelopes unflavored gelatin
Freshly ground black pepper	1 bunch fresh chives
2 stalks celery, diced	1 teaspoon minced fresh tarragon leaves
1 large carrot, diced	Sugar
1 leek, white part, diced	40 stalks white asparagus, peeled
1 onion, diced	
2 cloves garlic, minced	1 cup arugula or other small greens
Leaves of 1 sprig fresh thyme	1 cup Basic Champagne Vinaigrette (page 19)
1 bay leaf	
1 teaspoon coriander seeds, crushed	

1. Heat 2 tablespoons of the oil in a medium heavy-bottomed pot over medium-high heat until hot. Season the rabbit with salt and pepper and sear it in the pot until browned all over.

2. Add the celery, carrots, leeks, onions, and garlic to the pot and cook the vegetables, stirring frequently, for 5 minutes or so. Add the thyme, bay leaf, coriander seeds, pepper flakes, and Chicken Stock. Bring to a boil, then reduce the heat to medium-low. Simmer the rabbit until it is fork tender and the meat is nearly falling off the bones, about 1 hour, turning it every so often to ensure that it cooks evenly.

3. Using a slotted spoon, transfer the rabbit to a bowl to let rest until it is cool enough to handle. Meanwhile, increase the heat to medium-high and boil the broth in the pot until it has reduced by about half or to 4 cups, about 30 minutes. Discard the bay leaf.

4. Pick the rabbit meat from the bones and put it into a large bowl. Discard the bones.

5. Put ½ cup cold water into a small bowl, sprinkle in the gelatin, and set it aside for 3–5 minutes to let it soften and swell. Off the heat, add the gelatin to the broth and vegetables in the pot, stirring until it is completely dissolved.

6. Pour the broth and vegetables into the bowl with the rabbit meat. Chop one-quarter of the chives and add them to the bowl. Add the tarragon and season well with salt and pepper. Stir until well combined.

7. Prepare a 6-cup terrine mold by lightly greasing it with the remaining 1 tablespoon oil. Line the mold as smoothly as possible with a large sheet of plastic wrap, letting it drape over the sides by at least 2 inches. Spoon the rabbit mixture into the lined mold, cover it with another sheet of plastic wrap, and refrigerate the terrine for at least 1 day and as long as 3 days.

8. When you are ready to serve the rabbit terrine, cook the asparagus. Bring a large pot of water to a boil over high heat. Salt the water enough so that it tastes salty, then add enough sugar so that it tastes slightly sweet. Reduce the heat to medium-low, add the asparagus, and simmer until they are slightly limp, 10–15 minutes (unlike green asparagus, white asparagus need to take their time cooking). Taste a piece for doneness, and, if necessary, let simmer longer. Drain the asparagus, then plunge into a large bowl of ice water to stop the cooking. When they are cool, drain again and set them out on a clean dish towel.

9. Tip the rabbit terrine out of the mold, unwrap it, and slice it into ½-inch-thick slices.

10. Divide the asparagus and greens between the plates and dress with the Champagne Vinaigrette. Place 2 slices of the rabbit terrine on each plate.

RAGOUT OF ARTICHOKES, FAVA BEANS, AND MOREL MUSHROOMS

Serves 6–8

Artichokes can make a mess of things: you'll have to wash knives, cutting board, and hands very well after you prepare them so that they don't pass along a bitter aftertaste. Consequently, I try to prep and blanch my artichokes ahead, thus containing the mess. Ask your butcher for bacon ends, or use thick-cut sliced bacon.

Salt

2 lemons, halved

5 cloves garlic

1 sprig fresh rosemary

1 teaspoon crushed red pepper flakes

4 large artichokes

½ cup diced bacon, preferably from the bacon slab ends

1 bunch spring onions, white parts, halved lengthwise

1 cup shelled fava beans

1 cup fresh morel mushrooms, halved

¼ cup Basic Chicken Stock (page 13)

2 tablespoons heavy cream

Leaves from 1 sprig fresh tarragon, minced

Freshly ground black pepper

1 tablespoon butter

1. Bring a medium pot of salted water to a boil over medium-high heat. Squeeze the lemons into the boiling water and add the spent rinds. Crush 4 cloves of the garlic and add them, along with the rosemary and pepper flakes, to the pot.

2. Snap off and discard the outer layers of the sturdy green leaves from the artichokes, exposing the pale green interior leaves. Use a vegetable peeler to remove the tough, dark green outer layer from the stem. Cut off the top third of the artichokes with a large, sharp knife. Quarter the artichokes lengthwise; scoop out the fuzzy choke with a teaspoon and discard.

3. Add the artichokes to the pot of seasoned water and cook them for 10 minutes. Drain the artichokes and set them aside.

Fry the bacon in a medium heavy-bottomed pot over moderate heat for 5–7 minutes, stirring frequently. Thinly slice the remaining garlic clove and add it to the pot. Add the spring onions and artichokes and cook for 5 minutes. Add the fava beans and morels and cook until they are soft, about 5 minutes more.

4. Add the Chicken Stock, cream, and tarragon to the pot and let it simmer for 5 minutes or so. Season the ragout with salt and pepper. Remove the pot from the heat and stir in the butter.

SLOW-COOKED BABY GOAT WITH SPRING VEGETABLES

Serves 6–8

If baby goat proves difficult to find, substitute baby lamb. This kind of slow cooking requires particularly close attention at the beginning as well as at the end, but the extra attention will pay off in the most succulent meat ever.

4 pounds baby goat shoulder and shanks	2 anchovy filets, minced
Salt	4 tomatoes, peeled and diced, or 2 cups canned diced tomatoes
Freshly ground black pepper	Peel of 1 orange
1 teaspoon dried thyme	1 sprig fresh rosemary
1 teaspoon dried oregano	1 cup red wine
1 teaspoon crushed red pepper flakes	4 cups Basic Veal Stock (page 14)
¼ cup extra-virgin olive oil	½ pound baby carrots, peeled
1 cup small onions, blanched and peeled	½ pound baby turnips, peeled
4 cloves garlic, sliced	½ pound fingerling potatoes

1. Season the goat pieces by rubbing the salt, pepper, thyme, oregano, and red pepper flakes all over. Heat the oil in a wide heavy-bottomed pot over high heat until hot. Add the goat and sear until browned all over.

2. Add the onions to the pot, reduce the heat to moderate, cover, and cook until golden brown. Add the garlic, anchovies, tomatoes, orange peel, and rosemary and stir the browned bits stuck to bottom of the pot. Let the mixture simmer for a few minutes, then add the wine and Veal Stock.

3. Increase the heat to high and bring the liquid in the pot to a boil. Reduce the heat to medium-low and simmer the goat for about 1 hour, turning the meat every 15 minutes or so just to make sure it's cooking evenly.

4. Add the carrots, turnips, and potatoes to the pot, reduce the heat to low, and continue simmering the goat until the meat is fork tender and nearly falling off the bones, about 45 minutes more. Discard the orange peel and rosemary sprig and season the stew with salt and pepper.

WHITE CHOCOLATE AND MEYER LEMON SEMIFREDDO WITH VANILLA-POACHED BERRIES

Serves 6

A semifreddo, as its name implies, is an Italian almost-frozen dessert. This one is served on a layer of lemon cookie with a scattering of berries. It works best when the components are made well in advance and assembled just before serving. To unmold the semifreddo, dip the bottom of the mold into hot water and leave it there for a moment. Use whatever berries you have at your fingertips, as their seasons will vary.

FOR THE SEMIFREDDO
- 1 envelope unflavored gelatin
- 1 cup milk
- 1 vanilla bean
- 1½ cups white chocolate
- 1⅔ cups heavy cream
- 3 Meyer or regular lemons, zested and juiced

FOR THE BERRIES
- 1 cup sugar
- Zest of 1 lemon
- 2 vanilla beans, split
- ½ cup blueberries
- ½ cup blackberries
- ½ cup strawberries

FOR THE LEMON COOKIES
- 1½ cups powdered sugar, plus more for dusting
- 1½ cups ground almonds
- 1 teaspoon salt
- 2 cups unsalted butter, softened
- 2 eggs
- Zest of 2 lemons
- 3 cups all-purpose flour, sifted

FOR THE GARNISH
- 6 small sprigs fresh mint
- 1 handful shaved white chocolate

1. For the semifreddo, put 2 tablespoons water into a cup, sprinkle in the gelatin, and set aside to soften and swell, 3–5 minutes. Pour the milk into a small saucepan. Split the vanilla bean and scrape the seeds into the milk. Add the bean and bring the milk just to a boil over high heat. Remove from heat, discard the vanilla bean, add the softened gelatin, and whisk to dissolve gelatin. Strain through a fine sieve into a small bowl.

2. Put the white chocolate into a large bowl (saving some to shave for garnish). Slowly pour the hot milk over the chocolate, stirring constantly until the chocolate has melted. Set aside and allow to cool to room temperature.

3. Put the cream into a mixing bowl and beat until it forms soft peaks. Mix the lemon zest and juice into the cooled milk mixture, then fold in the whipped cream. Pour into a mold of whatever shape you prefer— rectangular or round—and freeze until set.

4. For the berries, while the semifreddo is in the freezer, make the vanilla-poached berries. Put ¼ cup water, the sugar, lemon zest, and split vanilla beans into a saucepan and boil for 5 minutes over medium-high heat, until the sugar has dissolved.

5. Add the blueberries and blackberries, reduce heat to low, and poach for 2 minutes. Remove from heat and add the strawberries. Let cool, then refrigerate.

6. For the lemon cookies, put the powdered sugar, almonds, and salt into a mixing bowl. Beat the butter in the bowl of a standing mixer fitted with a paddle until pale yellow and fluffy. Add the eggs, lemon zest, and sugar mixture and continue beating. Slowly add the flour while beating, until it is just incorporated. Wrap the dough in plastic wrap and refrigerate for 30 minutes to an hour before rolling out.

7. Preheat the oven to 325°. Sprinkle a work surface with a little powdered sugar and roll out the dough to a thickness of ⅛ inch. Cut 1 large cookie just the size of the semifreddo and cut the remaining dough into 6 small rounds. Place the cookies on a cookie sheet and bake until golden brown, 20–25 minutes.

8. Unmold the semifreddo and carefully place it on top of the large cookie. Slice into 1-inch pieces and serve each slice with a generous spoonful of the poached berries, mint leaves, shaved white chocolate on top, and an extra lemon cookie on the side. Add a white chocolate cigarette, if you like.

FIG CHAROSES

Serves 6

Our Southern contribution adds figs to the classic sweet apple-and-nut mixture that symbolizes mortar for the bricks the Jews made in Egypt.

¼ cup rice wine vinegar	½ cup diced pitted dates
¼ cup sugar	¼ cup chopped roasted pistachios
¼ cup white wine	
¼ cup diced onion	1 pinch ground allspice
1 apple, peeled, cored, and diced	1 pinch ground cardamom
1 cup diced dried figs	1 pinch ground cinnamon

1. Put the vinegar, sugar, and wine into a small saucepan and cook over moderate heat, stirring until the sugar dissolves. Add the onions and apples and cook until the onions are translucent, about 15 minutes.

2. Remove the pan from the heat, then stir in the figs, dates, pistachios, and ground spices. Set aside to let cool before serving.

HOMEMADE MATZOS

Serves 6

Homemade matzos are worlds better than the store-bought kind. Making them, however, involves a bit of a race against the clock because for the bread to be truly unleavened (as tradition requires), you have just 18 minutes to make the dough and get it into the oven before fermentation takes place. Have everything ready before you begin, and you'll find the result to be well worth it.

1 teaspoon kosher salt	2 cups whole-wheat flour (kosher for Passover)

1. Preheat oven to 500°. Put the salt and flour into the bowl of a standing mixer. Using the dough hook attachment, with the mixer set on medium speed, slowly add ¾ cup cold water and mix until the dough pulls away from the sides of the mixing bowl and forms a ball. Continue to work the dough with the dough hook for another 5 minutes.

2. Transfer the dough to a lightly floured surface, cut into 4 pieces, and flatten the pieces slightly. Roll the dough through a pasta machine, changing the settings on each pass and gradually rolling the dough thinner and thinner until it's as thin as possible without breaking.

3. Cut the rolled-out dough into smaller sheets; it will be easier to handle. Dock the dough by pricking it all over with either a fork or a pastry docker. Lay the sheets on nonstick cookie sheets and bake (in batches if necessary) until brown, about 5 minutes. Remove from oven, let cool, and serve with pride at the seder table.

The Passover table: New Orleans photographer
John Menszer shot this Krewe Seder, left, in
1998 at the home of Donna and David Mervis; 50
people attended.Above, our homemade matzos.

Gulf Coast Lamb

If you want to save a breed, eat the breed! That is my approach to our local Gulf Coast lambs—hardy youngsters that roam freely, grazing on grass and woodland vegetation, and thus develop a meat that is leaner, richer, and more flavorful than the rather bland, generic-tasting meat of sheep from factory farms. Our Gulf Coast lambs have been grazing here since the Spanish introduced them to Florida in the 1500s, and are one of the oldest and most resilient breeds in the country. These stalwart sheep bleated their way up through the Florida parishes to New Orleans's North Shore, mixing with other imported breeds along the way as they adapted to our extreme humidity and heat, evolving into the Gulf Coast population we know today. Also known as Florida Native or Louisiana Native, these white or tan sheep are comparatively small and nimble, with an open, wool-free face and legs and a lightweight fleece that helps them stay cool.

At one point they became endangered when the raising of sheep fell out of vogue in the South because most livestock farming was relegated to areas in the Midwest and Eastern plains states, where grain is produced. Fortunately, the current revival in sustainable agriculture and appreciation for animals reared with minimal intervention has meant that our Gulf Coast sheep are enjoying a well-earned revival of their own.

WHOLE ROAST GULF COAST LAMB

Serves 6–8

This roast lamb will take a little bit of love, but it sure gives it back. The idea is to braise the shoulder or shanks first, then stuff the braised lamb into a raw, butterflied leg of lamb and roast that. Once it's stuffed, make sure to truss the leg really well with kitchen string and roast it immediately.

FOR THE LAMB STUFFING
- 2 pounds lamb shoulder or shanks
- Salt
- Freshly ground black pepper
- 1 teaspoon dried thyme
- 1 teaspoon crushed red pepper flakes
- 2 tablespoons extra-virgin olive oil
- 1 onion, diced
- 3 cloves garlic, sliced
- 2 tomatoes, peeled and diced, or 1 cup canned diced tomatoes
- 1 sprig fresh rosemary
- 2 cups Basic Chicken Stock (page 13)

FOR THE LEG OF LAMB
- 1 5-pound deboned and butterflied leg of lamb
- Salt
- Freshly ground black pepper
- 4 cloves garlic, sliced
- 2 branches fresh rosemary, divided into small sprigs

1. For the lamb stuffing, season the lamb shoulder or shanks with salt, pepper, thyme, and pepper flakes. Heat the olive oil in a large heavy pot over high heat and sear the lamb on all sides until browned all over.

2. Add the onions to the pot, reduce the heat to moderate, and cook, stirring occasionally, until the onions are brown, about 10 minutes. Add the garlic, tomatoes, rosemary, and Chicken Stock, increase the heat to medium-high, and cook until the stock comes to a boil. Reduce the heat to low, cover, and cook until the meat is fork tender and falling off the bone, about 1½ hours.

3. Transfer the meat from the broth to a platter (set the broth aside for later); season with salt and pepper. Set the meat aside and let cool to room temperature.

4. For the leg of lamb, preheat the oven to 400°. Lay out the leg of lamb, skin side down, on a cutting board and season with salt and pepper.

5. Remove the cooled slow-cooked meat from the bones and arrange it in the center of the boneless leg of lamb (parallel to the short sides). Discard the bones. Beginning with a short side, roll the lamb around the slow-cooked meat, jelly-roll fashion, and tie it securely with kitchen string.

6. Using a paring knife, make small incisions in the tied-up roast. Stuff a slice of garlic or a sprig of rosemary into each incision and season the roast with salt and pepper. Put the lamb into a roasting pan and roast until the internal temperature is 130°, 30–40 minutes. Remove from oven and let rest 15 minutes.

7. While the lamb rests, reduce the broth of the slow-cooked meat by half over medium-high heat. Strain and serve it over slices of the stuffed leg of lamb.

BLOOD ORANGE CRÈME BRÛLÉE

Serves 8

This is a very simple, dairy-free Passover dessert that is easily prepared a day or so in advance. Just before serving, add the turbinado sugar and glaze the top with a small handheld torch or under a broiler.

1	cup ground almonds	6	egg yolks
2	cups blood orange juice	¼	cup turbinado sugar
⅔	cup granulated sugar		

1. Preheat the oven to 325°. Put the almonds, blood orange juice, and granulated sugar into a medium saucepan over medium-high heat. Bring to a boil, stirring until the sugar dissolves. Remove from heat and allow the almonds to steep in the orange juice for 5 minutes, then strain the juice through a fine sieve. Let the juice cool.

2. Whisk the egg yolks in a mixing bowl until they are thick and pale yellow. Continue whisking as you slowly add the strained orange juice.

3. Put eight 3-ounce ramekins into a 9-by-13-inch baking pan. Add enough hot water to the pan that it comes halfway up the sides of the ramekins. Fill the ramekins with the egg and juice mixture and bake until the custards have set in the center, 30–40 minutes.

4. Remove the pan from the oven, transfer ramekins to a wire rack, and allow to cool completely. Preheat the broiler. Sprinkle turbinado sugar on top of each custard and broil until the sugar melts, browns, and covers the top completely.

BECNEL'S ORANGE BLOSSOM FRITTERS WITH ORANGE BLOSSOM HONEY

Serves 8

If you're lucky enough to get your hands on some fresh orange blossoms, make these quick fritters, or scatter a couple of blossoms over the Blood Orange Crème Brûlée.

1	cup flour	24	sprigs orange blossoms
1	pinch salt	½	cup powdered sugar
1	pinch granulated sugar	½	cup orange blossom honey
1½	cups club soda		
3–4	cups canola oil		

1. Whisk together the flour, salt, and granulated sugar in a mixing bowl. Add the club soda and continue whisking until just smooth.

2. Heat the oil in a medium heavy-bottomed saucepan over high heat until it reaches 350°. Dip each of the orange blossom sprigs into the batter and fry until golden brown, about a minute on each side.

3. Allow the fried blossoms to drain on paper towels. Dust with powdered sugar and serve with a bowl of honey for dipping.

Sweet: Beekeeper Adrian Juttner, left, suits up and tends our bees behind La Provence. Orange blossom fritters, above. Top right, Passover hosts Alan and Diane Franco just before the birth of their son. Blood oranges at the Becnel farm, right.

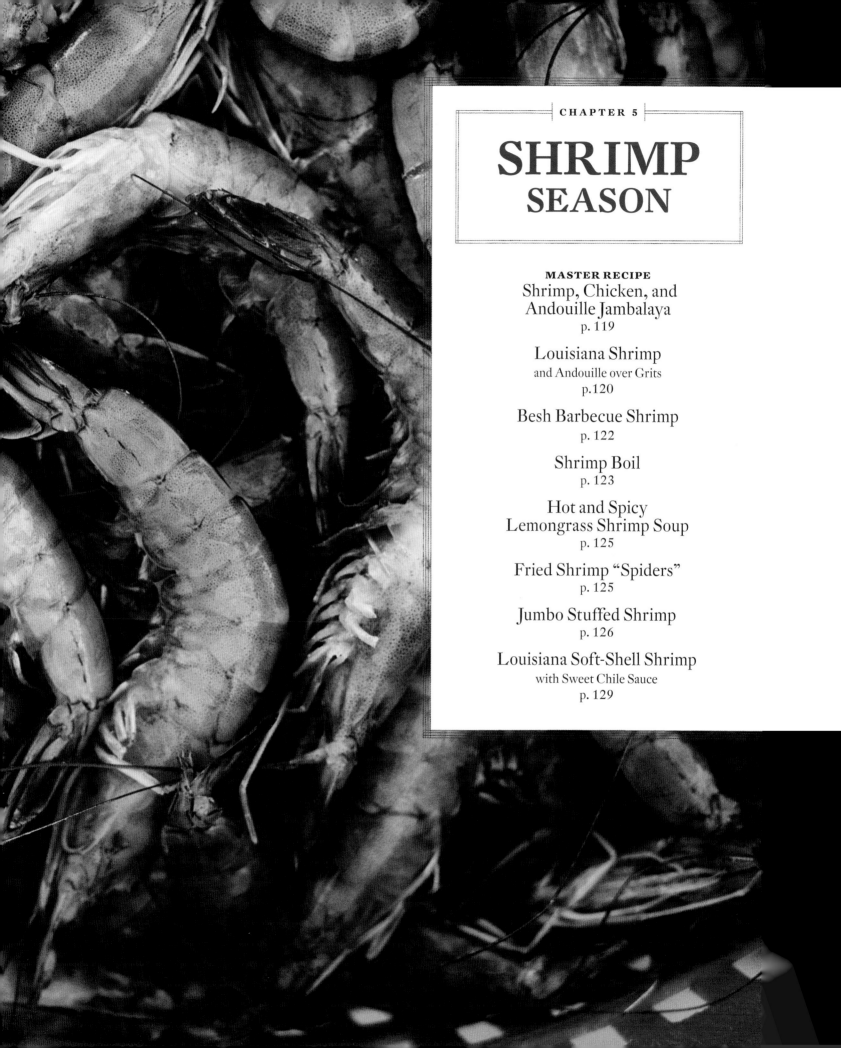

Shrimp boats: Boys with miniature shrimp luggers, above, at Chauvin, Louisiana, 1940s; The Historic New Orleans Collection. The real thing heads out on Bayou Jean Lafitte, right. Aimee Cappy, with daughter Abby, right, on their shrimp boat. Top right, my friend and chief shellfish supplier, Brian Cappy of Kenney's Seafood; jumbo shrimp, below. Far right, sturdy rope for hauling shrimp nets.

Troubled Waters

"Elbow deep in a mud-filled picking box, I knew we weren't cut out for the shrimping business."

My first shrimping trip was with Mr. Mike Reilly, a Louisiana transplant from upstate New York, who was an airline pilot with my father years after playing football for Navy with Roger Staubach. Behind his house on Bayou Paquet on the North Shore of Lake Pontchartrain he kept a boat, which, at least in my memory, resembled the *African Queen*. Well, on this monumental day, Mr. Reilly took me and my father on the *African Queen*'s first shrimping voyage so that Mike could show Dad and me how to really catch shrimp. Just minutes from Mike's house, we took a right onto Bayou Liberty and began to trawl in the shallows along the banks of the lake, dragging a big net behind the boat,

Wild shrimp: Shrimp coming off the boat on a conveyor belt is immediately weighed on the docks at Bayou Jean Lafitte, above. Right, vivid boiling spices await shrimp at Kenney's Seafood in Slidell.

which soon became heavy with shrimp. Great; this is pretty easy, I thought—that is, until it came time to pull in the net. We pulled and we pulled the dead weight of the mud-packed net up into the picking box, and soon it became clear we weren't cut out for the shrimping business. Removing the bycatch from the muddy nets was the worst. I don't know who was more pained, me or the crabs, mullet, and minnows that were caught up in the muck. Later, I learned that all we'd needed to do was to accelerate the motor and wash all the mud from the nets, leaving just those prized shrimp, clean and ready to be picked and sorted into baskets on the deck of the boat. But the experience did give birth to a profound respect for those who toil in these salt marsh bays, trawling for our glorious shrimp.

Shortly after the hurricanes Katrina and Rita of 2005, I was amazed to learn that many of our resilient shrimpers had been able to move their boats out of the path of the storms as they approached. Consequently, they saved our industry. After the storms, the shrimpers returned to find an overabundance of shrimp but no docks left to sell their catch, nowhere to buy fuel, and, most critical, no ice to keep the shrimp fresh. Unlike other threatened wild species, it wasn't the shrimp that needed saving; it was the shrimping business itself. Working with Louisiana's Department of Wildlife and Fisheries, we knew we had to get word out that the shellfish was safe, but what we desperately needed was ice. Shell Oil Company came up with the money to give us the ice machines the shrimpers needed to survive.

Our shrimping families are an integral part of our coastal communities, and their survival requires family involvement on every level. Without the help of a close-knit family, there is very little money to be made in shrimping. Much of their difficulty comes from competition from cheap imports—the irresponsible practice of harvesting lesser-quality, farm-raised shrimp from waters that aren't tested, by people who are working for essentially slave wages.

I pay particularly close attention to the origins of any shrimp we buy, making sure that all of them are wild American shrimp. I will cook the shrimp differently depending upon their variety and size. Royal reds that are caught offshore in deep waters are very salty and have the lush flesh of a lobster, so I like to eat them steamed, with melted butter and no added salt. I find big jumbo white shrimp best for the grill or a sauté. I love the smaller brown shrimp for my étouffées, gumbos, and shrimp and okra stews. Perhaps the most treasured is the soft-shell shrimp, a delicacy that requires your finding a trusted shrimper to sort them for you from the picking box.

W E HAD JUMBO brown shrimp in the summer as kids, and white shrimp in the fall. Mom and I loved shrimp. Dad enjoyed them, but Mom and I loved them, just because they are so easy to cook. We'd eat shrimp creole over white rice, sautéed jumbo shrimp with garlic and pasta, shrimp remoulade, and shrimp cocktail, which Mom would serve in little cups nestled in crushed ice. We would combine leftover boiled shrimp with mayonnaise, mustard, hard-boiled eggs, and chopped onions for the best shrimp salad you could imagine. Like our fresh fish, our shrimp often came from generous friends. When we did buy it, we'd get a hundred pounds or so, which meant that Mom and I would have a long night ahead of us peeling shrimp and putting them up in our deep freezer, covering the shrimp tails with water and freezing them in containers that we'd make from milk jugs with the top halves cut off, so that we could cook those beautiful local shrimp all year long.

Love boat: Cause for celebration, the blessing of the shrimp fleet in Chauvin, Louisiana, at a festival in the 1970s.

One big pot: A special jambalaya spade, top, helps stir sausage in the cast-iron pot. Cooked jambalaya, above. Jambalaya ingredients, from left, bay leaves, bacon, lard, salt, andouille sausage, thyme, cayenne pepper. Right, Jambalaya Queen at a festival in Gonzales, Louisiana, 1970s.

MASTER RECIPE

SHRIMP, CHICKEN, AND ANDOUILLE JAMBALAYA

Serves 12–15

Both the French and the Spanish have had their influence on our famous rice-based, paella-like jambalaya. As we do with a crawfish boil or a *cochon de lait* (suckling pig), we make jambalaya for a great gathering of folks, often cooking it outdoors over a gas or log fire. Try to find a large (three- to five-gallon) seasoned cast-iron pot, or use the heaviest pot you can get your hands on. A good-size pot is well worth the investment for making so many of these one-pot specialties we love to cook down here. We even have a long-handled, cast-iron spade for stirring the Jambalaya pot.

2 pounds bacon, diced

3 pounds andouille sausage, diced

½ cup lard

2 pounds fresh pork sausage, removed from casings

8 skinless, boneless chicken thighs, roughly cut into 1-inch cubes

Salt

Freshly ground black pepper

6 large onions, diced

4 bell peppers, seeded and diced

10 stalks celery, diced

12 cloves garlic, minced

9 cups converted Louisiana white rice

2 teaspoons dried thyme

2 dried bay leaves

3 tablespoons pimentón de la Vera or smoked paprika

2 teaspoons cayenne pepper

1 tablespoon celery salt

6 cups canned crushed tomatoes

6 cups Basic Chicken Stock (page 13)

5 pounds Louisiana white shrimp, or other wild American shrimp, peeled and deveined

3 bunches green onions, chopped

1. First, you'll need to heat a very large pot (3–5 gallons) over high heat until it is hot, then reduce the heat to moderate. This will allow the heat to be uniform all over, preventing those little hot spots that are likely to burn.

2. Render the bacon with the sausages and the lard in the hot pot, stirring slowly with a long wooden spoon or a spade. While the pork is rendering, go ahead and season the chicken thighs with salt and black pepper.

Add the chicken to the pot, stirring, and cook until the chicken becomes golden brown, about 5 minutes.

3. After the chicken has browned, add the onions to the pot and allow them to caramelize, about 15 minutes. Add the bell peppers, celery, and garlic and cook for about 5 minutes. Continue stirring from time to time so that everything in the pot cooks evenly.

4. Next add the rice, thyme, bay leaves, pimentón, cayenne, 2 tablespoons salt, 1 tablespoon black pepper, and the celery salt to the pot and cook, stirring often, for 3 minutes.

5. Increase the heat to high and add the tomatoes and Chicken Stock to the pot. Bring the stock to a boil. Reduce the heat to medium-low, cover, and simmer for 15 minutes.

6. While the rice is cooking in the covered pot, season the shrimp with salt and pepper and save them, along with the green onions, to be added at the last minute.

7. After the rice has simmered for 15 minutes, go ahead and remove the lid from the pot and fold in the shrimp and green onions. Turn off the heat and let everything continue to cook in the hot covered pot for an additional 10 minutes. Remove the lid, fluff the jambalaya, and serve!

LOUISIANA SHRIMP AND ANDOUILLE OVER GRITS

Serves 6

This is one of the most satisfying shrimp dishes. You needn't cook the shrimp long; make them in batches and be sure to keep a close eye on them so that they don't overcook. After you've sautéed the shrimp on both sides, remove them from the skillet with tongs and return them to the pot once they're all cooked to the same degree.

FOR THE GRITS

- 1 teaspoon salt
- 1 cup white stone-ground organic grits (page 362)
- 2 tablespoons butter
- ½ cup mascarpone cheese

FOR THE SHRIMP

- 2 tablespoons olive oil
- 36 jumbo Louisiana or other wild American shrimp, unpeeled
  Basic Creole Spices (page 13)
  Salt
- ⅓ cup minced andouille sausage
- 2 cloves garlic, minced
- 1 shallot, minced
- 2 piquillo peppers (roasted red Spanish peppers in a jar)
- 1 tablespoon chopped fresh thyme leaves
- 2 cups Basic Shrimp Stock (page 13)
- 2 tablespoons butter
- 1 teaspoon fresh lemon juice
- 2 cups canned diced tomatoes
- 1 tablespoon chopped fresh chives
- ½ cup fresh chervil sprigs

1. For the grits, bring 4 cups water with the salt to a boil in a medium-size saucepan over high heat. Slowly pour the grits into the boiling water, stirring constantly. Reduce the heat to low. Stir the grits often to make sure they don't stick to the bottom of the pot. Simmer the grits until all the water has been absorbed and they become soft, about 20 minutes. Stir in the butter and mascarpone. Remove from heat and place a piece of plastic wrap directly on the surface of the grits in the pot to keep a crust from forming.

2. For the shrimp, heat the olive oil in a large skillet over moderate heat. Season the shrimp with Creole Spices and salt. Sauté the shrimp until they begin to brown but are not cooked all the way through. Remove the shrimp as they cook and set aside.

3. In the same skillet, sauté the andouille, garlic, shallots, piquillo peppers, and thyme until they become aromatic, about 5 minutes. Add the Shrimp Stock and bring to a simmer. Stir in the butter and reduce the sauce until it's nice and thick, 3–5 minutes.

4. Return the shrimp to the skillet and cook for an additional 5 minutes. Add the lemon juice, diced tomatoes, and chives.

5. Spoon a heaping ¼ cup of the grits into the center of each of 6 large bowls. Arrange 6 shrimp in the middle of each bowl of grits. Spoon sauce around the shrimp and garnish each bowl with fresh chervil.

Jumbo shrimp: A Louisiana treasure, above. Shrimp and grits make Kerry Seaton, who runs Willie Mae's, right, very happy.

Shrimp

Louisiana is the number-one shrimping state in the country; we harvest tens of millions of pounds of the curvaceous crustaceans every year. The majority of these are brown shrimp (*Farfantepenaeus aztecus*), which are small, sweet, and mostly landed offshore during May and June, and the larger, more intensely flavored white shrimp (*Litopenaeus setiforus*), which are in season from the month of August onward, when they make their way closer to shore from deeper, cooler waters. Some of the less common shrimp species we encounter are the seabob, pink, rock, and royal red. When folks come to August, they want those big, meaty shrimp that they can't find easily, but for étouffées, shrimp creole, and bisques, I like the sweeter, less iodine-y flavor of brown shrimp.

The irony is that that the third- and fourth-generation shrimping communities along our coastline managed to survive Katrina and Rita only to be seriously endangered by the staggering quantities of cheap imports against which they cannot compete, given rising fuel costs. The number of Louisiana shrimpers has shrunk by half since 2000, so the Seafood Marketing Board is helping those remaining shrimpers fight back, teaching them how to direct-retail their catch and most important, to emphasize the superlative quality of these local, sustainably harvested Gulf shrimp. It's not just the critters we need to protect here but also the spirit of our shrimping community. So, always buy wild shrimp, preferably from Louisiana.

BESH BARBECUE SHRIMP

Serves 6

Where I come from, barbecue shrimp has nothing to do with barbecue sauce or even a grill, for that matter. Growing up, we'd cook our shrimp whole—head, tail, shells, and all—in a frying pan with lots of black pepper, lemon juice, a little Worcestershire, and, of course, a ton of butter. The heads and shells really make this dish, giving it the deep, nutty flavor you can get only from toasted shrimp shells. We'd suck out that flavor with our teeth, pulling off the shells with our fingers—a messy and delicious feast. This version is a bit more complex but is well worth the added preparation time because you can make the sauce base ahead and store it in the refrigerator or freezer until you're ready for the shrimp. It's easier to eat, too!

FOR THE SAUCE BASE
- 1 tablespoon olive oil
- 2 cups shrimp heads and shells
- ½ cup Worcestershire
- 2 tablespoons cracked black pepper
- 2 tablespoons Basic Creole Spices (page 13)
- ½ teaspoon whole cloves
- 2 bay leaves

Juice of 1 lemon

FOR THE SHRIMP
- 2 pounds medium Louisiana or wild American shrimp, peeled and deveined
- Salt
- Cracked black pepper
- 1 cup sauce base (left)
- 1 cup heavy cream
- 1 cup butter

1. For the sauce base, heat the olive oil in a medium saucepan over high heat, add the shrimp heads and shells, and cook, stirring often, for 5 minutes.

2. Add the Worcestershire, black pepper, Creole Spices, cloves, bay leaves, and lemon juice along with 2 cups water and bring to a boil. Once the liquid is boiling, reduce heat to moderate and simmer until it has reduced by half. Strain and reserve.

3. For the shrimp, season the shrimp with a little salt and lots of pepper. Put the shrimp and the sauce base, cream, and butter in a large cast-iron skillet over high heat. Bring the sauce to a boil and cook for 5 minutes.

SHRIMP BOIL

Serves 6–8

This is the recipe we use to boil shrimp for all our basic cold shrimp dishes, such as Shrimp Remoulade (page 348). For a typical Louisiana shrimp boil, use the recipe for Crawfish Boil (page 28), substituting shrimp for the crawfish and adding corn on the cob as we do here (left).

½ cup salt
¼ cup sweet paprika
1 teaspoon cayenne pepper
1 teaspoon garlic powder
¼ cup fresh lemon juice
4 bay leaves
1 small onion, sliced ¼ inch thick
1 head garlic, halved crosswise
1 sprig fresh thyme
1 tablespoon black peppercorns
1 tablespoon ground coriander
3–4 pounds jumbo Louisiana or wild American shrimp, unpeeled

1. Put the salt, paprika, cayenne, garlic powder, lemon juice, bay leaves, onions, garlic, thyme, peppercorns, and coriander into a large pot with 2 gallons water. Bring to a boil over high heat and boil for about 10 minutes. Add the shrimp and simmer for 5 minutes. Remove the pot from the heat and leave the shrimp in the hot water until they are just cooked through, 5–10 minutes.

4. Remove the shrimp from the skillet and arrange on a platter or in individual bowls. Reduce the sauce by half until it's a rich mocha color. Pour the sauce over the shrimp and serve with French bread.

2. Strain the shrimp and peel them when they are cool enough to handle. Use a paring knife to remove the dark vein that runs down the back of each shrimp before proceeding with your recipe.

HOT AND SPICY LEMONGRASS SHRIMP SOUP

Serves 6

Add rice or vermicelli to this simple soup and it becomes a lovely main course. Make the soup ahead by preparing the recipe through step 3; the strained broth will keep in the refrigerator up to two days.

½ pound medium head-on Louisiana or wild American shrimp	2 teaspoons fish sauce
	1 tablespoon sambal chile paste
2 tablespoons canola oil	Salt
2 tablespoons minced peeled ginger	12 okra, halved lengthwise
2 cloves garlic, minced	¾ cup mung bean sprouts
2 stalks lemongrass, trimmed and minced	16 peeled cherry tomatoes
2 green onions, chopped	¾ cup diced pineapple
2 tablespoons sugar	Leaves from 6 sprigs fresh cilantro
¼ cup rice wine vinegar	
1 cup pineapple juice	Leaves from 6 sprigs fresh Thai basil
3 cups Basic Shrimp Stock (page 13)	
¼ cup dried shrimp	Leaves from 6 sprigs fresh mint

1. Peel the shrimp, removing heads and tails and reserving the shells. Use a paring knife to remove the dark vein on the back of each shrimp. Set the cleaned shrimp aside.

2. Heat 1 tablespoon of the oil in a large saucepan over high heat. Add the shrimp shells, heads, and tails and cook for a few minutes, stirring often. Reduce the heat to moderate and add the ginger, garlic, lemongrass, and green onions. While you continue to stir, add the sugar and vinegar and cook until the liquid evaporates. Increase the heat to high and add the pineapple juice and Shrimp Stock. Bring the broth to a boil, then reduce the heat to moderate and let the broth simmer for 5 minutes.

3. Add the dried shrimp, fish sauce, and chile paste to the pan and simmer for 30 minutes. Remove from the heat and strain through a fine sieve into a bowl.

4. Heat the remaining tablespoon of oil in the same pan over high heat. Season the shrimp with salt and sear on both sides, then add the okra, mung bean sprouts, tomatoes, pineapple, and strained shrimp broth.

5. Season the broth with salt, simmer for 5 minutes, and serve garnished with cilantro, basil, and mint.

FRIED SHRIMP "SPIDERS"

Serves 6

When jumbo shrimp are plentiful, we use every part of the creature, even frying up the heads with their spidery "legs" for a crunchy nibble.

FOR THE SAUCE	1 cup buttermilk
1 cup Basic Sauce Ravigote (page 19)	1 cup flour
	1 cup cornmeal
1 tablespoon chopped fresh chives	1 teaspoon Basic Creole Spices (page 13)
1 teaspoon Creole mustard	1 quart canola oil
2 dashes Tabasco	Salt
FOR THE SHRIMP HEADS	Freshly ground black pepper
18 jumbo shrimp heads	

1. For the sauce, mix the Sauce Ravigote with the chives, mustard, and Tabasco in a bowl; reserve.

2. For the shrimp heads, separate the shells from the "legs" by lifting up the back of the shrimp head and pulling while you hold the body with the legs attached. (Save the shrimp head shells for stock and the shrimp tails for another recipe.)

3. Put the shrimp heads in a bowl and pour the buttermilk over them. In another bowl, whisk together the flour, cornmeal, and Creole Spices. Remove the shrimp heads from the buttermilk and dredge in cornmeal mix.

4. Heat the oil in a deep skillet until it reaches 350°. Fry the cornmeal-coated shrimp until golden, about 3 minutes. Remove the shrimp "spiders" from the oil and drain on paper towels. Season with salt and pepper and serve with the now jazzed-up Sauce Ravigote on the side.

Tabasco

There's an old joke about Tabasco: everybody has a bottle in their cupboard, and it's still the same bottle. But Tabasco never lasts that long in Louisiana. Though some folks swear by Crystal Hot Sauce, and bottles of "Slap Ya Mama" and "Bayou Butt Burner" show up at every corner grocery, Tabasco is in a league of its own. In the 1860s, Edmund McIlhenny, a banker, keen gardener, and early foodie, planted seeds of Mexican or Central American *Capsicum frutescens*, variety *tabasco*, at his home on Avery Island, southwest of New Orleans. This petite but punchy pepper is a cayenne-type chile with a Scoville Unit heat range of from 30,000 to 50,000, just below that of the killer habanero. McIlhenny's tinkering with the pepper gave birth to a sauce that became so popular with locals that in 1868 he was persuaded to market it at a dollar a bottle.

Today, once the peppers have ripened to a deep, fiery red, they're picked and crushed into a mash and aged for three years in white oak barrels, sealed beneath a layer of Avery Island salt. Then the fermented mash is blended with high-grain, natural vinegar, strained, and bottled. The seeds of Tabasco's peppers are still grown on the Avery Island estate, which remains home to the McIlhenny family, but today those seeds are planted mostly in Latin America; then the peppers are brought home for making Tabasco.

JUMBO STUFFED SHRIMP

Serves 6

You'll end up with a lot of stuffing, but this dish is all about overstuffing the shrimp. The olive oil–drenched bread crumbs almost melt into a crust.

2 tablespoons butter	1 teaspoon sambal chile paste
2 shallots, minced	Salt
1 clove garlic, minced	Freshly ground black pepper
1 stalk celery, minced	
2 tablespoons flour	½ cup dried bread crumbs
½ pound medium Louisiana or wild American shrimp, peeled and chopped	¼ cup grated Parmesan cheese
½ pound crabmeat, picked over	⅓ cup extra-virgin olive oil
1 green onion, chopped	Leaves from 1 sprig fresh thyme
½ cup Basic Shrimp Stock (page 13)	18 jumbo Louisiana or wild American shrimp, peeled, heads and tails left on
½ cup fresh bread crumbs	

1. Preheat the oven to 425°. Melt the butter in a medium skillet over medium-high heat. Add the shallots, garlic, and celery and cook, stirring often, until the vegetables are soft, about 5 minutes.

2. Sprinkle the flour into the skillet and stir until mixed into the vegetables. Add the chopped medium shrimp, crabmeat, and green onions. Slowly add the Shrimp Stock, stirring until sauce thickens; remove from heat. Add the fresh bread crumbs and chile paste; season with salt and pepper. Set aside.

3. Mix together the dried bread crumbs, Parmesan, olive oil, and thyme in a small bowl. Using a paring knife, butterfly the jumbo shrimp by making a deep incision through the shell and down the back of each shrimp. Remove the vein and take care to keep the heads and tails intact. Season with salt and pepper and place back side up on a cookie sheet.

4. Generously stuff each jumbo shrimp with the shrimp mixture and top with bread crumbs. Bake until golden, 12–15 minutes.

Drying shrimping nets: A magical moment on the water; photo: G.E. Arnold, The Historic New Orleans Collection.

SALT AND PEPPER LOUISIANA SOFT-SHELL SHRIMP WITH SWEET CHILE SAUCE

Serves 6

I love fried soft-shelled anything, and this light batter can be used to fry just about anything. As kids, if we caught soft shells or sorted them from the picking box, we'd save them for frying. Nowadays, I've got shrimping friends who'll do the sorting for me. I love the Vietnamese idea of wrapping fried shrimp in fresh herbs—Thai basil, mint and/or cilantro, and then lettuce leaves—and dipping them into the sauce: it's like fireworks for the palate.

FOR THE SWEET CHILE SAUCE

- ½ cup rice wine vinegar
- ¼ cup Vietnamese fish sauce
- ¼ cup sugar
- 3 tablespoons fresh lime juice
- 1 clove garlic, peeled
- 2–3 teaspoons sambal chile paste

FOR THE SHRIMP

- 1 egg
- 1 cup iced soda water
- 1 cup flour
- ¼ teaspoon salt
- 1 pinch cayenne pepper
- 18 jumbo soft-shell shrimp
- Salt
- Freshly ground black pepper
- 1 quart canola oil

1. For the sweet chile sauce, purée the vinegar, fish sauce, sugar, lime juice, garlic, chile paste, and ½ cup water in a blender or a food processor. Don't worry about straining the sauce; just pour it into a cup and set it aside until you're ready to serve it.

2. For the shrimp, beat the egg with a whisk in a large mixing bowl. Add the ice-cold soda water (iced water is important because it helps the batter adhere to the shrimp). Whisk together the flour, salt, and cayenne in a small bowl, then slowly whisk the seasoned flour into the egg and water mixture until just combined. Don't overmix, or the batter will be tough.

3. Season the soft-shell shrimp with salt and pepper, then toss into the batter.

4. Heat the oil in a medium deep, heavy pot over high heat until it reaches 350°. Use tongs to lift each shrimp carefully out of the batter and into the hot oil. Cook in batches of 6, so as not to crowd the pot, until the shrimp are golden brown; drain on paper towels. Serve with the sweet chile sauce.

CHAPTER 6

CREOLE TOMATOES

Salad of Heirloom Tomatoes,
Cheese, and Country Ham
p. 136

Cherry Tomato Five-Minute Sauce
p. 138

Crabmeat-Stuffed Tomatoes
p. 141

Terrine of Cherokee Purple Tomatoes
p. 142

Green Tomato and Pepper Jam
p. 143

Shrimp Creole
p. 144

Chilled Tomato Soup with Tapenade
p. 146

Fried Snow White Tomatoes with Aïoli
p. 149

Farm to table: Jim Core, top, among his Creoles. A happy tomato vendor, above; photo: Josephine Sacabo, 1978, The Historic New Orleans Collection. A beaming Gladys Core, right; a just-picked Creole awaits the mayonnaise, far right.

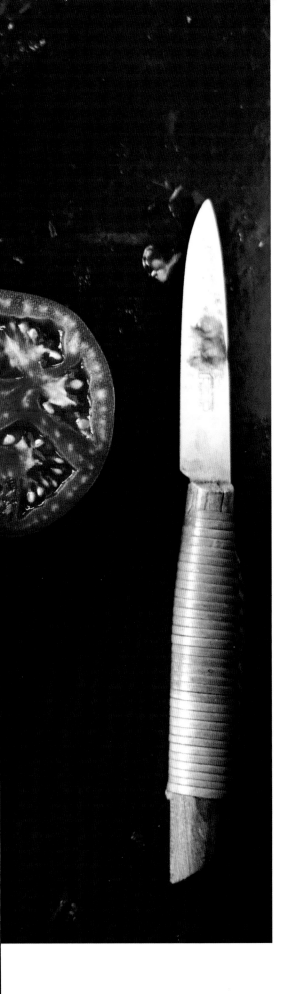

Call It Creole and It'll Sell

"Bunny bread and a thick slice of Creole tomato, salt, pepper, and an abundance of Blue Plate mayonnaise. Now, that's living!"

The Creoles of my childhood were ugly and deformed, split to the point of bursting. Picked the day they went to market or set on the windowsill to wait for whichever meal came next—that's what these tomatoes were good at. Creole tomatoes should be eaten warm, right off the plant, a thing I still look forward to like a child. I'm not saying that I don't love herbs and fancy cheeses, but a good ol' ripe Creole doesn't need any help; it just needs to be eaten.

The Creoles of my childhood were all grown in the St. Bernard or Plaquemines parishes, which flank the Mississippi south of New Orleans pretty

Extended family: Jim Core, center, in his tomato fields at Folsom, Louisiana, enlists help for the harvest.

much all the way to the Gulf of Mexico. That fertile farmland was formed by hundreds of years of rich silt deposits that the mighty Mississippi brought downstream. Cattle, a gift from the king of Spain, and brought here in 1779 by the Isleños, or Canary Islanders, once grazed on these same lands. Descendants of the Isleños still grow many of our Creoles today. This rich soil, with its low acidity, makes our tomatoes particularly sweet tasting; our moderate climate gives us a gloriously long growing season.

TODAY, CREOLE TOMATOES have become self-conscious; they're just a little too smooth and unblemished for me. Instead, we work with farmers like Jim Core (though there are few like him!) who grow terribly sweet, pretty, and ugly tomatoes in St. Tammany Parish, on New Orleans's North Shore. Jim's tomatoes are thin skinned and picked the day they go to market; they never sit on a grocery shelf or see the inside of a refrigerator. Each one is picked and carefully washed in artesian-well water by his beautiful wife, Gladys, and her vivacious sister, Gay Redler, on the same plot of land that Jim Core's great-grandfather once farmed.

I got to know Jim Core years ago through the Crescent City Farmers Market, the group that organized the first of our seven flourishing farmers' markets. We were brought together through the chefs Susan Spicer and Frank Brigtsen, who organized a charity fund-raising event to pay for the intricate foot surgery Jim required when he sustained a life-threatening injury on the farm. Now, Jim Core doesn't even limp.

A tough old bird, Jim Core was an airborne soldier who fought in the rice fields and jungles of Southeast Asia, but he never talks about that. At first glance he seems the quintessential family farmer, but look closer and you'll find him far wiser and shrewder than the stereotype. Jim and I got to be close after the fund-raiser. He was the first farmer who would grow specifically for me. While other farmers were stuck on iceberg lettuce, Jim Core would listen to the chefs, find out what they needed, and grow the varieties that no one else in the community had ever heard of. Our relationship was cemented when, in the summer prior to Katrina, we partnered with Kendall-Jackson Winery, which has an organic farm in Sonoma that grows about 175 heirloom varieties. I couldn't understand why we couldn't grow some of those here, so Jim Core planted 68 varieties (where before he'd grown only half a dozen). We guaranteed to buy what he grew, and for the first time he had a built-in market.

Tools of the trade: Rakes and brooms in the Core's shed, below. Gladys's sister, Gay Redler, washes a rainbow of peppers in the farm sink.

THE NEXT YEAR, Jim Core found new tomato sources himself, and the money he made from that summer right before the Katrina crisis just about got him through the storm. Because he's a crackerjack farmer, he knows which varieties work for him. Jim Core still grows a Creole variety called Celebrity. But as he puts it, you can call anything Creole and it'll sell. He also grows Red Brandywine, Purple Calabash, Purple Russian, Japanese Black Trifele, Cuban Yellow Grape, and Chocolate Cherry tomatoes and Silver Queen corn and foot-long beans. I don't know whether Jim would ever see himself as the Tomato Man, the kind books are written about, but he sure belongs in this one. When I cook with his beautiful vegetables, I handle them in a way that pays respect to Jim and all the work it takes his family to get them to me. Gladys and Gay do a showbiz sister act at their booth at the Uptown Farmers' Market every Tuesday. Beautifully turned out and carefully made up, they draw customers like sunshine or honey: "Hey, Miss Lisette! Hey, Chantelle! You want the good ones? You sure you don't want the bad ones? You enjoy them, now. We love you to death." Jim Core just chuckles and reminds them, "While y'all are out there soaring like eagles, remember who put the wind beneath your wings!"

SALAD OF HEIRLOOM TOMATOES, CHEESE, AND COUNTRY HAM

Serves 8

When shopping for this salad, don't worry about finding the exact varieties I list here; just use the ripest local tomatoes you can find. For the most beautiful salad, look for a range of colors, shapes, and sizes. I love paper-thin slices of country ham, but prosciutto, jamón Serrano, or your favorite salami will work equally well.

2 large Cherokee Purple tomatoes

2 Green Zebra tomatoes

2 Black Prince tomatoes

2 Pineapple tomatoes

4 Snow White tomatoes

4 green grape tomatoes

1 pint yellow or red currant or pear tomatoes

Salt

Freshly ground black pepper

¼ cup extra-virgin olive oil

3 tablespoons balsamic vinegar

2 cloves garlic, minced

1 anchovy filet, minced

1 teaspoon sugar

½ teaspoon crushed red pepper flakes

Smallest leaves from 1 branch fresh basil

4 ounces ricotta salata cheese

8 pieces very thinly sliced country ham or prosciutto

1. First wash the tomatoes and core all but the smallest ones. Then, depending on their size, slice, quarter, or halve the tomatoes or leave them whole, slicing the larger ones thickly (about 4 slices each). Arrange them on one big serving platter or divide them evenly between 8 individual plates. Season the tomatoes with a touch of salt and pepper.

2. Whisk together the olive oil, vinegar, garlic, anchovies, sugar, pepper flakes, and a pinch or two of salt in a small bowl. Drizzle the vinaigrette over the tomatoes and scatter basil leaves on them.

3. Finally, coarsely crumble the cheese over the tomatoes, then arrange the slices of country ham on top of and around the tomatoes.

Creole Tomatoes

Much mystique surrounds the identity of the famed Creole tomato. Turns out it is not so much a variety as an idea of a tomato, evoking a memory of the field-picked, just-ripe tomatoes of our childhood, before hybrids and industrial farming took the flavor away. Experts say the definition comes down to geography: any red, ripe tomato grown in the state of Louisiana, but most often in the southeast in the parishes along the Mississippi, can be deemed a Creole. It can be grown from any seed variety, such as the Celebrity, favored by Jim Core, or those newer, hardier varieties, like Amelia and Christa. Historically, St. Bernard and Plaquemines parishes were tomato central, but following Katrina the area shrank to the upper Plaquemines.

Today, more than 250 growers cultivate the almost 500 acres of Louisiana that are dedicated to this buxom fruit so fundamental to Creole cooking. The crops are mostly sold locally at wholesale warehouses, farmers' markets, roadside stands, and supermarkets, and there is rarely enough of a surplus to cause a Creole ever to head out of state. Nowadays, some of us feel that the Creole is looking a little too pretty and uniform, but in general locals will tell you with pride that a Creole tastes the way a real tomato should.

CHERRY TOMATO FIVE-MINUTE SAUCE

Makes 1 quart

This ultrasimple sauce is one of my favorite basic preparations. Its vibrancy depends on the freshest, ripest tomatoes. I favor the intensely flavorful cherry tomatoes, but any small, sweet tomato works well. The sauce changes with the addition of ingredients; serve it chilled with onions, peppers, and lime for a wonderful gazpacho, or heat it and then toss with pasta. The added touch of sugar does the job of balancing the spices and acids.

¼ cup extra-virgin olive oil	2 teaspoons crushed red pepper flakes
2 quarts ripe cherry tomatoes, halved	4 cloves garlic, thinly sliced
Leaves from 1 branch fresh basil	Salt
1 teaspoon sugar	Freshly ground black pepper

1. Heat the oil in a large sauté pan over high heat. Add the tomatoes, basil, sugar, pepper flakes, and garlic and cook until tomatoes come to a boil. Cook for 5 minutes more, crushing the tomatoes with the back of a wooden spoon.

2. Use a food mill to purée the sauce, or push the tomatoes through a strainer into a bowl with a rubber spatula. Discard solids. Season the purée with salt and pepper.

3. Pour the puréed tomatoes through a canning funnel into a quart jar. Use as soon as possible.

Making the sauce: From right, quickly cooking the tomatoes, Jenifer pushes heated tomatoes through a food mill, pouring the finished sauce into jars.

Father's Day in Slidell:
My Dad, Ted, holds court,
above. Top right, crabmeat-
stuffed tomatoes. Right,
my in-laws, Patrick and
Barbara Berrigan, with
daughter Erin. My mother,
Imelda.

CRABMEAT-STUFFED TOMATOES

Serves 6

If you don't have the time or the inclination to peel the tomatoes, use the juiciest tomatoes you can find, slice and season them, top with the crabmeat and basil, and enjoy.

6 ripe medium to large Creole or other ripe tomatoes in season Salt	2 tablespoons fresh lemon juice
½ cup mayonnaise	1 teaspoon Dijon mustard
1 small branch fresh basil leaves, 6 small leaves reserved for garnish, the rest finely chopped	2 cups jumbo lump crabmeat, picked over Basic Creole Spices (see page 13) 3–6 chive or garlic chive blossoms, optional

1. To peel the tomatoes, bring a medium pot of water to a boil over high heat. Core the tomatoes, then score the bottoms by making a small *X* in each. Blanch 3 tomatoes at a time for exactly 5 seconds per batch, moving them around with a pair of tongs or a slotted spoon. Transfer the tomatoes, cored side down, to paper towels to let drain and cool briefly, then peel off the skin and discard.

2. Using a teaspoon and starting at the core, carefully scoop out the center of the tomatoes, creating a bowl. Cut off bottom third of the tomatoes and set aside (you'll use them as lids to top the stuffed tomatoes). Season the tomatoes with a little salt.

3. Mix the mayonnaise, chopped basil, lemon juice, and mustard together in a medium bowl. Add the crab, stirring gently so as not to break up the meat. Season the crab salad with Creole Spices and salt. Stuff the tomatoes with the crab salad, add a a basil leaf or two, and chive blossoms, if using. Set a tomato lid on top of each one.

TERRINE OF CHEROKEE PURPLE TOMATOES

Serves 12

This terrine might seem somewhat involved, but it's not much more difficult than those old-fashioned tomato molds that used tomato juice and gelatin. Here, we're dehydrating the tomatoes slightly to intensify their flavor, then binding them together in a terrine—just an update on an old-time idea.

10	pounds Cherokee Purple or other large, meaty heirloom tomatoes
2	cloves garlic, minced
1	teaspoon crushed red pepper flakes
1	teaspoon sugar
	Salt
½	cup extra-virgin olive oil
	Freshly ground black pepper
3	envelopes unflavored gelatin
	Balsamic vinegar
	Tapenade (page 146)
	Basil leaves for garnish

1. Preheat the oven to 300°. To peel the tomatoes, bring 1 gallon water to a boil in a large pot over high heat. Core the tomatoes, then score the bottoms by making a small *X*. Blanch several tomatoes at a time for exactly 5 seconds per batch, moving them around with a slotted spoon or a pair of tongs. Transfer the tomatoes to paper towels to let drain, cored side down, and let cool briefly, then peel off the skin and discard.

2. Quarter the tomatoes from top to bottom, then trim off the center rib from each quarter, removing seeds.

3. Set 4 cups of the tomatoes aside. Arrange the remaining tomatoes in a single layer on cookie sheets. Season them with the garlic, red pepper flakes, sugar, and salt, then drizzle them with the oil. Transfer the pans to the oven and bake the tomatoes for 30 minutes.

4. Purée the reserved 4 cups tomatoes in a blender until smooth. Strain the purée through a sieve into a medium saucepan and season well with salt and pepper. Bring the purée just to a simmer over medium-low heat.

5. Remove the saucepan with the purée from the heat. Whisk the gelatin into the tomato purée until it's completely dissolved, about 1 minute. Set purée aside at room temperature.

6. Remove the tomatoes from the oven and transfer them with a slotted spatula to paper towels, setting them in a single layer to drain off the excess oil and juices. You may need to change the paper towels several times to absorb the moisture.

7. To assemble the terrine, line a 6-cup terrine mold with a large sheet of plastic wrap, smoothing it down so that there are no wrinkles. Allow the wrap to drape over the edges by at least 4 inches. Spread 2 tablespoons of the tomato purée on the bottom of the

terrine. Arrange the tomatoes lengthwise in the terrine and completely line the bottom of the mold with a single layer of the tomato pieces. Spread 2 tablespoons of the purée over the tomatoes and arrange another layer of tomatoes over the purée. Continue this process, layering the purée and the tomatoes in the mold (and taking care not to have any gaps in the layers of tomatoes), until the terrine is filled to the top. Drape the plastic wrap over the filled mold and refrigerate the terrine until it is completely set, about 24 hours.

8. Turn the terrine out of the mold, unwrap it, and slice it into ½-inch-thick slices. Serve each slice of tomato terrine with a drizzle of balsamic vinegar, a small spoonful of Tapenade, small purple basil leaves, and a touch of extra-virgin olive oil.

GREEN TOMATO AND PEPPER JAM

Makes 2 cups or 1 pint jar

It's not just that we love green tomatoes in the South; it's that, at the end of the season, there are always so many of them that we have to come up with novel ways to use them. Green tomatoes are great for preserving because they're firm; they'll hold up to cooking and absorb the flavors of the spices. This instant jam will keep in the refrigerator for weeks.

4 black peppercorns	¼ cup aged sherry vinegar
1 teaspoon mustard seed	⅓ cup sugar
1 teaspoon coriander seed	1 tablespoon fresh orange juice
¼ teaspoon cumin seed	1 teaspoon fresh lemon juice
1 small strip orange zest	1 teaspoon minced seeded jalapeño pepper
1 small strip lemon zest	Salt
2 ½ pounds green tomatoes	

1. Put the peppercorns, mustard seed, coriander seed, and cumin seed, along with the orange and lemon zest, on a piece of cheesecloth and gather it into a pouch to make a spice bag. Tie it closed with kitchen string.

2. Peel tomatoes with a vegetable peeler, seed and dice them. Put the tomatoes, vinegar, sugar, orange juice, lemon juice, jalapeños, a pinch of salt, and the spice bag into a heavy-bottomed saucepan over medium-high heat and bring to a boil. Stir occasionally with a wooden spoon.

3. Reduce the heat to low and simmer until almost all of the liquid has evaporated. The mixture should be soft, moist, and spreadable. Remove and discard the spice bag. Transfer the jam to a sterilized jar with a lid (page 240) and refrigerate for several weeks.

SHRIMP CREOLE

Serves 12–15

Traditionally a roux-and-tomato-based dish, Shrimp Creole in my new version has Vietnamese influences; it's spicy and sweet, full of herbs and flavor. Any ultraripe tomatoes will work. The amounts given feed a typical Sunday supper at my house; for six to eight, halve the ingredients, but don't worry too much: there's a lot of forgiveness.

- 5 pounds jumbo Louisiana or wild American shrimp, peeled and deveined
- Salt
- Freshly ground black pepper
- 1 tablespoon minced fresh lemongrass
- ½ cup olive oil
- 3 medium onions, diced
- 10 cloves garlic, thinly sliced
- 1 stalk celery, diced
- 1 bell pepper, red, green, or yellow, seeded and diced

- 5 pounds overripe Brandywine or other heirloom tomatoes, peeled, seeded, and chopped
- 1 bay leaf
- ¼ teaspoon ground allspice
- 1 tablespoon crushed red pepper flakes
- Leaves from 2 branches fresh basil, chopped
- Leaves from 1 sprig fresh mint, chopped
- Sugar
- 6–8 cups cooked Basic Louisiana White Rice (page 15)

1. Put the shrimp into a large bowl, season with salt and pepper, then mix in the lemongrass. Heat ¼ cup of the oil in a large deep skillet over moderate heat. Add the shrimp, stirring and tossing them with a spatula. Sauté until they turn pink, about 2 minutes. Remove the shrimp from the pan and set aside while you make the sauce.

2. Into the same skillet with the oil and shrimp juices, put the remaining ¼ cup oil and the onions, garlic, celery, and bell peppers and cook, stirring constantly with a wooden spoon, for about 2 minutes.

3. Add the tomatoes. Reduce the heat to medium-low and when the sauce comes to a simmer add the bay leaf, allspice, and red pepper flakes. Simmer for 10 minutes.

4. Add the shrimp back to the skillet along with the basil and mint. Cook for a minute or two. Season with salt and pepper. If the sauce tastes too tart, add a little sugar to balance the flavor. Remove the bay leaf. Serve over steamed Louisiana white rice.

Shrimp love tomatoes: Quickly seared shrimp await sauce, left. Cases of Creole tomatoes, below.

CHILLED TOMATO SOUP WITH TAPENADE

Serves 6

This is the place to use the finest aged sherry vinegar to brighten the flavor of the ripest tomatoes. I love using old vinegar because its acids have mellowed and truly complement the tomatoes' natural sweetness.

FOR THE SOUP

- ¼ cup extra-virgin olive oil
- 1 white onion, minced
- 3 cloves garlic, minced
- 3 pounds ripe Creole or heirloom tomatoes, roughly chopped
- 1 red bell pepper, seeded and chopped
- 2 tablespoons aged sherry vinegar
- Leaves from 1 sprig fresh thyme
- Leaves from 1 branch fresh basil

Salt

Freshly ground black pepper

- 1 tablespoon sugar

FOR THE TAPENADE

- 4 cloves garlic
- ½ cup pitted black olives
- 2 anchovy filets
- Leaves from 1 sprig fresh thyme
- Juice of 1 lemon
- 1 cup extra-virgin olive oil

1. For the soup, heat the oil in a large heavy-bottomed pot over medium-high heat. Add the onions and garlic, stirring with a wooden spoon, and cook for a moment without browning, just until the onions soften. Add the tomatoes and bell peppers, reduce the heat to moderate, and simmer, stirring often, for 15 minutes.

2. Add the vinegar, thyme, and basil. Remove from the heat and purée in a food mill or a food processor. Season with salt and pepper. If the sauce tastes too tart, add a little sugar to balance the flavor. Transfer the soup to a container with a cover and refrigerate until the soup is chilled, about 4 hours.

3. For the tapenade, purée the garlic, olives, anchovies, thyme, and lemon juice to a paste in a food processor. With the machine running, slowly drizzle in the olive oil. Feel free to omit the anchovies if you prefer; it's all a matter of taste.

4. Pour the soup into chilled soup bowls and top with a generous spoonful of the tapenade.

Showtime: Gladys Core meets her public at the Uptown Farmers Market.

Bountiful: A wooden trug of just-harvested heirloom tomatoes, above. Fried snow white tomatoes with aïoli, left.

FRIED SNOW WHITE TOMATOES WITH AÏOLI

Serves 6–8 as hors d'oeuvres

For this dish, I love to find small tomatoes still on the vine. The stem not only looks great but works well when you're handling the delicate tomatoes, which burst the moment you bite into one. Snow White is just one of many small and intensely sweet varieties of tomato; you can substitute any sweet cluster tomatoes.

1 quart olive or vegetable oil	24–36 Snow White or other small tomatoes, preferably on the vine
1 cup flour	
1 pinch salt	1 cup Basic Aïoli (page 17)
1½ cups club soda	

1. Heat the oil in a deep heavy-bottomed pot over medium-high heat to 350°. Meanwhile, make a tempura-style batter by whisking the flour and salt together in a mixing bowl. Then add the club soda, whisking gently to keep the batter fluffy. The batter will be thin.

2. Cut the tomatoes into small clusters with scissors. Rinse the tomatoes and pat them dry. Working in batches, dip the tomatoes into the batter, coating them all over, then carefully slip them into the hot oil. Deep-fry the tomatoes until the batter is lacy, crisp, and golden brown, about 1 minute. Using metal tongs or a slotted spoon, carefully transfer the tomatoes to paper towels to let drain.

3. Put the aïoli into a small bowl and serve alongside the tomatoes for dipping.

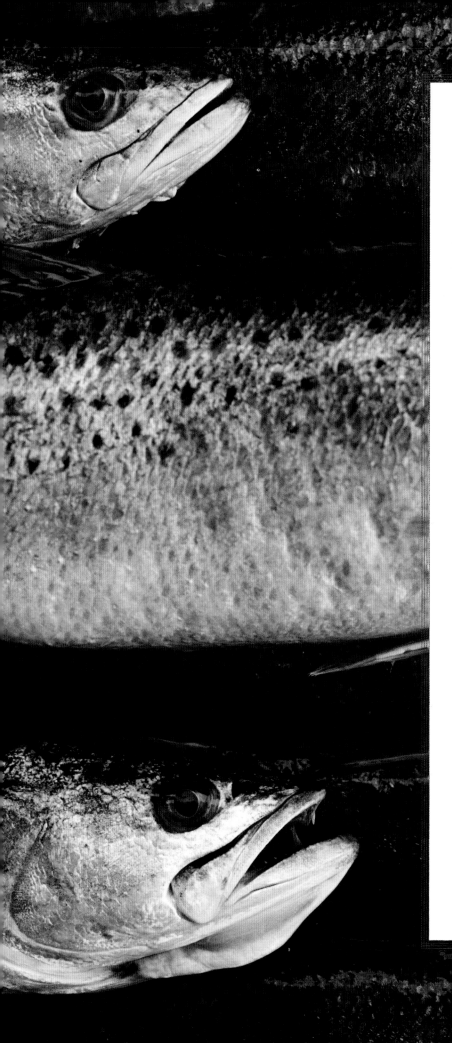

SPECKLED TROUT & REDFISH

We Fish to Eat

"The worst thing about combat in the first gulf war was that the smell of toasted almonds meant a chemical attack."

The aroma of toasted almonds and brown butter—Mom's trout amandine—is my foremost food sense memory. When that smell whiffed through the house, it meant that Dad and Mike Reilly had been fishing, that the trout had been fileted, seasoned, dredged in flour, and sautéed in butter with sliced almonds, parsley, and lemon juice. What an irony that those comforting memories were sullied by the threats we Marines were trained to counter from that madman Saddam Hussein.

Where I come from, you eat speckled trout and other fish because they taste good. We fish primarily to eat, so you go fishing when you're in the mood to eat fish. Our trout really aren't trout at all; they're spotted weakfish—shimmering silver with black specks, two

Memories: Clockwise from top left, me with a mortar on the Kuwaiti–Saudi border, in Desert Storm, 1990; hanging speckled trout; vintage image of boys about to go fishing feels familiar, photo: The Historic New Orleans Collection. Left, a just-caught flounder awaits stuffing; cane poles rigged with bobbers; Blake Boyd catches a croaker from his family's dock on Lake Pontchartrain.

large fangs, and sweet white, flaky flesh, best when eaten within a day or two of the fishing trip. They are not related to that highfalutin species that hangs out around posh mountain resorts, to be fished with expensive long rods and dry flies. Now, I did grow up fly-fishing, but that was only for panfish. I have tried fishing for those snob trout like rainbows, brookies, browns, and cutthroats, but I just don't get it. The speckled trout is hardly ever caught and then released. A good fishing trip is defined not by the wicked fight the fish put up just before it was set free. Instead, our success is measured by how many ice chests we filled. Nor do I understand people who view fishing as an art form, or practice it as a way to perfect their casting. I've fished with JB Mahoney most of my life, and he's never once commented on my cast. We just fish. And occasionally complain about gnats or whatnot.

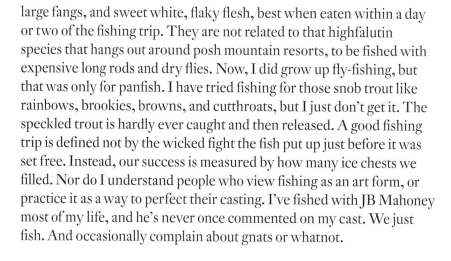

I CAN'T SAY THAT my mother has ever bought fish from a fishmonger; our seafood shops sell mainly shrimp, crawfish, crab, oysters, and a few offshore fish like tuna, amberjack, and lemonfish. As for the other great fish in these fertile waters, well, most folks have friends who fish, and so it was with restaurants as I was coming up. I will never forget when the state finally started cracking down on restaurants for buying fish—or even getting free fish—from unlicensed fishermen. Chefs were arrested and sent to jail for serving the freshest fish! Of course that publicity worked in favor of the chefs and their business prospered because of it. Speckled trout certainly isn't the only fish we eat, but it's by far the most popular. Every year the trout move out of deep waters into the estuaries for spawning and every year anglers like my friends will be right there following them. We do favor trout, but we're happy to catch black drum, sheepshead, white trout, and croaker, and we'll catch the self-same redfish that became so famous two decades ago when Chef Paul Prudhomme's blackened redfish craze spread out across the land. I love a redfish not much bigger than three pounds, so it fits perfectly in the pan where it will be smothered in a Creole "gravy"—a stew of onions, garlic, and Creole tomatoes spiced with a touch of black pepper and cayenne, and a bit of allspice in there for good measure—and baked in the oven.

As a little boy I'd prefer croaker to anything, mainly because they were easy to catch and the

Sunrise: I love to fish at the crack of dawn at Marshdown on Bayou Liberty. Inset, casting into the brackish waters of Lake Ponchartrain.

Holy mackerel: No, really, those are prize tarpon hanging behind the nuns at a fishing rodeo at Grand Isle, Louisiana, 1960; photo: Manuel C. DeLerno, The Historic New Orleans Collection.

law would let you keep them and eat them regardless of size. For starters, Dad would cut us poles from the cane that grows wild on the side of the road and hang them from a tree, where they'd stay for a few weeks until they were completely dry. Then he'd tie us a line with a hook and a cork bobber, which was all you needed for a day of fun. Dad would load several of us in the little 15-foot skiff and take us down the rigolets to the edge of Lake Borgne. We'd usually pull over near a shrimper and buy a couple pounds of live shrimp for bait. My best memories are of fishing around an inshore oil platform that was a natural reef for any indigenous fish. It was quite remarkable how I'd only have to put a piece of shrimp on a hook and drop the hook near one of the pilings; in no time I'd have a croaker or sheepshead for sure.

I did learn how to fly-fish as a teenager, but it was never about the form. I did it just well enough to plop a popping bug out in front of a largemouth bass or a small fresh water panfish, like sunfish, bluegill, perch, bream, or sacalait (crappie), which we'd eat the same way we ate croaker: we'd remove the scales and guts, make an incision alongside both the pectoral and the dorsal fin, dredge the fish in a little egg wash and then in a flour-and-cornmeal mix, and fry them up in a pan with a half inch or so of peanut oil. When those fish came out of the pan, all they needed was a little salt, a dash or two of Tabasco, and a squeeze of lemon. Nothing fancy for croaker or panfish. They were as good as any other fish, with half the effort and none of the affectation.

TROUT PONTCHARTRAIN

Serves 6

Of course the filets of any flaky, white fish will work fine here; so will most any mushroom. I'm a fanatic for the wild varieties like chanterelles, morels, porcinis, black trumpets, hedgehogs, and hen of the woods, but back in the day even button mushrooms did the trick.

1 cup flour

1 tablespoon Basic Creole Spices (page 13)

4 eggs

½ cup milk

3 cups panko bread crumbs

6 speckled trout filets

Salt

Freshly ground black pepper

3 tablespoons extra-virgin olive oil

2 tablespoons butter

1 handful fresh wild mushrooms, sliced

1 shallot, minced

1 clove garlic, minced

½ teaspoon crushed red pepper flakes

1 cup jumbo lump crabmeat, picked over

1 teaspoon fresh lemon juice

2 dashes Tabasco

2 tablespoons chopped fresh chives and/or the petals of chive blossoms

1 cup Basic Sauce Hollandaise (page 17)

1. Combine the flour and Creole Spices in a wide dish. Beat the eggs and milk together in another wide dish. Put the bread crumbs into a third wide dish.

2. Season the fish filets with salt and pepper. Dredge them in the seasoned flour, dip them into the egg wash, then dredge them in the bread crumbs.

3. Heat the olive oil in a large skillet over medium-high heat. Working in batches, cook the fish until golden brown on both sides, about 3 minutes per side. Transfer the fish as done to paper towels to drain.

4. Pour off any remaining oil from the skillet. Reduce the heat to moderate. Add the butter and wild mushrooms and cook for a couple of minutes. Add the shallots, garlic, and pepper flakes and cook, stirring frequently, until the shallots and garlic are soft but have not taken on any color, 3–5 minutes. Add the crabmeat, lemon juice, and a little bit of salt and cook until the crab is just heated through, 3–5 minutes, keeping the crabmeat from breaking up. Season with Tabasco, salt, and pepper. Fold in the chopped chives.

5. Divide the fish between 6 warm plates, spoon Sauce Hollandaise on each, and top with a heaping spoonful of the crab and mushrooms. Serve more Sauce Hollandaise in a small bowl on the side.

Fishing party: A family sets out for a day of fun, 1928; photo: W. Knighton Bloom Pictures, Amistad Research Center.

TROUT AMANDINE

Serves 6

In traditonal French cooking, a whole fish would be lightly dredged in flour and cooked in butter. In New Orleans we prefer the skinless trout filet. Properly browning the butter makes all the difference. Don't rush it; take your time swirling the butter in the pan so that the milk solids brown and give off the signature, nutty aroma that is heightened once you add the almonds. Add the lemon juice and serve while the sauce is still foamy.

---

1 cup milk

1 cup flour

1 teaspoon Basic Creole Spices (page 13)

6 5–7-ounce skinless speckled trout filets

Salt

Freshly ground black pepper

8 tablespoons butter

½ cup sliced almonds

Juice of 1 lemon

2 tablespoons minced fresh parsley

1. Put the milk into a wide dish. Put the flour and Creole Spices into another wide dish and stir to combine. Season the fish filets with salt and pepper, dip them into the milk, and dredge in the seasoned flour.

2. Melt 4 tablespoons of the butter in a large skillet over medium-high heat. Add the filets and cook on each side until golden brown, about 3 minutes per side. Transfer the fish to a serving platter.

3. Add the remaining 4 tablespoons butter to the same skillet over medium-high heat. Swirl the skillet over the heat so that the butter melts evenly and cook until the butter turns brownish, 5–7 minutes. Reduce the heat to medium-low, add the almonds, and cook, stirring gently, until the nuts are toasty brown, about 3 minutes. Add the lemon juice, parsley, and a dash of salt.

4. Spoon the browned butter and almonds over the fish and serve.

VARIATION

TROUT MEUNIÈRE

Follow the steps above, omitting the almonds.

Speckled Trout

Freshness and delicacy are the best things about our trout, and although they're fine fried, I prefer to dredge the filets in a bit of flour and quickly sauté them over high heat in a touch of butter or olive oil. Like flounder and sole, which are similarly delicate, the speckled trout must be carefully handled; it would disintegrate without flour. Also known as spotted sea trout, speckled trout is, in fact, a member of the weakfish family (*Cynoscion nebulosus*), which includes croaker, black drum, and red drum. Speckled trout can be discovered at the end of a fishing line along the Eastern seaboard from Virginia south, but they are the most abundant and the best protected in the Gulf of Mexico. Here in South Louisiana, they seek out brackish water for spawning, and once their minuscule planktonic eggs hatch into larvae, they settle into one of the many sheltered pockets that our marshes and estuaries provide, safe from predators. By the time these carnivores are strong enough to venture out, they are armed with two canine teeth, which make it all the easier for them to dine on shrimp; they move on to small fish as their speed and appetite grow. Speckled trout eventually disperse into oyster beds, open bayous, and channels, letting the current wash tasty pickings their way. We love it that speckled trout are fished recreationally, never commercially. Pan-frying one of these boys is the perfect finale to a day well spent.

Looks fishy in there: On this romantic tributary of Lake Pontchartrain, we'll catch everything from bass to croaker.

CHARCOAL-GRILLED REDFISH WITH CORN AND GINGER SALAD

Serves 6

I like to leave the scales on the fish as a buffer against the hot coals. Substitute any fish that'll take the heat: striped bass, drumfish, or grouper.

6 ears corn, shucked	2 green onions, chopped
12 cherry tomatoes, halved	2 teaspoons sugar
4–6 large redfish filets, skin and scales left on	½ teaspoon crushed red pepper flakes
½ cup extra-virgin olive oil	¼ cup rice wine vinegar
Salt	1 teaspoon fresh lemon juice
Freshly ground black pepper	Leaves from 1 sprig fresh mint, chopped
2 cloves garlic, minced	Leaves from 1 sprig fresh basil, chopped
2 teaspoons minced peeled fresh ginger	Leaves from 1 sprig fresh cilantro, chopped

1. Light a charcoal or gas grill. Grill the ears of corn over the hot coals until the kernels are golden brown, about 5 minutes. Cut the corn kernels off the cobs and set them aside; discard the cobs. Grill the cherry tomatoes, cut side up, for 30 seconds and set aside.

2. Rub the redfish filets with 1–2 tablespoons of the olive oil and season them with salt and pepper. Put the fish on the grill, skin side down, over moderately hot coals, cover the grill with the lid, and grill the fish until the flesh pulls away easily from the skin, about 10 minutes. Using a long metal spatula, slide the fish filets off their skins and transfer the fish to a platter.

3. Heat the remaining olive oil in a large skillet over medium-high heat. Add the garlic, ginger, and green onions and cook, stirring frequently, until the onions begin to soften, 2–3 minutes. Add the grilled corn and cherry tomatoes, the sugar, pepper flakes, vinegar, lemon juice, mint, basil, and cilantro and cook, stirring often, until the corn is heated through, 3–5 minutes. Spoon the warm corn and tomatoes over each fish filet and serve.

MOM'S REDFISH COURTBOUILLON

Serves 4–6

My father had a way of slicing a whole fish along the dorsal fin so that, as it cooked, the flesh would just lift from the bone, which made it quite easy to handle with just a serving spoon and fork. Much of the time in Louisiana, a courtbouillon (pronounced CU-boo-yon) looks more like a variation of bouillabaisse, using fish filets. But I think slow-cooking the whole fish on the bone yields a much better-tasting dish. Ask your fishmonger to prepare the fish gutted and scaled, and to remove its gills.

---

1 **5-pound redfish**	¼ **teaspoon ground allspice**
Juice of 1 lemon	¼ **teaspoon ground coriander seed**
Salt	
Freshly ground black pepper	3 **bay leaves**
½ **cup canola oil**	2 **cups Basic Shrimp Stock (page 13)**
½ **cup flour**	1 **pound medium Louisiana or wild American shrimp, peeled**
2 **onions, chopped**	
2 **blue crabs, quartered**	
1 **bell pepper, seeded and chopped**	1 **cup shucked oysters**
2 **stalks celery, chopped**	1 **pound jumbo lump crabmeat, picked over**
4 **cloves garlic, minced**	
6 **tomatoes, peeled and diced**	3 **green onions, chopped**
Leaves from 1 sprig fresh tarragon, minced	3 **dashes Worcestershire**
	Tabasco
1 **teaspoon crushed red pepper flakes**	4 **cups cooked Basic Louisiana White Rice (page 15)**

1. Preheat the oven to 300°. To keep the fish from curling up in the roasting pan while cooking, score both sides of the redfish about ¼ inch deep in a couple of places between the pectoral fins and the tail and along both sides of the dorsal fin.

2. Put the fish into a roasting pan just large enough for it to lie flat. Season the fish all over with the lemon juice, salt, and pepper and set aside.

3. Pour the oil into a large heavy-bottomed saucepan and stir in the flour. Cook over moderate heat, stirring constantly, until the roux becomes deep brown and has a nutty aroma, about 15 minutes.

4. Add the onions and blue crab quarters to the roux and cook, stirring frequently, for 5 minutes. Add the bell peppers, celery, garlic, and tomatoes. Increase the heat to medium-high and bring to a boil, stirring every so often.

5. Add the tarragon, pepper flakes, allspice, coriander, bay leaves, and Shrimp Stock to the saucepan and bring to a boil, stirring frequently. Season with salt and pepper, then pour over the redfish in the roasting pan, cover the pan with foil, and bake the fish for about 40 minutes.

6. Scatter the shrimp, oysters, lump crabmeat, and green onions around the fish in the pan and return the pan to the oven. Bake the fish, uncovered, until it begins to flake from the bone, about 15 minutes more.

7. Add the Worcestershire, a little Tabasco, and salt and pepper to the tomato–shellfish gravy in the roasting pan. Use a large spoon and fork to portion the fish, serving it with the gravy over the rice.

Family affair: Above, my dad, Ted, in his serious fishing hat. My mother, Imelda, in 1988. She taught me to cook fish.

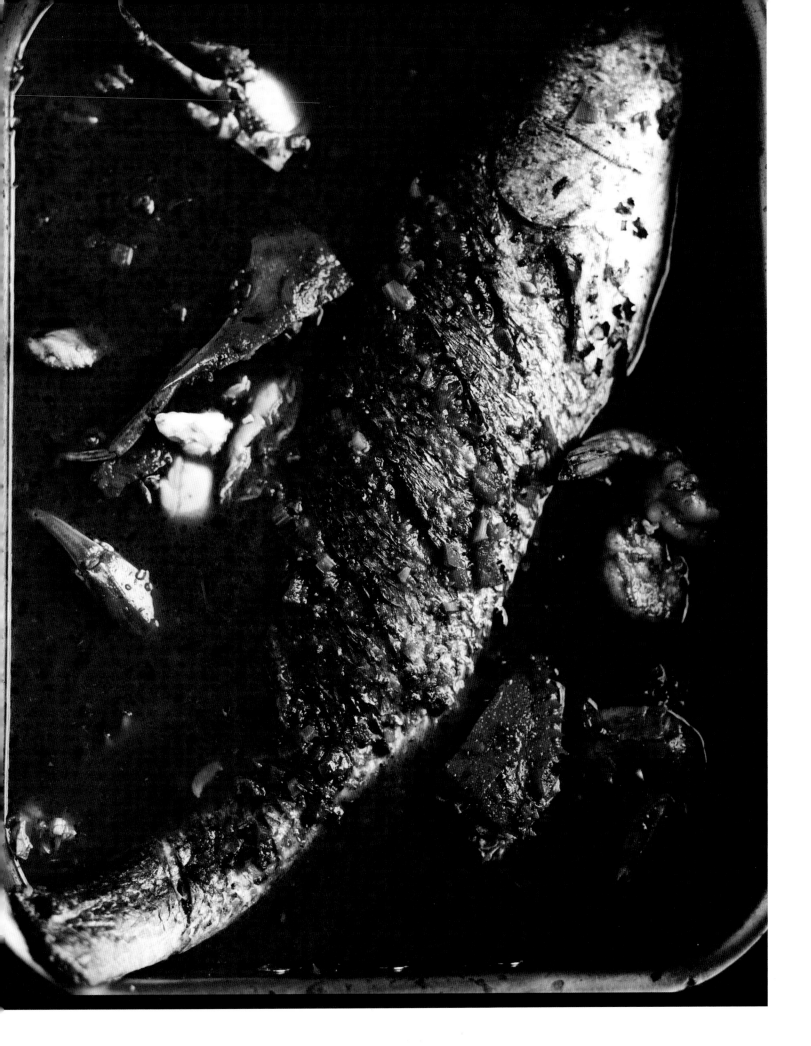

CRAB-AND-SHRIMP-STUFFED FLOUNDER

Serves 6

It's a very intricate job to remove the bones of the fish and keep the fish intact, but I'll walk you through it. If all else fails, filet the fish completely and place one filet in the pan, then a layer of stuffing, and top with the second filet.

3 large flounder	Leaves from 2 sprigs fresh thyme
4 tablespoons extra-virgin olive oil	Salt
1 onion, chopped	Freshly ground black pepper
1 bulb fennel, chopped	½ cup diced white bread
1 stalk celery, chopped	½ cup dried bread crumbs
3 cloves garlic, thinly sliced	¾ cup Basic Fish Pan Sauce (page 15)
1 teaspoon crushed red pepper flakes	Juice of 1 lemon
¼ cup Basic Shellfish Stock (page 13)	1 teaspoon Creole mustard (page 362)
1 pound crabmeat, picked over	Leaves from 1 sprig fresh tarragon, minced
1 pound small Louisiana or wild American shrimp, peeled and chopped	4 tablespoons butter

1. Working with one flounder at a time, put the fish on a cutting board, dark side facing up and positioned with the head facing away from you. Now, your goal is to make a boneless pocket for stuffing the fish. Using a sharp, flexible boning knife, make an incision, deep enough to hit the backbone, down the center of the flounder from head to tail. Now make 2 cuts perpendicular to the long cut, one behind the head, the second in front of the tail. You should now have cuts in the shape of a capital *I*.

2. Working on the left side of the center cut, slide the knife between the flesh and the bone and carefully cut the flesh back, exposing the bones, until you have a long, wide flap of flesh that's still attached to the fish along the belly. Repeat this process, cutting another flap that remains attached along the top of the fish.

3. Leaving the head and tail on, carefully slide the knife between the exposed bones and the flesh beneath, cutting the whole backbone out from the flesh beneath it. Now you have a fileted fish with a boneless pocket for stuffing. Repeat with each flounder and set them aside.

4. Preheat the oven to 400°. Heat 2 tablespoons of the olive oil in a large skillet over moderate heat. Add the onions, fennel, celery, and garlic and cook, stirring often, until the vegetables are soft, 5–10 minutes. Add the pepper flakes, Shellfish Stock, crabmeat, shrimp, and thyme and cook, stirring occasionally, for 10 minutes. Season with salt and pepper, then add the diced bread and bread crumbs. Check to make sure the stuffing is well-seasoned.

5. Spoon one-third of the stuffing into the pocket of each flounder and fold the flaps of fish over the stuffing. Season the fish with salt and pepper and drizzle each with some of the remaining olive oil.

6. With the remaining olive oil, grease a baking sheet large enough to accommodate the stuffed flounder in a single layer and place the stuffed flounder on it, stuffed side up. Cover the pan with foil and bake the fish for 20 minutes.

7. Meanwhile, put the Fish Pan Sauce into a small saucepan and boil over medium-high heat until reduced by half, 7–10 minutes. Add the lemon juice, mustard, tarragon, and butter. Remove the pan from the heat and stir the sauce until the butter has melted. Season the sauce with salt and pepper and set aside.

8. Remove the flounder from the oven, uncover the pan, and return the flounder to the oven to bake for 5–7 minutes more. Serve the flounder with the sauce on the side.

Stuffing a flounder:
Counterclockwise, from top left, first make a cut the length of the fish; next remove the backbone, creating a pocket; stuff the pocket with crab and shrimp. Above, the glorious fish just out of the oven.

PAN ROAST OF LEMONFISH WITH GINGER–PEA RISOTTO

Serves 6

Lemonfish, or cobia, is very lean. Brown only three steaks at a time to keep the pan from cooling and steaming the fish. You want to caramelize the the outside so the fish browns, but stays rare inside. The risotto should be creamy and loose.

FOR THE SAUCE

- 3 cups fresh orange juice
- 8 tablespoons cold butter, cubed
- Salt

FOR THE RISOTTO

- 4 cups Basic Chicken Stock (page 13)
- 2 tablespoons extra-virgin olive oil
- 1 onion, minced
- 2 tablespoons minced peeled fresh ginger
- ½ teaspoon crushed red pepper flakes
- 1 cup Arborio rice
- 2 cups sugar snap peas, thinly sliced on the bias
- ½ cup whipped cream
- 3 green onions, very thinly sliced on the bias
- 2 tablespoons butter
- 2 tablespoons freshly grated Parmesan cheese
- Salt

FOR THE FISH

- 4 tablespoons extra-virgin olive oil
- 6 6-ounce lemonfish steaks
- Salt
- 1 cup flour
- 1 handful small fresh cilantro leaves and/or fresh garlic chive blossoms

1. For the sauce, put the orange juice into a medium heavy-bottomed saucepan and gently boil over moderate heat until reduced to ¼ cup. Reduce the heat to low and whisk in the cold butter, one cube at a time, whisking constantly until each cube of butter has melted and been incorporated into the sauce before adding more. Season the orange–butter sauce with salt and keep it on a warm spot on the stove.

2. For the risotto, bring the Chicken Stock to a simmer in a medium pot over moderate heat. Heat the olive oil in a wide shallow saucepan over moderate heat. Add the onions and cook until soft, 5–10 minutes. Add the ginger and pepper flakes and cook until fragrant. Stir in the rice and cook, stirring frequently, until slightly toasted, 2–3 minutes.

3. Ladle the hot Chicken Stock into the rice, 1 cup at a time, stirring frequently and waiting until the liquid has been absorbed before adding more. Continue to cook the rice in this way for about 15 minutes, then add the sugar snap peas and cook until tender, 1–2 minutes. Stir in the whipped cream and cook until it has reduced by half, 3–5 minutes. Add the green onions, turn off the heat, then stir in the butter and the cheese. Season with salt. Keep the risotto warm in a warm spot on the stove.

4. For the fish, heat 2 tablespoons of the olive oil in a large skillet over high heat. Season both sides of the fish steaks with salt, then dredge them in the flour. Carefully lay 3 fish steaks in the skillet, then give the skillet a shake to make sure the fish doesn't stick to the bottom. Reduce the heat to moderate. Cook the fish until a golden brown crust has formed on the bottom, about 3 minutes, then use a spatula to flip the fish over. Reduce heat to medium-low and cook for 1–2 minutes longer. Drain the fish on paper towels. Wipe out skillet and repeat with the remaining olive oil and fish steaks.

5. Spoon equal portions of the warm orange–butter sauce into the middle of 6 deep warmed soup bowls. Divide the risotto evenly between the bowls, spooning it into the center of the butter sauce so that the sauce spreads evenly to the edges of the bowl. Place lemonfish on the risotto and scatter the cilantro leaves and/or garlic chive blossoms on top.

BREADED RED SNAPPER WITH SHRIMP, FENNEL, AND ORANGES

Serves 6

The bread in this dish is really a paper-thin, crispy crust that adheres to each portion of fish. A good trick is to roll the bread slices through a pasta machine to get them as thin as possible. My idea is that with each bite you'll have the sensation of the crispy bread, the luscious fish with the velvety hollandaise, and the crunchy, tangy salad on top.

1   bulb fennel

4   oranges

12 jumbo wild American shrimp, boiled, peeled, and halved lengthwise

¼   cup Basic Lemon Vinaigrette (page 18)

1   pinch cayenne pepper

1   pinch sugar

    Salt

    Freshly ground black pepper

6   slices white bread, crusts removed

    Leaves from 1 sprig fresh tarragon, minced

6   6-ounce skinless red snapper filets

2   tablespoons extra-virgin olive oil

1   cup Basic Citrus Hollandaise (page 17)

1   handful fresh chives, chopped

    Small sprigs from 1 branch fresh dill

    Petals from 2 chive blossoms

1. For the salad, slice the fennel as thinly as possible using a mandoline or a very sharp knife. Put the fennel into a medium bowl.

2. Using a sharp knife, prepare the oranges by first cutting off the top and bottom of each. Then stand the orange on one end and slice off the peel and white pith from top to bottom, cutting around the entire orange, removing as much peel as possible and leaving as much flesh as you can.

3. Working over the bowl with fennel to catch the juices, cut out each fleshy fruit segment from between the membranes on each side. Squeeze any remaining juice left from the pulp into the same bowl. Discard the pulp.

4. Add the shrimp, Lemon Vinaigrette, cayenne pepper, and sugar to the fennel and orange segments and season with salt and pepper. Toss well and set the salad aside.

5. Using a pasta machine or a rolling pin, flatten each slice of bread to a thickness of ⅛–¹⁄₁₆ inch. Lay the slices of bread out on a work surface and sprinkle each slice with the minced tarragon.

6. Season the fish with salt and pepper and place each filet on top of one of the slices of bread. Using a sharp knife, cut around the perimeter of the fish so that the bread perfectly matches the dimensions of the filet.

7. Heat the olive oil in a large skillet over moderate heat. Place the pieces of prepared fish in the skillet, bread side down, and cook until the bread is golden brown, about 4 minutes. Carefully turn the filets over and cook the fish until it is lightly browned and just cooked through, 3–4 minutes longer.

8. On each of 6 plates, make a pool of a couple of tablespoons of Citrus Hollandaise and place one of the "breaded" filets on top, bread side up. Spoon some of the fennel–orange salad over each fish filet and scatter some of the chives, dill, and chive blossoms on top.

Local catch: Unloading redfish, drum, sheepshead, and speckled trout at a dock in Bucktown, within New Orleans city limits, in the 1980s; photo: Kathy Bloodworth.

RARE SEARED TUNA WITH CRUSHED FIGS

Serves 6

This is a never-fail way to eat our yellowfin tuna, which can be a little dry if it's not handled and cooked properly. Be sure to cut the steaks as thick as one and a half to two inches so that you can get a good sear and not overcook the tuna. Crushed figs are as wonderful with this tuna as they are with veal or pork chops.

½ cup soy sauce

½ cup granulated sugar

1 teaspoon sambal chile paste

6 4–6-ounce yellowfin tuna steaks, each 1 ½–2 inches thick

1 tablespoon extra-virgin olive oil

1 pint fresh figs, quartered

1 shallot, minced

1 teaspoon minced peeled fresh ginger

1 clove garlic, minced

1 tablespoon rice wine vinegar

2 teaspoons brown sugar

Leaves from 4 sprigs fresh cilantro, minced

Salt

Freshly ground black pepper

1. Stir together the soy sauce, granulated sugar, and chile paste in a wide dish. Add the tuna steaks and turn in the marinade until well coated. Set the tuna steaks aside to let marinate, turning them a few times, for 5–10 minutes. Drain the tuna steaks.

2. Heat the olive oil in a large skillet over high heat. Working in two batches, sear the tuna steaks on each side until they are mahogany in color, 2–3 minutes. Transfer the steaks to a plate as they are done.

3. Return the skillet to moderate heat. Add the figs, shallots, ginger, garlic, rice wine vinegar, and brown sugar and cook for 3 minutes, crushing the figs with a wooden spoon and stirring frequently. Add the cilantro and season the crushed fig mixture with salt and pepper.

4. Serve a couple of spoonfuls of the crushed figs with each tuna steak.

LOUISIANA BLACKFISH WITH SWEET CORN AND CAVIAR

Serves 6

Blackfish is a wonderful delicacy, white and flaky, a fish that doesn't need much coaxing. (Striped bass or snapper is a good substitute.) I like to combine blackfish with my friend John Burke's Louisiana caviar roe from local paddlefish and bowfin, or choupiquet, from the Atchafalaya River.

FOR THE CORN PUDDING
- Cooking spray
- 2 cups heavy cream
- 2 cups (from 7–8 ears) Silver Queen corn kernels
- 1–2 pinches cayenne pepper
- Salt
- 8 eggs

FOR THE SAUCE
- 2 cups Basic Fish Pan Sauce (page 15)
- 2 stalks lemongrass, chopped
- 1 cup (from 3–4 ears) Silver Queen corn kernels
- 1 tablespoon butter
- Salt

FOR THE FISH
- 2 tablespoons extra-virgin olive oil
- 6 4-ounce blackfish filets
- Juice of 1 lemon
- Salt

FOR THE CORN AND CRAB SAUTÉ
- 6 ears baby corn, blanched and sliced into rounds
- 1 cup jumbo lump crabmeat, picked over
- 2 tablespoons butter
- 1 dash Tabasco
- Salt
- 2 tablespoons (or more) Louisiana Caviar (page 362)
- Leaves from 2 sprigs fresh chervil
- Leaves from 2 sprigs fresh dill

1. For the corn pudding, preheat the oven to 275°. Spray six 2–3-ounce ramekins with cooking spray and set aside.

2. Put the cream and corn into a large saucepan and bring to a boil over medium-high heat. Reduce the heat to moderate and simmer for 5 minutes. Pour the corn and cream into a blender and purée until smooth. Add the cayenne and salt. With the motor running, add the eggs through the feed hole in the blender lid, blending the purée until the eggs are completely incorporated.

3. Divide the corn purée between the prepared ramekins. Set the ramekins in a pan large enough to hold them and fill the pan with enough hot water so that it comes halfway up the side of each. Bake the corn puddings until they are set, about 20 minutes. Remove the puddings from the hot water bath and set aside.

4. For the sauce, put the Fish Pan Sauce, lemongrass, and corn into a medium saucepan and simmer over moderate heat for 15 minutes. Add the butter and season with salt. Strain the sauce through a fine sieve into a small saucepan, discarding the solids. Keep the sauce warm in a warm spot on the stove.

5. For the fish, heat the olive oil in a large heavy-bottomed skillet over moderate heat. Score the skin of each blackfish filet in several places, then season the filets with lemon juice and salt.

6. Cook the fish in the skillet, skin side down, until it is not quite cooked through, about 4 minutes. Turn the fish over and cook on the flesh side for about 2 minutes more. (The cooking times depend on the desired level of doneness; I'm always wary of overcooking.) Transfer the fish to paper towels to drain.

7. For the corn and crab sauté, return the skillet used for frying the fish to medium-high heat. Add the corn, crab, and butter and sauté until hot. Add the Tabasco and season with salt. Set aside.

8. Unmold the corn puddings into each of 6 wide warmed soup bowls. Place a fish filet over each pudding. Put a heaping spoonful of the corn and crab sauté over each piece of fish.

9. To froth the warm sauce, use an electric hand mixer and half-submerge the beaters in the sauce. Beat on high speed until a froth forms. Ladle the froth around the fish in each bowl.

10. Top each dish with a small dollop of Louisiana Caviar and sprigs of chervil and dill and chive blossoms if you like.

Fry 'em up in a pan: Croaker sizzles in a cast-iron skillet. Right, returning from a fishing trip.

PAN-FRIED CROAKER WITH SWEET CORN HUSH PUPPIES AND COLE SLAW

Serves 6

I grew up eating whole fried fish and still love it with hush puppies fried in the fishy oil. Scoring the fish will help you peel the flesh off the bone more easily. Besides croaker, any small panfish, like bass, bream, or sacalait (crappie), works well.

FOR THE HUSH PUPPIES

- 1 cup flour
- 1 cup cornmeal
- 1 tablespoon sugar
- 1 tablespoon baking powder
- 1 teaspoon salt
- 1 egg
- ¾ cup milk
- ½ cup corn kernels
- 1 green onion, finely chopped
- 1 teaspoon crushed red pepper flakes

FOR THE COLE SLAW

- 1 small head cabbage, shredded or thinly sliced
- 1 white onion, minced
- 1 carrot, shredded
- 1 cup mayonnaise
- ¼ cup sugarcane or cider vinegar
- ¼ cup sweet pickle relish
- ¼ cup sugar
- 1 tablespoon Creole mustard
- ½ teaspoon celery salt
- Salt
- Freshly ground black pepper

FOR THE FISH

- 4 cups cornmeal
- 1 tablespoon Basic Creole Spices (page 13)
- 4 cups flour
- 4 cups buttermilk
- 6 1-pound croaker gills removed
- Salt
- Freshly ground black pepper
- 6 cups canola oil
- 1 cup Basic Sauce Remoulade (page 19)

1. For the hush puppies, sift together the flour, cornmeal, sugar, baking powder, and salt in a large bowl. Add the egg and milk and mix well. Fold in the corn kernels, green onions, and pepper flakes. Cover and refrigerate for 30 minutes.

2. For the cole slaw, put the cabbage, onions, carrots, mayonnaise, vinegar, relish, sugar, mustard, and celery salt into a medium bowl and toss well. Season with salt and pepper. Cover and refrigerate until ready to use.

3. For the fish, combine the cornmeal with the Creole Spices and 2 cups of the flour in a wide pan. Put the remaining 2 cups of flour into another wide pan and the buttermilk into a third wide pan.

4. To keep the fish from curling up while cooking, score both sides of each fish about ¼-inch deep in a couple of places between the pectoral fins and the tail and along both sides of the dorsal fin, then season the fish with salt and pepper. Dredge each fish in the flour, then let it soak in the buttermilk for a minute or so. Lift the fish from the buttermilk and dredge it in the seasoned cornmeal.

5. Heat the canola oil in a wide heavy-bottomed pot over medium-high heat until the temperature reaches 350° on a candy thermometer. Deep-fry one or two fish at a time until they are golden brown on both sides, 12–15 minutes (since the fish are fried whole, they'll cool the oil down considerably once you add them to the hot oil, so they'll take a bit longer to fry than you'd normally expect). Transfer the fish to paper towels to let drain and season them with salt.

6. Fry the hush puppies in batches by dropping heaping tablespoonfuls of the batter into the same 350° oil used for frying the fish. Fry them, turning periodically, until they are golden brown, about 3 minutes per side. Drain on paper towels.

7. Transfer the fish, hush puppies, and cole slaw to individual platters and serve with a bowl of Sauce Remoulade on the side.

POMPANO WITH JUMBO SHRIMP AND TWO CELERIES

Serves 6

Be sure to have the purée and shellfish jus ready once you start the pompano. This fish can get dry, so be careful to cook it just to medium.

FOR THE PURÉE
- 1 bulb celery root, diced
- 1 Yukon Gold potato, diced
- 1 onion, chopped
- 2 cloves garlic, crushed
- Salt
- ½ cup heavy cream

FOR THE JUS
- 1 cup Basic Shellfish Stock (page 13)
- 4 tablespoons cold butter, cubed
- Salt
- Freshly ground black pepper

FOR THE FISH
- 6 6–7-ounce pompano filets
- Salt
- 1 cup flour
- 2 tablespoons extra-virgin olive oil
- 1 tablespoon butter

FOR THE SALAD
- 3 tablespoons extra-virgin olive oil
- 2 cloves garlic, thinly sliced
- 12 jumbo wild American shrimp, peeled and deveined
- Salt
- 2 cups yellow celery leaves
- ¼ cup Basic Pepper Jelly Vinaigrette (page 19)

1. For the purée, put the celery root, potatoes, onions, and garlic into a large saucepan. Add enough cold water to cover the vegetables and add several pinches of salt. Bring to a boil over high heat. Reduce the heat to medium-low and simmer until the celery root and potatoes are tender, about 30 minutes. Drain the vegetables and transfer them while still very hot to the work bowl of a food processor. Add the cream and purée the mixture until smooth. If the purée is a bit stiff, add a little more cream. Season with salt. Transfer the purée to a bowl, cover with plastic wrap, and keep warm in a warm spot on the stove.

2. For the jus, put the Shellfish Stock into a small saucepan and boil over moderate heat until it has reduced to 2 tablespoons, 5–7 minutes. Reduce the heat to low and whisk in the cold butter, one cube at a time, whisking constantly until each cube of butter has melted and been incorporated into the sauce before adding more. Season with salt and pepper and set aside.

3. For the fish, score the skin of each pompano filet in several places. Season the fish with salt and dredge in the flour. Heat the olive oil and the butter together in a large skillet over medium-high heat. Sauté the fish filets, skin side down, until golden brown, then turn them over and continue cooking until golden brown on the second side, 3–5 minutes per side. Transfer the fish to a large plate and set aside.

4. For the salad, put the olive oil, garlic, and shrimp into the same skillet used for frying the fish and cook over moderate heat until the shrimp are cooked through, 3–5 minutes. Season with salt. Transfer the shrimp to a medium bowl and set aside.

5. Toss the celery leaves with the Pepper Jelly Vinaigrette in a small bowl and set aside.

6. To serve, put a couple of spoonfuls of the celery root purée on each of 6 plates and top each with a pompano filet, skin side up. Drizzle a spoonful of the shellfish jus around the purée and fish on each plate. Set 2 shrimp on top of each piece of fish, then place a tuft of the celery leaves on top of the shrimp.

Fishing spots: A typical fishing camp on Lake Catherine, above. Boys on the Boyd family pier, right, await sunset and the speckled trout. Piers extend great distances from shore camps into the waters of Lake Pontchartrain.

In their own backyards:
Vietnamese farmers like Lieu V. Nguyen, right, in east New Orleans live very much the way they did in their homeland, cultivating small plots to feed their community. Bottom, farmer Thang Nguyen and his wife. Below, a woman irrigates her garden from a canal; photo, Mark J. Sindler, The Vietnamese Documentary Project. Top right, long squash grows on a trellis.

The Fruits of Their Labor

"We would so much rather spend our produce dollars in our community than send them out of state."

When I returned home after my years in the Marine Corps, my mother kept urging me to go to church, telling me that I had to meet the new priest: I'd just love him, he could hear my confessions. And I'm thinking, I've just spent way too much time in a hot desert, in a Muslim country with no alcohol, no women, and no life. How much sinning does she think I could get up to? To appease my mother, I finally relented and walked into the church of my childhood to meet this nice young man. Well, needless to say, Father Ken Harney was not what I'd imagined. Old, salty, and loud, he had served three tours in Vietnam with the marines. He invited me into his office, where we smoked and laughed and told stories. When he asked

whether I wanted him to hear my confession, I agreed and headed into the church. But he said, "Aw, hell, I can do it right it here." So he kept on chain-smoking as I came up with a couple of boring sins, until he said, "That's nothing. You need to come back when you've got some better sins." I knew this was the start of a great friendship.

Father Ken had joined the priesthood late, after the military and years of service in Vietnam, where he'd met Father Vien Nguyen at seminary. Back in New Orleans, they became the best of friends and would cook together at a small camp just outside the city. Father Ken told me often about Father Vien, about the food they cooked, about how I had to meet him. Years pass. Father Ken marries Jenifer and me. We leave and come back, have babies, have more, and before you know it, Hurricane Katrina distracts us all. Not long thereafter, Ken Harney died suddenly of cancer. Flash forward to the one-year anniversary of the storm, and I'm surprised to be invited to a dinner at Leah Chase's Dooky Chase restaurant for President George Bush and Mrs. Bush, local dignitaries, government officials, and . . . the Vietnamese priest, the Reverend Vien The Nguyen. At last we meet face to face. After two minutes, I understand why Father Ken wanted us to know each other.

Heart of Vietnam: Mark J. Sindler, who photographed the Versailles community of east New Orleans from 1978 to 1985 for his Vietnamese Documentary Project, made the iconic photo, opposite, of a newly settled couple. Below, the visionary Father Vien The Nguyen; photo: Kim Bourgault. Bottom, squash in the verdant fields.

FATHER VIEN IS a visionary, a true leader, and he has a dream, a life plan for the Vietnamese community in Orleans Parish: The Urban Farm. On 28 acres of once storm-ravaged wasteland, he envisions a multiple-use farm and market, where children can play while their grandparents work, keeping it all close to home. Across the street is a retirement center. There's been a small Vietnamese market on Saturdays in the area for years, but it suffered with the loss of many backyard farms following Katrina. His parish was one of the hardest hit when the flood-waters came through, and it's still pretty desolate land, home to coffee roasting plants and the Michoud space center, which manufactures fuel tanks for space shuttles. But to thousands of Vietnamese Americans who arrived here in the mid-1970s, east New Orleans was the land of opportunity.

After Katrina, Father Vien hatched his plan. He knew there were aging members who continued their business of fishing; he saw families still farming their own land, growing their produce, and selling the surplus in small markets. After Katrina, universities

Community: Top, a Christmas fair in the Vietnamese community featured a ring toss on live ducks; photo: Mark J. Sindler, The Vietnamese Documentary Project. Above, land destroyed by Hurricane Katrina is the site of the future Urban Farm. Opposite, grilled watermelon, tomato, and goat cheese salad (recipe, page 184).

involved with the recovery heard about Father Vien's idea for The Urban Farm. MIT helped with the business plan, Tulane and LSU worked on design; the University of Montana supplied a composting program.

And that's where we come in. My team and I, and especially Steve McHugh, who grew up on a farm in Wisconsin, have become partners in the project, providing assistance with growing crops, bringing in master gardeners to teach intensive farming. We have committed to purchase their seeds, and we have guaranteed to buy back the fruits of their labor. When Steve and I came to present our ideas to the farmers at a lunch in the social hall of the Mary Queen of Vietnam Church, the first thing we saw was Father Vien hacking up a cooked chicken with a cleaver. After I tasted the chicken that had been washed with whiskey, rubbed with garlic and salt, and steamed, I thought, Sure glad he's a priest and not a chef!

I STOOD AT A long table where farmers—some in their 80s, old souls in baseball caps with well-worn hands, many who did not speak English—were seated among the younger generation of beautifully educated Vietnamese Americans. I told them why we wanted to support The Urban Farm. I explained the economics of buying produce and meat out of state and shipping it in: "It sounds insane, I know, but we need tiny vegetables. We would so much rather spend our dollars in our community than send it to Ohio and pay FedEx charges. We could buy every duck you raise. If I didn't have four restaurants and four sons and a demanding wife, I'd be raising ducks." Father Vien, laughing, stands up to translate all this.

The farmers' response has been amazing. They love swapping ideas and working with us on our small farms, in Lacombe, Folsom, and Bush parishes. I'm thrilled to meet monthly with Father Vien, Father Luke Nguyen, and the project director, Peter Ngyuen. Of course I schedule these meetings at mealtimes so I get to taste the good father's Mea Culpa Chicken, with garlic, chile, lime, and lemongrass purée; Spanish mackerel, smothered in onions and chiles and cooked for 72 hours; and bitter melon soup. I thank heaven for this community. How can my cooking not be influenced by these new flavors of New Orleans?

Watermelon

Watermelon is king in Washington Parish, which is situated across the lake on the North Shore of New Orleans. Around here, you wouldn't consider eating a watermelon unless it came from Washington Parish, which is where more than 100 growers are concentrated, producing such varieties as Jubilee, Summer Flavor, and Starbrite. These melons are unparalleled, as they are picked close to home and eaten fresh from the farm, not like supermarket melons that were harvested weeks ago, refrigerated, and shipped somewhere far away.

A watermelon should be picked when it is ripe and bursting with flavor, and one way to tell its farm origins is to check for a warm yellow patch caused by its lying in the sandy soil, growing heavy and juicy in the sun.

Watermelon (*Citrullus lanatus*) may be 92 percent water, which explains why it was cultivated in Africa as early as 2000 B.C., but it also contains a nutritious dose of lycopene, amino acids, potassium, and vitamins A, B, and C. In watermelon season, my children eat a watermelon a day. They chomp through chunky wedges of it just as it comes, but also love watermelon soup and watermelon sorbet. You can make the same things with all the other melons we raise, such as fragrant Charentais and canteloupe. Another simple variation is to make an all-natural granita. Just purée the watermelon, freeze the purée in a shallow pan, and then scrape it out and serve it.

GRILLED WATERMELON, TOMATO, AND GOAT CHEESE SALAD

Serves 6

The hotter the grill, the better the grill marks will be on the watermelon slices (photo, page 183). I like to brush spicy Pepper Jelly Vinaigrette over the melon before it's grilled because the sugars quickly caramelize, imparting incredible flavor. Feel free to substitute whatever vinaigrette you have on hand.

¼ cup Basic Pepper Jelly Vinaigrette (page 19)

6 large slices seedless watermelon, ½ to 1 inch thick, rind removed

⅓ cup extra-virgin olive oil

2 tablespoons balsamic vinegar

1 clove garlic, minced

1 pinch sugar

Leaves from 1 sprig fresh basil, chopped

Salt

Freshly ground black pepper

2 cups cherry tomatoes (mixed colors and varieties)

2 or 3 handfuls young lettuces

½ cup fresh goat cheese

Fresh herbs such as chives, chive blossoms, chervil, parsley, and dill

1. Light a charcoal or gas grill. Brush the Pepper Jelly Vinaigrette over each watermelon slice. Let the watermelon marinate for a few minutes before placing on the hot grill. Grill each side of the watermelon slices for several minutes, remove, cut into large serving pieces, and arrange on a platter.

2. Whisk together the olive oil, vinegar, garlic, sugar, and basil in a small mixing bowl. Season with salt and pepper. Add the tomatoes and toss to coat them well, then scatter them over the grilled watermelon pieces on the platter. Toss the lettuces in the vinaigrette remaining in the bowl.

3. Crumble the goat cheese over the tomatoes and watermelon. Scatter the dressed lettuces, then the fresh herbs, over the salad.

A watermelon a day: The Besh boys, from left, Andrew, Luke, Jack, and Brendan, out in back of our house, can't get enough of their favorite fruit.

NO. 690; FRENCH MARKET.

Market central: Not so long ago (1955), the French Market in the Quarter was a bustling center of produce and not just the tourist draw it is today; photo: Clarence John Laughlin, The Historic New Orleans Collection. Right, the ripest vegetables at the Uptown Farmers Market.

AUGUST CHOPPED SALAD

Serves 6

This is one of those dishes that's always on the August menu; its ingredients change with the seasons. Picture yourself walking through your market, shopping for small amounts of whatever colorful combination of vegetables catches your eye. In the winter, the salad is made with root vegetables; come summer, it gets lots of tiny heirloom tomatoes. In other seasons, we combine fruit with the vegetables and toss everything in a Champagne Vinaigrette. The ingredients below are only a suggestion.

3 golden beets	1 bulb fennel
3 candy-stripe beets	2 small radishes
3 red beets	1½ cups Basic Champagne Vinaigrette (page 19)
1 cup rice wine vinegar	
½ cup sugar	1 cup pomegranate seeds
Salt	
1 cup chanterelle mushrooms	½ grapefruit, sectioned
	1 satsuma tangerine, sectioned
6 baby carrots, of different sizes and colors	1 cucumber, seeded and shaped with a melon baller
6 baby turnips	
1 small Yukon Gold potato, peeled and diced	1 cup sunflower sprouts
	1 cup pea sprouts
	6 sprigs fresh dill
6 stalks asparagus	6 sprigs fresh chervil
2 artichokes	
2 cups canola oil	

1. Put each color of beet into separate pots with enough water to cover and bring to a boil over medium-high heat. (Cooking them separately allows the beets to maintain their individual colors.) Cover and simmer until beets are fork tender, about 30 minutes.

2. While beets are cooking, make the beet marinade by mixing the rice wine vinegar and sugar together in a pot. Cook over moderate heat, stirring occasionally, until the sugar has dissolved, about 5 minutes. Remove from heat.

3. Drain the beets and, when they are cool enough to handle, peel. Halve each beet and transfer to the marinade, and allow to marinate for at least 4 hours.

4. Fill a large pot with water and add a generous pinch of salt. Cover and bring to a gentle boil over moderate heat. Blanch the chanterelles, baby carrots, baby turnips, potatoes, and asparagus separately and in that order, until each vegetable is just soft—al dente. Use tongs or a strainer to transfer the vegetables to a large bowl filled with ice water. Cool quickly, remove from the water and drain, then blot the vegetables dry with paper towels.

5. Remove and discard the tough outer leaves of the artichokes, leaving only the palest, tender green leaves. Slice off about 2 inches of the leaves' thorny tips. Peel the stem and trim off the brown end. Cut the artichokes in half lengthwise. Use a spoon to scrape out and discard the fuzzy chokes. Cut each artichoke in half lengthwise again, then into 3 pieces. Heat the oil in a small deep skillet to 350°. Fry the artichoke pieces until golden on all sides, about 7 minutes. Remove from the oil and let drain on paper towels.

6. Thinly slice the fennel and radishes with a sharp knife or use a mandoline.

7. Remove beets from their marinade, discard the marinade, and arrange on 6 plates.

8. Toss the chanterelles, carrots, turnips, potatoes, asparagus, artichokes, fennel, and radishes separately in the Champagne Vinaigrette and then arrange a few of each on top of the beets on each plate.

9. Evenly divide the pomegranate seeds, grapefruit sections, satsuma sections, and cucumber balls between the plates.

10. Toss the sunflower sprouts and pea sprouts in the Champagne Vinaigrette and scatter them, along with the dill and chervil, over each salad.

Okra

When I was a kid, I couldn't understand why they didn't sell fried okra in movie theaters instead of popcorn! Here's the deal about okra: it's a very personal vegetable, and every New Orleans cook thinks she or he has the best way of preparing it. That's in the South, mind you, as it often gets a bad rap in other parts of the country because of its tendency to break down and become sticky and mushy if it's not treated properly.

These delicately ridged and tapered green pods, sometimes called ladies' fingers, are a member of the mallow family and are bursting with tiny seeds as well as the glutinous compounds that make okra such a natural thickener for soups and gumbos.

In fact, the name for okra (*Hibiscus esculentus*) comes from Africa, the continent where it most likely originated. In Angola it is known as *ki h gombo*, and it migrated west with the Portuguese slave trade under the name *quingombo*, which was shortened in the West Indies to *gumbo*. Do you want to know my grandmother's secret for keeping okra from getting slimy? Add a capful of white vinegar while it stews, to give it just the right touch of acidity. But I wouldn't add acidity to something like a gumbo, as I want the okra, the filé, and the roux to have that slightly gelatinous consistency.

CORNMEAL-FRIED OKRA

Serves 6

When buying okra, look for smaller, greener spears. Good frozen okra will work fine, especially if it is presliced. This recipe yields a thin fried crust, but if you prefer a thicker crust, all you have to do is double-dip the okra, repeating steps 1 and 2 before you fry the okra rounds.

1 pound okra, sliced into ½-inch-thick rounds	2 teaspoons Basic Creole Spices (page 13)
1 cup buttermilk	1 quart canola oil
1 cup cornmeal	Salt
1 cup flour	

1. Put the okra and the buttermilk into a mixing bowl and toss together.

2. Whisk together the cornmeal, flour, and Creole Spices in another mixing bowl. Lift the okra from the buttermilk and toss it in the cornmeal mixture until well-coated.

3. Heat the oil in a medium saucepan until it reaches 350° on a candy thermometer. Fry the okra in the oil—in batches, only a third at a time, so that you don't crowd the pan—until golden brown, 5–7 minutes. Remove the okra from the oil with a slotted spoon or strainer and let drain on paper towels while frying the next batch. Season with salt and serve hot.

STEWED OKRA AND TOMATOES

Serves 6

I love to find the smaller, greener okra and leave them whole. Just trim the stem end off; that way they're more tender and a bit less stringy. If you've got larger okra, slice them in rounds. Cooking the okra and tomatoes separately and combining them at the end allows the best flavors of each to come through.

- 6 large handfuls fresh small okra
- 2 tablespoons baking soda
  Salt
- ¼ cup extra-virgin olive oil
- 6 large tomatoes, peeled and diced
- 4 cloves garlic, thinly sliced
- 1 teaspoon crushed red pepper flakes
- 1 teaspoon sugar
  Leaves from 1 sprig fresh oregano, chopped
  Leaves from 1 sprig fresh basil, chopped
  Freshly ground black pepper
- 1 recipe Basic Louisiana White Rice (page 15)

1. Bring a gallon of water to a boil in a large pot. Add the okra, baking soda, and 2 tablespoons salt. Cook the okra at a hard boil for 5 minutes. Strain the okra and plunge it into a large bowl of ice water. Once it's cool, drain the okra and set aside.

2. Heat the olive oil in a medium skillet over medium-high heat until warm, then add the tomatoes and garlic and cook for several minutes. Add the pepper flakes and sugar and cook for 10 minutes, stirring constantly. Add the oregano, basil, and okra, reduce the heat to medium-low, and cook for an additional 3–4 minutes.

3. Season the stew with salt and pepper. Serve with hot rice.

TEMPURA-FRIED SQUASH BLOSSOMS WITH CRABMEAT STUFFING

Serves 6

There's nothing better than just-picked squash blossoms, fried and served with this dressing. If you can't find crabmeat, just omit it. Use only a bit of stuffing, or it will all fall out. For the garlic cloves, feel free to substitute a bulb of green garlic or young garlic in season.

FOR THE TOMATO–GARLIC DRESSING

- 1 large tomato, peeled and diced
- 4 cloves garlic
- ¾ cup mayonnaise
- ¼ teaspoon Tabasco
- ½ teaspoon rice wine vinegar
- Leaves from 1 sprig fresh basil

FOR THE SQUASH BLOSSOMS

- ¾ cup Basic Sauce Ravigote (page 19)
- 1 cup jumbo lump crabmeat, picked over
- ½ cup fresh bread crumbs
- ¼ teaspoon crushed red pepper flakes
- 12 large squash blossoms
- 1 cup flour
- 1 egg
- 1 teaspoon Basic Creole Spices (page 13)
- 2 cups canola oil

1. For the Tomato–Garlic Dressing, purée the tomatoes, garlic, mayonnaise, Tabasco, vinegar, and basil together in a blender or a food processor. Transfer to a small bowl, cover, and refrigerate.

2. For the squash blossoms, fold together the Sauce Ravigote with the crabmeat, bread crumbs, and pepper flakes in a mixing bowl. Use a small spoon to carefully fill each squash blossom with the crabmeat stuffing. Refrigerate the stuffed blossoms for at least 1 hour.

3. Whisk together the flour, egg, and Creole Spices with 1 cup cold water in another small mixing bowl.

4. Heat the canola oil in a medium saucepan over high heat until it reaches 350° on a candy thermometer.

Carefully dip each squash blossom into the batter, making sure that the excess batter drips off before putting the blossom into the hot oil. Do this one at a time and be careful not to fry more than 3 blossoms at a time. Fry the cold blossoms on both sides until golden brown, 3–5 minutes per side. Allow them to drain for a moment on paper towels.

5. Serve with the Tomato–Garlic Dressing on the side for dipping.

SILVER QUEEN CORN, ORZO, AND CRABMEAT MACQUE CHOUX

Serves 6–8

Originally a Native American dish, macque choux came from the Choctaws, who called it Matache, meaning spotted. Cajun patois twisted its name to sound French, but macque choux never contained cabbage—*choux*. Any sweet corn at its peak of ripeness works well. Be careful not to cook the corn at a high temperature; we don't want it to brown. Cook it slowly so that the corn and shallots soften. Substitute wild mushrooms for the summer truffle or omit it.

- 6 ears Silver Queen or other ripe corn, shucked
- 2 tablespoons butter
- 2 shallots, minced
- 2 cloves garlic, minced
- 1 teaspoon crushed red pepper flakes
- 1 pound jumbo lump crabmeat, picked over
- 2 cups cooked orzo pasta
- 1 cup Basic Crab Pan Sauce (page 15)
- 1 tablespoon chopped fresh chives
- ¼ summer truffle, sliced
- 2 tablespoons freshly grated Parmesan cheese
- Salt

1. Cut the corn kernels off the corncobs and set aside.

2. Melt the butter in a large skillet over moderate heat. Add the corn and shallots and cook gently, stirring occasionally, until the corn is tender and the shallots are translucent, 5–10 minutes.

3. Add the garlic and red pepper flakes to the pan and cook for a few minutes longer. Add the crabmeat and cook just until heated through. Stir in the orzo and the Crab Pan Sauce. Increase the heat to high and bring to a boil.

4. Reduce the heat immediately to low, add chives, truffles, and Parmesan, and simmer for a few minutes. Season with a little salt.

CALDO

Serves 10–15

The Isleños (Islanders) came to the sultry, flat marshlands of St. Bernard Parish from the Canary Islands, off the coast of Morocco, over 200 years ago. They brought a version of the Spanish stew *puchero*, which they renamed *caldo* and made with vegetables from their South Louisiana harvest. Caldo is a slow-cooked soupy stew that always includes pork, often pickled.

¼	cup extra-virgin olive oil	1	sweet potato, peeled and diced
2	large yellow onions, diced	1	Yukon Gold potato, peeled and diced
1	bell pepper, seeded and diced	1	large handful green beans, chopped
1	stalk celery, diced	1½	gallons Basic Chicken Stock (page 13)
2	cloves garlic, minced	2	bay leaves
3	ham hocks	1	teaspoon cayenne pepper
2	cups lima beans	½	teaspoon ground allspice
2	large handfuls mustard greens, chopped		Salt
1	cup diced whole tomatoes, fresh or canned		Freshly ground black pepper
1	cup corn kernels		

1. Heat the olive oil in a large heavy-bottomed pot over moderate heat. Add the onions, bell peppers, celery, and garlic and cook, stirring until the vegetables are soft, about 15 minutes.

2. Add the ham hocks, lima beans, mustard greens, tomatoes, corn, sweet potatoes, Yukon Gold potatoes, and green beans and mix with the cooked vegetables.

3. Add the Chicken Stock, bay leaves, cayenne, and allspice. Increase the heat to high and bring the soup to a boil. Reduce the heat to low and gently simmer the caldo until all the vegetables are soft and the ham hocks are tender, about 1½ hours.

4. Season with salt and pepper. Remove the ham hocks from the soup, pull the meat from the bones, shred the meat, and return it to the soup. Serve it up in bowls.

ROASTED RED GYPSY PEPPERS, ARUGULA, AND COUNTRY HAM SALAD

Serves 6

If you can't find red gypsy peppers, substitute red bell peppers (or even a jar of Spanish piquillo peppers, drained, in which case you'd omit the roasting step).

12 red gypsy peppers or red bell peppers	1–2 pinches sugar
2 tablespoons extra-virgin olive oil	2 teaspoons red wine vinegar
3 cloves garlic, thinly sliced	Salt
1 green onion, chopped	Freshly ground black pepper
Leaves from 1 sprig fresh basil, chopped	2 cups arugula or other salad greens
1 teaspoon smoked paprika	2 tablespoons Basic Pepper Jelly Vinaigrette (page 19)
½ teaspoon crushed red pepper flakes	12 very thin slices country ham or prosciutto

1. Preheat the oven to broil. Rub the peppers with 1 tablespoon of the olive oil and place them on a cookie sheet. Roast the peppers in the oven until they are blistered and slightly charred, 5–10 minutes. Set the peppers aside to let them cool to room temperature.

2. Meanwhile, combine the remaining 1 tablespoon oil, the garlic, green onions, basil, smoked paprika, pepper flakes, sugar, vinegar, and salt and pepper in a medium bowl and set the vinaigrette aside.

3. Peel the blistered skin off the peppers with your fingers, or use a paring knife to trim skin that doesn't pull away easily. Cut the peppers in half lengthwise, then remove and discard the stem and seeds. Add the cleaned peppers to the bowl with the vinaigrette.

4. Toss the arugula with the Pepper Jelly Vinaigrette in another medium bowl.

5. Divide the peppers, country ham, and arugula evenly between 6 plates and serve.

GRILLED LSU FIG SALAD WITH RICOTTA AND ENDIVE

Serves 6

Experts at LSU, Louisiana State University, continue to delight us by developing new and succulent varieties of fig, like LSU Purple and LSU Gold. Of course you can use whatever ripe figs you can find in season. Sometimes just touching a fig to a grill brings out new flavors. The Lavender Honey Vinaigrette is subtle enough not to overpower the figs yet sweet enough to balance the endive's slight bitterness.

9 Purple figs, halved	½ cup ricotta salata cheese, crumbled
9 Gold figs, halved	1 small handful chives, chopped
6 tablespoons Basic Lavender Honey Vinaigrette (page 19)	Salt
4 cups red and yellow endive lettuces, halved lengthwise	Freshly ground black pepper

1. Light a charcoal or gas grill. Toss the figs with half the Lavender Honey Vinaigrette in a small mixing bowl, then grill them over high heat for just 2 minutes on each side. Place them on individual plates or serving platters.

2. Using the same bowl, toss the endive with the remaining vinaigrette and serve over and around the grilled figs.

3. Crumble the cheese over the figs, scatter the chives over the top, and season with salt and a grind or two of black pepper.

CHARENTAIS MELON, MUSCAT WINE, AND WILD BERRIES

Serves 6

If you have an ice cream machine and the inclination, you can easily freeze the muscat, or any favorite dessert wine, with the puréed berries as I do here, or make the purée without the berries. Easier still, drizzle the melon with muscat just before you serve it with fresh berries and mint.

1 cup wild berries, such as blueberries, strawberries, raspberries, or blackberries	½ liter, about 2 cups, muscat de Beaumes-de-Venise or other dessert wine
	3 Charentais melons
	6 small sprigs fresh mint

1. Purée ½ cup of the berries along with the wine in a blender or food processor. Transfer to a quart-size pan and freeze completely, about 2 hours.

2. Just before serving, halve the melons and remove the seeds. Trim the rind flat on the bottom of each melon so that it will sit upright on the plate.

3. Scrape the surface of the frozen wine and berries with a large spoon to make shaved ice. Generously fill each melon's cavity with the frozen wine. Garnish the melon with the remaining berries and tiny leaves of fresh mint.

Melons of Washington Parish: Watermelon, cantaloupe, honeydew, Charantais, and gala, above. Muscat wine and wild berries fill Charantais melon, left.

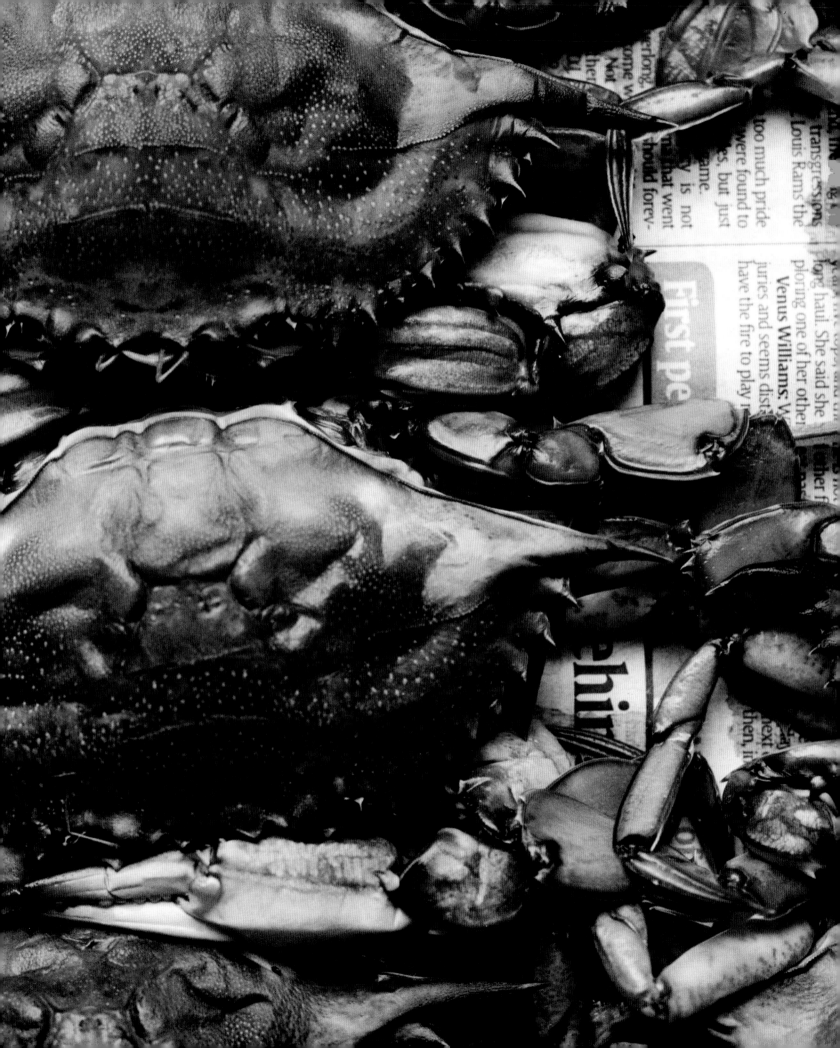

How to eat a crab: My sister-in-law, Kim Bourgault, above, loves to eat crab. Clockwise from top left, removing the top shell and the dead man's fingers, turning it over and removing the apron, breaking it in half to reveal the prize: lump crabmeat. Left, serving crabs at a booth at a New Orleans food festival in the 1970s.

Blue Crabs and the Fourth of July

"We'd hear the crabs were running, which meant they had grown fat and there were plenty of them."

I'd just love it whenever Dad would pack us all into the Chevy overflowing with hoop net traps, chicken necks, and two ice chests—one filled with Barq's root beer and Big Shot soda, one empty, just waiting for the crabs we'd catch. We'd hear that the crabs were running at a certain time or near a certain bridge. Nobody I knew could keep a secret, especially one that involved where and when crabs are running. It is imprinted on my memory that crabs run around the Fourth of July. What could be more American? We'd settle ourselves on a designated bridge, a transistor radio playing a baseball game, probably Tulane or our minor-league Pelicans; we'd share po'boy sandwiches

Crabbing: Blue crabs straight from Lake Pontchartrain, ready for the boil, above. Netting crabs lakeside, about 1941; photo: Charles L. Franck Photographers, The Historic New Orleans Collection.

for lunch. Only a few restaurants sold boiled seafood in those days, and when you had five siblings and an airline pilot father who traveled as much as mine did, well, we didn't go out all that often. So, when we heard the crabs were running, we knew we'd better get out there and catch us some.

WE'D DO OUR crabbing from a bridge so that we could lower the net down into the water beneath, securing the net to the bridge with a length of twine, baiting our crab nets with chicken necks. Don't ask me why we use chicken necks to bait every net or snare; we just do, and it happens to work well. Sometimes, we'd tie a piece of twine to a lone chicken neck, lower it into the shallow waters, and, if we were lucky, catch one crab at a time. Hoop nets, though, were a much more effective way of harvesting them in quantity.

Dad would have a Dixie or a Falstaff while he waited impatiently for the crabs to begin running into his particular nets, which he hung on one particular nail in his own particular fashion. At home, he kept his nets carefully stowed away next to the fly rods, hunting bows, and a variety of his other toys that were off-limits to me. It wasn't until years later that I'd help myself to those same nets come Independence Day, as I tried to assert my own independence at the Besh house.

The Fourth of July wasn't the only time to crab, of course. We had half a year to do that, but Dad had the patience of the Great Santini, which meant he could sit still for only so long before he'd take off to walk down the seawall, where he'd toss his nets or use his spinning rod and a spoon to land a flounder for dinner. Hmmm, flounder stuffed with crabmeat; how good would that be?

IT WASN'T UNTIL high school that I began crabbing with friends. We'd set a line of proper wire crab traps baited with fish heads out by Lakefront Airport, dodging afternoon thunderstorms under the C-Brook Bridge, in the industrial canal. In later years, we did our crabbing by boat, which increased our yield if not our pleasure. Dad's nets no longer exist, and I don't even know whether they still make those hoop types, but I sure need to find an acceptable substitute, as my four boys are in dire need of building their own memories of crab season.

The sweet and salty waters of Lake Pontchartrain gave us sustenance and identity. The lake was the place to cross to get away from the city—they say that because of the pine trees the temperature is at least ten degrees lower on the North Shore—and it is the perfect habitat for our big, fat blue crabs. I don't know of a better-tasting crab out there. These creatures—which are caught, boiled, picked, packed, and sent all around the country—are superb in a crab boil. When they shed their shells, those soft shells most certainly end up battered with cornmeal and pan-fried. We used to call crab gills dead man's fingers, and we knew for sure you'd die if you ate them. Years later, of course, it dawned on me that you really won't die, but still, I have never eaten a crab gill. Becoming a proficient crab sheller was imperative if you wanted to eat these wonderful creatures, because nobody was about to peel a crab for you.

Today, I handle our crabs in a similar way. We boil them, pick them, stuff them, and roast them. Soft shells and busters—which are soft shells as they burst out of their shells—are usually fried or cooked into a bisque or used to season a gumbo or flavor redfish courtbouillon. Not one little morsel of crab is ever wasted. If anything has changed, it's the fact that I now wear shoes on those long, hot summer days, and the Great Santini and I no longer go crabbing together the way we once did.

Secrets of a crab boil: A sachet of such spices as black pepper, coriander seed, mustard seed, cayenne pepper, allspice, bay leaves, and others delivers its authentic perfume to our cooked crabs.

Blue Crab

Blue crab is the delicacy of New Orleans. It is to Lake Pontchartrain what sturgeon is to the Caspian Sea. This crustacean (officially called *Callinectes sapidus*, which translates as "beautiful swimmer" and "tasty") is the most common American crab and ranges all along the East Coast from Delaware south. In fact, most of our Louisiana crabs are shipped back up North. Crabbing is a much more lucrative business than shrimping, as there is no rival import for live crab, so our fishermen can get a premium price, especially for soft shells. For these, you have to catch them when they are about to molt, put them into a tank, and basically not take your eyes off them. Once the old shell cracks, the soft-shell critters crawl out and they must be shipped immediately, before the new shells harden (in just a matter of hours).

Crabs can shed their shells some 20 times in their lifetime, each event marking a little growth spurt! Blue crabs are the most common and commercially fished crab. But if you're crabbing for fun, you'll discover fiddlers, mud crabs, or wharf crabs. Blue crabs are mild tasting, similar in flavor to Dungeness, just not as big. It's easy to get picked crabmeat at good fish markets—picking's tedious to do at home. For me, it's all about the crab boil: our stuffed crab shells and crab bisque can be made from the boiled crabs, so nothing is wasted.

CRAB BOIL

Serves 8

A crab boil, like its cousin the crawfish boil, is a great excuse for a casual party. Afterward, the seasoned, boiled crab and its succulent juices can be turned into many other dishes, such as Stuffed Blue Crab Grandmère (recipe, page 207).

2 cups kosher salt

1 package Zatarain's Crab Boil

5 lemons, halved

3 tablespoons cayenne pepper

5 whole heads garlic, halved

5 small onions, halved

3 stalks celery, cut into large pieces

3 pounds smoked sausage, cut into 4-inch lengths

8 ears corn, shucked and halved

2 dozen jumbo blue crabs or 3 dozen medium blue crabs

1. Fill a very large pot with 10 gallons water, leaving plenty of room for all the other ingredients. Bring the water to a boil with the kosher salt, boiling spices, lemons, cayenne, garlic, onions, and celery. Reduce the heat and allow to simmer for 10 minutes.

2. Add the smoked sausage and corn. Simmer for 15 minutes.

3. Next add the crabs and simmer for an additional 10 minutes. Turn off the heat and let the crabs sit for 15–20 minutes before straining them out of the boiling liquid.

4. Pour the crabs, corn, and sausage onto a table covered with newspaper, and let everyone dig in!

MASTER RECIPE

CRAB BISQUE

Serves 8–10

Sautéing the shells—be they crab, shrimp, or crawfish—is the true secret to a good rich bisque and the key to its signature nutty flavor. The farther west you go in Louisiana, the less cream and the more rice you'll find in the bisque.

¼ cup olive oil

10 hard-shell blue crabs

2 tablespoons flour

2 onions, chopped

4 cloves garlic, chopped

1 stalk celery, chopped

¼ cup raw white rice, finely ground in a food processor

1 sprig fresh thyme

1 bay leaf

1 teaspoon crushed red pepper flakes

1 tablespoon tomato paste

¼ cup brandy

6 cups Basic Shellfish Stock (page 13)

2 cups heavy cream

2 dashes Worcestershire

2 dashes Tabasco

Salt

Freshly ground black pepper

1. Heat the olive oil in a large soup pot over high heat. Crush the whole crabs with a rolling pin, then add them to the pot. Cook, stirring frequently with a wooden spoon, for 15 minutes.

2. Stir the flour into the pot, mixing it into the oil and crabs. Then add the onions, garlic, and celery. Reduce the heat to moderate and cook, stirring often, for 15 minutes.

3. Add the ground rice, thyme, bay leaf, pepper flakes, and tomato paste, stirring to mix well. Cook for another 5 minutes. Add the brandy and cook, stirring constantly, for 5 more minutes.

4. Increase the heat to medium-high and stir in the Shellfish Stock and heavy cream. Bring the bisque to a boil. Reduce the heat to medium-low and simmer for 25 minutes.

5. Remove the pot from the heat. Purée the bisque in a blender, then strain through a fine sieve. Season with Worcestershire, Tabasco, salt, and pepper.

VARIATIONS

CRAWFISH BISQUE

Substitute 3 pounds whole or live crawfish, cleaned in fresh water, for the 10 crabs and proceed with the recipe.

SHRIMP BISQUE

Substitute 1 pound shrimp heads, shells, and tails for the 10 crabs and proceed with the recipe.

Classic: Octavia Strickland, left, with a tureen of our prize soup.

CRABMEAT MAISON

Serves 6–8

Picking crabmeat is an art: you've got to get the hang of extracting the meat from the shell without crushing the crabmeat, making it stringy instead of light and lumpy. Before you mix the crabmeat with other ingredients, make sure that it's been properly picked through by feeling for shell bits. Here, jumbo lumps of crab are loosely held together with the rich and briny Sauce Ravigote.

- 2 hard-cooked eggs, peeled and minced
- 1½ cups Basic Sauce Ravigote (page 19)
- 1 tablespoon Creole mustard (page 362)
- 1 shallot, minced
-   Leaves of 1 sprig fresh tarragon, minced
- 1 small handful chives, minced
- 1 teaspoon capers, rinsed and chopped
-   Juice of 1 lemon
- 1 pound jumbo lump blue crabmeat
-   Salt
-   Tabasco
- 3 handfuls seasonal lettuces
- 2 tablespoons Basic Walnut Oil Vinaigrette (page 19)
-   Leaves from fresh herbs, such as dill or chive blossoms

1. Mix together the eggs, Sauce Ravigote, mustard, shallots, tarragon, chives, capers, and lemon juice in a mixing bowl. Fold in the crab, taking care not to break up the large lumps of meat. Season with salt and Tabasco.

2. Toss the lettuces with the Walnut Oil Vinaigrette in a mixing bowl.

3. Put a large spoonful of Crabmeat Maison on each of 6–8 salad plates. Arrange a tuft of dressed greens on top of the crabmeat and scatter the fresh herbs over the top.

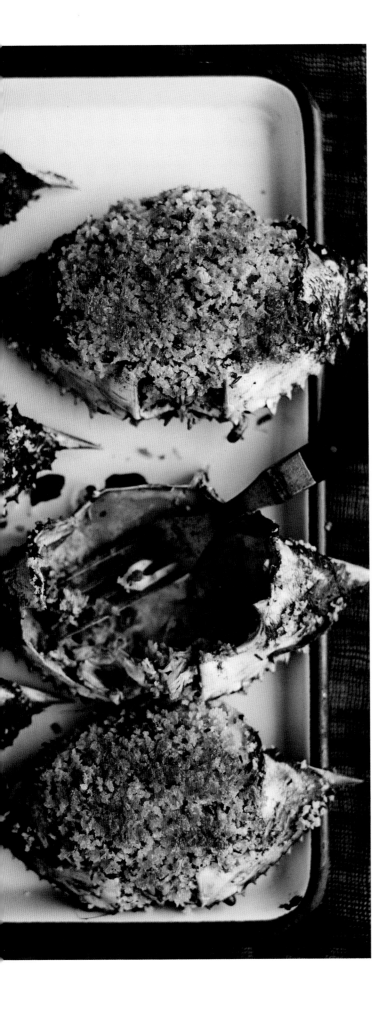

STUFFED BLUE CRABS GRANDMÈRE

Serves 6

I like to use the leftover crabs from a crab boil (page 202) for this simple preparation. Keep as much juice as you can in those shells, stuff them, and bake them until they're golden brown and hot in the middle.

2 cups picked blue crabmeat	2 pinches ground allspice
2 shallots, minced	2 pinches Basic Creole Spices (page 13)
1 green onion, chopped	Salt
1 clove garlic, sliced	6 blue crab top shells
½ cup mayonnaise	¼ cup extra-virgin olive oil
½ cup fresh bread crumbs	¼ cup grated Parmesan cheese
Leaves from 1 sprig fresh tarragon, minced	½ cup dried bread crumbs
1 teaspoon crushed red pepper flakes	

1. Preheat oven to 400°. Mix together the picked crabmeat, shallots, green onions, garlic, mayonnaise, fresh bread crumbs, tarragon, pepper flakes, allspice, and Creole Spices in a mixing bowl. Season with salt. Divide the crabmeat stuffing between the individual crab shells.

2. Mix together the olive oil, Parmesan, and dried bread crumbs in a small bowl. Sprinkle the bread crumbs over the stuffing in the crab shells. Arrange the crab shells on a baking sheet. Bake until golden, 12–16 minutes.

GNOCCHI WITH JUMBO LUMP CRABMEAT AND TRUFFLE

Serves 6

It's very important to make these dumplings while the potatoes are still hot, so that their heat will cook the egg yolks slightly; this makes for lighter dumplings because they'll require less flour. Use just enough flour to form the dough into a ball. Rolling the dough on a grooved board with your thumb makes those sauce-catching indentions on the surface of the gnocchi.

2 medium Yukon Gold potatoes, peeled and quartered	1 pinch ground nutmeg
	1 cup Basic Crab Pan Sauce (page 15)
3 egg yolks, lightly beaten	½ pound jumbo lump blue crabmeat
3 tablespoons butter	1 small black truffle, shaved
¾ cup flour, plus more for dusting	¼ cup shaved Parmesan cheese
Salt	
1 pinch white pepper	

1. Put the potatoes into a small saucepan, cover with cold water, and bring to a boil over high heat. Once boiling, reduce the heat to medium-low and simmer until the potatoes are soft when pierced with a fork, about 20 minutes.

2. Strain the potatoes, return them to the pot, and dry out the potatoes by shaking them over low heat for a minute or two. Transfer the potatoes to a potato ricer or a food mill and press the potatoes through into a mixing bowl.

3. Add the egg yolks and 1 tablespoon of the butter to the warm riced potatoes and mix well. Next, fold the flour, a pinch of salt and white pepper, and the nutmeg into the potatoes until a manageable dough is formed. You may need more flour or less, depending on the moisture content of the potatoes.

4. Separate a fist-size ball of dough from the rest and gently roll the dough with your hands on a lightly floured surface until you've formed a rope about an inch thick. Cut into 1-inch lengths, then roll each piece into a ball. Continue until all the dough is used. Working quickly, shape dumplings on a gnocchi board, or gently press each piece with the tines of the back of a fork to groove the gnocchi.

5. Bring a large pot of lightly salted water to a gentle boil over medium-high heat. Drop the gnocchi, in two batches, into the simmering water. Once the gnocchi float to the surface, allow them to cook for 30 seconds more.

6. While the gnocchi are cooking, heat the Crab Pan Sauce in a large skillet over moderate heat. Scoop the cooked gnocchi out of the water with a slotted spoon and transfer them to the skillet with the Crab Pan Sauce. Now add the crabmeat, the remaining 2 tablespoons butter, and the truffle slices. Serve immediately, topping each portion with a little shaved Parmesan.

Steps to perfect gnocchi:
Below left, ricing the cooked potatoes. The dough, below, made from the cooked potatoes, eggs, flour, and nutmeg, ready for cutting. Bottom, cutting the dough into portions. Top right, making gnocchi groovy by rolling bits of dough on a ridged board (or on the back of a fork). Bottom right, the cooked gnocchi tossed with crabmeat, truffles, and Parmesan.

BUSTER CRAB BLT

Serves 6

Busters are crabs in the process of shedding their shells, so they're not yet soft shells. To clean soft shells, lift up both sides of the top shell and trim away the gills with kitchen shears or a paring knife. Then trim off about a half inch of the face of the crab; this will minimize those air pockets that cause crabs to splatter while frying. As for peeling the tomatoes, it's a bit of a pain in the neck, but the result is well worth the effort. Think of this as a refined, soft-shell crab po'boy.

6 buster crabs or small soft-shell blue crabs, cleaned

Salt

Freshly ground black pepper

1 cup buttermilk

2 cups mixed tiny tomatoes, such as currant, grape, pear, or cherry tomatoes

4 tablespoons Basic Walnut Oil Vinaigrette (page 19)

Leaves from 1 sprig fresh basil, chopped

2 tablespoons butter, softened

6 1-inch-thick slices French bread, halved

1 cup flour

1 cup yellow or white cornmeal or corn flour

1 teaspoon Basic Creole Spices (page 13)

3 cups canola oil

2 tablespoons Basic Sauce Remoulade (page 19)

2 cups mixed baby greens or sprouts

Leaves from 6 sprigs fresh chervil

Leaves from 6 sprigs fresh dill

1. Season the crabs with salt and pepper. Pour the buttermilk into a bowl, add the crabs, and set aside to marinate for a few minutes.

2. Bring a small pot of water to a boil over high heat. While the water heats, make a tiny incision on the stem end of each tomato. Drop the tomatoes into the boiling water. Remove them immediately and cool in a bowl of ice water. Slip the skins from the tomatoes.

3. Put the peeled tomatoes into a bowl along with 2 tablespoons of the Walnut Oil Vinaigrette, the basil, and salt and pepper. Toss together until the tomatoes are well coated.

4. Preheat the broiler. Butter the bread slices, arrange on a baking sheet, and toast under the broiler, turning once, until golden on both sides. Set aside.

5. Mix together the flour, cornmeal, and Creole Spices in a small bowl.

6. Heat the oil in a skillet over high heat until it reaches a temperature of 350° on a candy thermometer. Remove the crabs from the buttermilk and dredge in the seasoned flour. Fry the crabs, turning once, until golden brown on both sides, 6–7 minutes. Remove crabs from skillet and drain on paper towels.

7. Place a slice of toasted bread on each of 6 plates (or arrange on a platter). Spoon marinated tomatoes onto the bread slices, then pile the fried crabs on the tomatoes. Dollop a teaspoon of Sauce Remoulade on each crab.

8. Toss the baby greens with the remaining 2 tablespoons Walnut Oil Vinaigrette in the same bowl used for the tomatoes. Place a handful of greens on each crab, then scatter chervil and dill leaves and top with a piece of toast.

BUSTERS AND GRITS

Serves 6

If you have difficulty finding buster crabs or small soft shells, you can use large soft shell crabs, quartered, and they'll make a great dish.

Salt

1 cup white corn grits (page 362)

6 tablespoons butter

½ cup mascarpone cheese

Freshly ground black pepper

½ cup milk

4 eggs, beaten

1 cup cornmeal

½ cup flour

1 teaspoon Basic Creole Spices (page 13)

1 quart canola oil

6 small soft-shell blue crabs, cleaned (see note opposite)

1 cup Basic Crab Pan Sauce (page 15)

3 cloves garlic, minced

1 green onion, chopped

2 dashes Tabasco

1. Bring 4 cups lightly salted water to a boil in a medium heavy-bottomed pot over high heat. Slowly pour the grits into the boiling water, stirring constantly. Reduce the heat to low. Stir the grits often to make sure they don't stick to the bottom of the pot. Simmer until all the water has been absorbed and the grits become soft, about 20 minutes.

2. Stir in 3 tablespoons of the butter and the mascarpone. Season with salt and pepper. Remove from heat and place a piece of plastic wrap directly on the surface of the grits to keep a crust from forming.

3. Whisk together the milk, eggs, cornmeal, flour, and Creole Spices in a medium bowl until smooth.

4. Heat the canola oil in a deep skillet over high heat until it reaches a temperature of 350° on a candy thermometer. Dip the crabs in the cornmeal batter, then fry the crabs, turning once, until golden brown on both sides, about 7 minutes. Remove crabs from skillet and drain on paper towels. Season with salt and pepper.

5. Heat the Crab Pan Sauce along with the garlic and green onions in a small saucepan over moderate heat.

6. Bring to a boil, stir in the remaining 3 tablespoons butter and the Tabasco, and season with salt and pepper. Once you've added the butter, remove from heat.

7. Spoon grits into a large serving bowl. Ladle a generous amount of sauce around the grits, then put the fried soft shells on top of the grits.

SPICY CRABMEAT WITH VEGETABLE PASTA

Serves 6–8

You can substitute store-bought chile oil for the chile paste, but I prefer to use the best extra-virgin olive oil I can find and emulsify the chile paste in the skillet with Cherry Tomato Five-Minute Sauce. Add more chile paste to suit your taste.

1 cup cherry tomatoes
1 recipe Basic Homemade Pasta (page 16) or dried linguine or spaghetti
  Salt
½ cup extra-virgin olive oil
1 small zucchini, thinly sliced
1 small yellow squash, thinly sliced
1 small Japanese eggplant, thinly sliced
1 clove garlic, minced
  Freshly ground black pepper
1 pound jumbo lump blue crabmeat, picked over
1 cup Cherry Tomato Five-Minute Sauce (page 138)
1 heaping teaspoon sambal chile paste
  Leaves of 1 sprig fresh basil, chopped

1. Bring a small pot of water to a boil over high heat. While the water heats, make a tiny incision on the stem end of every tomato. Drop the tomatoes into the boiling water. Remove them immediately and cool in a bowl of ice water. Slip the skins from the tomatoes.

2. Meanwhile, cook the pasta in a large pot of boiling salted water over moderate heat until just tender, 3–12 minutes depending on whether you are using fresh pasta or dried. Drain the pasta.

3. Heat 2 tablespoons of the olive oil in a large skillet over medium-high heat and sauté the zucchini, yellow squash, and eggplant until soft, about 7 minutes.

4. Add the garlic and peeled tomatoes to the skillet. Season with a little salt and pepper. Add crabmeat, Cherry Tomato Five-Minute Sauce, and cooked pasta. Toss everything together, then add 6 tablespoons of the olive oil and the chile paste. Cook for 5 minutes then remove from the heat. Add the basil just before serving and season again with salt and pepper.

CRABMEAT AND FROG ÉTOUFFÉE

Serves 8

Wild frogs' legs benefit from long, slow cooking; just make sure that they don't cook so long that the meat falls from the bone. Check periodically to keep the sauce from scorching and to test for doneness. And, yes, you can use frozen frogs' legs.

½ cup canola oil
½ cup flour
1 pound frogs' legs
  Salt
  Freshly ground black pepper
1 onion, chopped
1 stalk celery, chopped
1 bell pepper, seeded and chopped
4 cloves garlic, minced
1 tablespoon tomato paste
¼ teaspoon cayenne pepper
1 bay leaf
  Leaves from 1 sprig fresh thyme
2 cups Basic Shellfish Stock (page 13)
1 pound blue crab claw meat, picked over
  Tabasco
4 cups cooked Basic Louisiana White Rice (page 15)

1. Heat the oil in a large saucepan over moderate heat. Stir in the flour and cook the roux, stirring frequently, until the flour has cooked and turned a blond color, about 5 minutes.

2. Season the frogs' legs on all sides with salt and pepper. Increase the heat to medium-high and sear the legs in the hot roux until they are brown on all sides, about 5 minutes. Add the onions, celery, bell peppers, and garlic and cook, stirring frequently, for 10 minutes.

3. Add the tomato paste and cook for 5 minutes. Add the cayenne, bay leaf, thyme, and Shellfish Stock. Reduce the heat to low, cover, and simmer for 20 minutes.

4. Add the crabmeat and season with Tabasco and salt and pepper. Serve over hot rice.

Fat of the crab:
Kenyatta Ashford,
above, tucks into grilled
corn slathered with
crab fat butter, left.

GRILLED CORN ON THE COB WITH CRAB FAT BUTTER

Serves 6

What we call crab fat is that yellowish delicacy found in and around the top shell of the crab, plus the orange crab roe. Flavored with the spicy crab boil, it's especially succulent on corn. Save the fat and freeze it after a crab boil, or make this butter when you're serving crabs as a main dish.

6 ears corn, husk and all
   Salt

6 tablespoons crab fat
   (saved from a dozen
   boiled crabs)

8 tablespoons butter,
   softened

1. Soak the corn overnight in a gallon of well-salted water.

2. Purée the crab fat and softened butter in a food processor. Transfer to a small bowl, cover with plastic wrap, and refrigerate until you are ready to use it.

3. Light a charcoal or gas grill. When the coals have burned down, grill the corn in the husk, turning several times, for 30 minutes. Test the corn by peeling back the husk and pressing the kernels with your fingers. The corn is done when tender to the touch.

4. Keep the corn warm on the side of the grill or in a very low oven. Peel the husks back and remove as many of the silks as you can. Slather the corn with the crab fat butter and season with a pinch of salt.

CHAPTER 10

CHANTERELLES & BLACKBERRIES

Foraging: Chef Todd Pulsinelli finds chanterelles deep in the wilds of the Honey Island Swamp, left. Top left, double-crusted blackberry pie (recipe, page 227). Above, mushrooms grow close to the gnarled roots of old live oak trees like this one in St. Charles Parish; photo: Whitsell, 1934. Blackberries, far right.

Out of the Kitchen and Into the Woods

"My goal is to get my cooks to talk about food the way my friends talk about food."

If you were to ask any of my friends why they're such good cooks, they'd say, "Because we're such good eaters." But I believe it's because we all grew up hunting and fishing and foraging, never far from the origins of our ingredients. I'm always looking for new and different ways to inspire the young chefs who come to work for me in New Orleans. Never before in America have we turned out so many well-educated cooks, but these days they come mostly from urban and suburban middle-class families and have never known hardship or the need for frugality. Most cooks grow up almost totally removed from the source of their food—from farming and the most elementary practices of harvesting and preserving; giving animals a better life is an alien idea to most of them. Yet I have never met a great chef who did not have a respect for the origins of their ingredients. So, over the years, I've found it very effective to take my cooks out of the kitchen and into the woods, face to face with mosquitoes, snakes, wasps, and all the creatures of the wild. The magic of hunting mushrooms and berries, I tell them, is to push yourself out of your comfort zone. That's when greatness is achieved. Foraging is a practice that was passed down to me by my grandparents and a wild Frenchman whom I worked for at an impressionable age. That crazy Frenchman, Philippe Parole, taught me how to pick chanterelle, oyster, and boletus mushrooms. It's scary to realize that now I'm the wild chef, and our cooks are the pupils.

THOUGH I GREW up stumbling around in the swamps among countless varieties of mushroom, the thought of eating one would never have crossed my mind. Wild mushrooms were *verboten*! Granddaddy made sure to instill in us the fear that we'd surely die if we ate one. Well, that all changed once I started working for Philippe. He was a notable chef in Baton Rouge, with a larger-than-life personality, always a ready joke, and an easy smile. I worked at his restaurant when I was 18, before I joined the Marines. It never even occurred to me to wonder why a great chef would have a restaurant in Baton Rouge. But the truth is, Philippe was cheap, too cheap to purchase wild mushrooms or berries or fish, for that matter. "Why should I buy them when God gives them away?" he'd ask.

We would forage for whatever we could find. He'd sell the mushrooms we gathered, and he even had me soak them in water so they'd weigh more! Whatever fish we'd catch would go on his menu as "sea bream." Consequently, I spent much of my summer fishing for trout and redfish and picking wild berries by day and turning it all into Refined French Cuisine by night. I'd hate to sound as if my late teen years were occupied with much profound thought, because surely they weren't, but foraging for those forbidden mushrooms did change the way I learned to appreciate foodstuffs.

Like finding a lost wallet or the car keys, finding the first mushroom is hitting pay dirt. You get into that ankle-high grass and the layers of leaves that act as mulch, and you start to really focus, trying to make out those veins of chanterelles. Finding one leads you to another because the spores scatter in patterns. When the conditions are right, they're right. In the middle of the summer, there's a type of tulip flower in the woods, but nothing else is the color of a chanterelle in the swamp. You can almost smell its apricot–black pepper perfume

Wild berries: The "blackberry woman," a Louisiana street vendor in a WPA photograph from 1940.

before you see it. Just as it does when he's hunting ducks or deer, the cook's mind races: what dish can I cook with this mushroom? Well, this one's small; maybe I should marinate it and put it in a salad. This one's bigger; I can trim it and sauté it and scatter the pieces on top of a redfish.

Unlike crawfishing, foraging for chanterelles is not a social activity: crawling around on your hands and knees in a dark, hot swamp, battling ticks and spiders and snakes. As soon as you have enough, you want to go home. Blackberries, too—and what we called huckleberries, which are actually elderberries—can be picked all over our low-lying swamps and sloughs if you defend yourself against their thorny brambles.

WE DON'T ISSUE disclaimers to any of our staff who regularly spend their Saturday mornings in the summer scouring God's country for tasty things to cook. Of course the harvest does not come without collateral damage. In fact, foraging is all about risk, especially since many of our young employees have no practical experience in the wild. It's not uncommon to happen upon a wild hog who's unhappy to see us, because she's just had a litter of little feral pigs. We've had a snake-bite or two that sure gave us a scare. So far, our worst mishap was a bite by a brown recluse spider on the tip of the nose of one unlucky sous-chef. Ouch! He didn't die, he wasn't permanently disfigured, but it did take some time before he looked like himself again. I'm not sure that he's ever returned to the Honey Island Swamp. But that's part of the lesson—you can't spend time in the wild without truly confronting it, and perhaps that's the beauty of it. These pilgrimages produce a kitchen brigade with a deeper appreciation for wild foods. In contrast to just opening boxes of mushrooms and berries from some purveyor a thousand miles away, when we cook with the things we forage, our food reflects the richness and soul of our experiences.

Backyard berries: In the woods behind our restaurant La Provence, in Lacombe, big, early-season blackberries grow in wild abundance.

CHANTERELLES, CHICKEN, AND DUMPLINGS

Serves 4

Often, when I roast a few chickens, I'll save those delectable chicken oysters (the little nuggets of the chicken back that look like oysters), or I'll use the meat from roasted chicken legs for this dish. For cooked chicken, don't brine the chicken first, reduce the amount of stock to one cup, and follow the process from step 2.

FOR THE CHICKEN

- ¼ cup sugar
- Salt
- 6 boneless skinless chicken thighs, cut into pieces
- 2 tablespoons extra-virgin olive oil
- 3 shallots, minced
- 2 cloves garlic, minced
- 1 teaspoon minced peeled fresh ginger
- 1 teaspoon crushed red pepper flakes
- 2 cups Basic Chicken Stock (page 13)
- 1 cup fresh chanterelle mushrooms, halved lengthwise
- Leaves from 1 sprig fresh thyme
- Leaves from 1 sprig fresh sage, chopped
- ½ cup shelled sweet peas or shucked, peeled fresh fava beans
- 1 tomato, peeled, seeded, and diced
- 2 tablespoons butter
- Freshly ground black pepper

FOR THE DUMPLINGS

- Salt
- 1 cup ricotta cheese
- 3 egg yolks
- 1 pinch nutmeg
- ⅓ cup flour
- Leaves from 4 sprigs fresh chervil

1. For the uncooked chicken, dissolve the sugar and ¼ cup salt together in 1 quart cold water in a medium bowl. Add the pieces of chicken thighs and let them marinate in the brine, refrigerated, for 1 hour. Drain the chicken and pat dry with paper towels. Discard the brine.

2. Heat the olive oil in a wide heavy-bottomed pot over high heat. Add the chicken and sauté until it is no longer pink. Add the shallots, garlic, ginger, and pepper flakes, reduce the heat to moderate, and cook for 5 minutes. Stir in the Chicken Stock and simmer until the liquid has reduced by nearly half, about 5 minutes.

3. Add the chanterelles, thyme, sage, peas, and tomatoes to the pot. Increase the heat to medium-high and cook, stirring often, for 5 minutes. Add the butter and season with salt and pepper. Cover and reduce the heat to low to keep the chicken and vegetables warm while making the dumplings.

4. For the dumplings, bring a medium pot of salted water to a boil, then reduce the heat to moderate to maintain a very gentle boil.

5. Combine the ricotta with the egg yolks, nutmeg, and ¼ teaspoon salt in a medium mixing bowl. Gradually stir in just enough flour to form a soft dough. Test the dumpling dough before adding more flour by dropping a small spoonful of the dough into the boiling water. Once the dumpling floats to the surface, let it poach for 45 seconds. If the dumpling breaks apart while cooking, you'll need to add a bit more flour to the dough and test again. Just don't overwork the dough, or it'll become tough.

6. Drop the remaining dough by teaspoonfuls into the boiling water and poach the dumplings for 45 seconds. As soon as they are done, use a slotted spoon to transfer the dumplings to the pot of chicken and vegetables.

7. Serve the chicken and dumplings in bowls and scatter the chervil on top.

Chanterelles

Every year since my high-school days, I can be found on hot and steamy mornings in the same swamp, just minutes from downtown New Orleans, in pursuit of wild mushrooms. Usually, we'll find them on sandy river bluffs on the North Shore of Lake Pontchartrain. Chanterelles (*Cantharellus cibarius*) love the roots of oak trees, where they grow in small enclaves under the canopy of this often flooded forest. During the dry summer, these ridgelines are quickly covered with thick grasses and ferns that offer the perfect growing conditions for mushrooms. Locating them means spending much time on your hands and knees. Where you find one mushroom, you'll find plenty, so tracking the elusive fungus is either feast or famine.

If you're a novice, make sure to forage with someone who really knows what he is doing. Because the correct identification of mushrooms can truly be a matter of life and death, you don't want to play around! There are many mushroom clubs around the country eager to share information; you can find state-by-state lists on the Internet through such organizations as NAMA (North American Mycological Association). One of the drawbacks to crawling on the sandy floor of our swampland is that you are not alone; we share the real estate with spiders, snakes, alligators, wild hogs, and many kinds of poisonous plants. Despite its perils, foraging pays off when you find that perfect little, tender chanterelle and inhale its woody, apricot perfume.

JAEGERSCHNITZEL (HUNTER'S CHOPS)

Serves 6

Cook only a couple of veal chops at a time (overloading the pan will turn them soggy) until they're brown and crisp.

- 2 cups dried bread crumbs
- Leaves from 1 sprig fresh thyme
- 1 teaspoon Creole Spices (page 13)
- 6 veal chops (either rib chops or T-bones)
- Salt
- Freshly ground black pepper
- 3 eggs, beaten
- 3 tablespoons canola oil
- 2 shallots, minced
- 2 cloves garlic, minced
- 1 cup halved chanterelle mushrooms
- ¾ cup Basic Chicken Pan Sauce (page 15)
- 1 tablespoon chopped fresh chives
- 1 pinch crushed red pepper flakes
- ½ teaspoon fresh lemon juice
- 2 tablespoons cold butter, diced

1. Mix together the bread crumbs, thyme, and Creole Spices in a large mixing bowl.

2. Season the veal chops with salt and pepper. Dunk the chops into the beaten eggs, then dredge in the seasoned bread crumbs.

3. Preheat the oven to 325°. Heat the canola oil in a large skillet over medium-high heat. Pan-fry the veal chops on both sides, in batches, until golden brown. Remove the veal chops from the skillet, drain on paper towels; transfer to a baking sheet and place in the oven.

4. In the same skillet over medium-high heat, cook the shallots, garlic, and mushrooms for 5 minutes, stirring frequently. Reduce the heat to moderate. Add the Chicken Pan Sauce, chives, pepper flakes, and lemon juice. Reduce the sauce by half, 7–10 minutes.

5. Remove the skillet from the heat. Stir in the butter and season with salt and pepper. Remove the veal chops from the oven and serve them with a heaping spoonful of the chanterelle mushroom sauce.

SALAD OF GRILLED BOBWHITE QUAIL AND CHANTERELLES

Serves 6

Be careful not to overcook the mushrooms; just heating them up will soften them considerably. Then toss them in the sherry vinaigrette. Use whatever wild mushrooms you can find, but nothing beats the woodsy, peppery aroma of dainty chanterelles.

- 6 semiboneless bobwhite quail
  Salt
  Freshly ground black pepper
- 2 tablespoons Basic Pepper Jelly Vinaigrette (page 19)
- 4 tablespoons extra-virgin olive oil
- 1 shallot, minced
- 1 clove garlic, minced
- 2 cups small chanterelle mushrooms
- 2 tablespoons sherry vinegar
- 2 tablespoons hazelnut oil
- 1 teaspoon sugar
  Leaves from 1 sprig fresh thyme
- 1 handful chives, minced
- 2 cups bitter greens or other tiny lettuce leaves

1. Season the quail with salt and pepper and brush on all sides with the Pepper Jelly Vinaigrette. Let marinate for 20 minutes or so. Light a charcoal or gas grill. When the coals have burned down to a moderate heat, grill the quail on both sides until brown, about 8 minutes. Remove from the grill and set side.

2. Heat 1 tablespoon of the olive oil in a medium pan over moderate heat. Cook the shallots and garlic until soft, about 3 minutes. Add the chanterelles and cook for about 4 minutes. Remove the pan from the heat and transfer the chanterelles to a mixing bowl.

3. Add the sherry vinegar, the remaining 3 tablespoons olive oil, hazelnut oil, sugar, thyme, and chives to the bowl; toss together until well mixed. Season with salt and pepper.

4. Use a slotted spoon to scoop up the chanterelles from the bowl and divide equally between 6 salad plates. Place 1 grilled quail on each plate.

5. Add the greens to the same mixing bowl and toss to coat in the sherry vinaigrette remaining in the bowl. Divide the greens between the plates.

CHANTERELLE MUSHROOM TARTLETS AND PORK CRACKLINS SALAD

Serves 6

If you braise the pork bellies a day or so ahead, this dish becomes much easier. Prepare the basic pie dough according to directions, and "blind bake" or prebake the tartlets for a few minutes until they are blond in color, then fill them with the mushrooms. Feel free to make just one large nine-inch tart instead of six individual tartlets.

FOR THE CRACKLINS

- 2 pounds skinless pork belly
- 2 onions, chopped
- 1 carrot, chopped
- 3 cloves garlic, crushed
- 1 stalk celery, chopped
- 1 cup white wine
- 3 sprigs fresh thyme
- Salt
- ½ teaspoon crushed red pepper flakes
- 1 tablespoon hoisin sauce
- 1 tablespoon Steen's cane syrup (page 362)
- 2 tablespoons rice wine vinegar
- 2 tablespoons canola oil
- 1 tablespoon Asian sesame oil
- ¼ teaspoon cayenne pepper
- Freshly ground black pepper

FOR THE TARTLETS

- 3 tablespoons rendered bacon fat
- 1 onion, thinly sliced
- 4 cups (4–6 ounces) fresh chanterelle mushrooms, halved lengthwise
- Salt
- Freshly ground black pepper
- 5 eggs, beaten
- 2 cups heavy cream
- 6 3–4-inch round pie shells, or 1 9-inch pie shell, blind-baked using Basic Pie Dough recipe (page 16)
- 1 shallot, minced
- 2 cloves garlic, minced
- Leaves from 1 sprig fresh thyme
- ¼ cup Basic Veal Stock (page 14)

FOR THE SALAD

- 2 cups frisée lettuce
- 2 tablespoons Basic Walnut Oil Vinaigrette (page 19)

1. For the cracklins, preheat the oven to 325°. Put the pork belly, fat side up, into a deep roasting pan. Add the onions, carrots, garlic, celery, wine, thyme, ½ teaspoon salt, and pepper flakes. Pour in enough cold water to cover the pork belly by 1 inch. Tightly cover the pan with aluminum foil and braise the pork in the oven for 6 hours.

2. Remove the pan from the oven and allow the pork belly to cool completely before uncovering the pan. Cut the pork belly into 6 equal portions and discard the braising liquid.

3. Whisk together the hoisin sauce, cane syrup, rice wine vinegar, canola and sesame oils, cayenne, and salt and pepper in a medium bowl. Add the braised pork belly pieces to the bowl and let them marinate while preparing the tartlets and salad.

4. For the tartlets, preheat the oven to 350°. Heat 2 tablespoons of the rendered bacon fat in a medium skillet over medium-high heat. Add the onions and sauté until they begin to brown. Add one-quarter of the chanterelles to the skillet, season with a little salt and pepper, and sauté, stirring often, for 5 minutes or so.

5. Whisk together the eggs and cream in a medium bowl. Add the cooked chanterelles and onions to the bowl and stir until well combined.

6. Divide the mushroom filling evenly between the 6 prepared tartlet shells or spoon into the 1 large shell, and place on a baking pan. Bake the tartlets until the crusts are golden brown and the filling has set, about 30 minutes. Let the tartlets rest a few minutes before removing them from the pans.

7. Heat the remaining 1 tablespoon rendered bacon fat in a medium skillet over medium-high heat. Add the remaining chanterelles and sauté them, stirring frequently, for 5 minutes. Add the shallots and garlic and sauté for 1 minute or so. Add the thyme and Veal Stock. Reduce the heat to low, season with salt and pepper, and simmer the mushrooms until the liquid has evaporated from the skillet.

HONEY ISLAND CHANTERELLE SOUP

Serves 6–8

This simple soup will work with whatever mushrooms you have at your fingertips. Add a bit more chicken stock if it's a touch too thick.

½ cup finely chopped bacon

1 onion, chopped

2 cloves garlic, minced

1 pound chanterelle mushrooms

1 large russet potato, peeled and diced

1 teaspoon crushed red pepper flakes

Leaves from 1 sprig fresh thyme

1 cup white wine

3 cups Basic Chicken Stock (page 13)

1 cup heavy cream

Salt

Freshly ground black pepper

2 tablespoons chopped fresh chives

1. Render the bacon in a large heavy-bottomed pot over moderate heat. Once the bacon has browned, remove it from the pot, leaving the rendered fat. Drain the bacon on paper towels.

2. Add the onions and garlic to the pot and cook in the bacon fat, stirring often, until the onions are translucent, about 5 minutes. Increase the heat to medium-high and add the chanterelles. Cook, stirring frequently, for 5 minutes.

3. Add the potatoes, pepper flakes, thyme, and white wine to the pot. Cook for several minutes until the wine has reduced by half. Add the Chicken Stock and cream and, when the soup comes to a boil, reduce the heat to medium-low. Cover and simmer until the potatoes are tender, about 20 minutes.

4. Purée the soup in a blender or a food processor. Strain through a fine sieve back into the pot. Season with salt and pepper. Thin with a little water or Chicken Stock if the soup is too thick. Serve with bacon and chopped chives scattered on top.

8. To finish the cracklins, heat a medium skillet over medium-high heat until hot. Sear the braised pork belly pieces, fat side down, until evenly browned, then turn them and brown them on the second side, about 3–5 minutes per side.

9. For the salad, toss the greens with the Walnut Oil Vinaigrette in a medium bowl.

10. To assemble each plate, place each tartlet (or slice of tart) on a plate and top with the sautéed mushrooms. Alongside the tart, put a piece of the pork cracklins and cover each with a mound of dressed frisée.

OLD-FASHIONED DOUBLE-CRUSTED BLACKBERRY PIE

Makes one 9-inch pie

This very pretty pie can be made as I've described below, or you can make a lattice crust by rolling a third of the dough out to the same thickness, cutting it in strips, weaving the strips in a lattice over the top of the pie, then crimping the dough and baking the pie. The filling itself is good stuffed into puff pastry and baked as a turnover.

4 cups blackberries	¼ cup flour
¾ cup sugar	1 recipe Basic Pie Dough (page 16)
2 tablespoons powdered pectin	1 egg
1 vanilla bean	2 tablespoons milk
2 tablespoons butter, softened	

1. Put the blackberries, sugar, pectin, and ½ cup cold water into a medium saucepan. Split the vanilla bean in half lengthwise and scrape the seeds into the saucepan. Add the pod to the saucepan.

2. Bring the berries to a boil over medium-high heat, stirring frequently. Reduce the heat to moderate and simmer, stirring occasionally, until the juices thicken enough to coat the back of the spoon, about 30 minutes. Remove the pan from the heat and let the berries cool for 30 minutes or so.

3. Preheat the oven to 375°. Grease a 9-inch ceramic or glass pie pan with the softened butter and dust it with some of the flour. Roll two-thirds of the pie dough out on a lightly floured surface to a ¼-inch thickness. Fit the dough into the prepared pan and trim off any excess dough from the edges.

4. Remove the vanilla bean pod from the cooled filling and discard; pour the filling into the prepared pie shell.

5. Roll the remaining third of the pie dough out on a lightly floured surface to a ¼-inch thickness and lay it over the berry filling. Crimp the edges of the dough together and make a few slits through the top crust to allow steam to escape while baking.

6. Bake the pie for 30 minutes. Beat the egg and milk together in a small bowl, then brush the top crust of the pie with the egg wash. Return the pie to the oven and continue to bake it until the crust is a deep golden brown, about 15 minutes more.

7. Transfer the pie to a wire rack to let cool until it is just warm or room temperature.

CORNMEAL WHITE CHOCOLATE BISCOTTI

Makes 24

These very simple sugar cookies have the crunchy consistency of biscotti. Make them a few days in advance and store them in an airtight container; they won't dry out.

1 pound unsalted butter, softened	2 cups all-purpose flour, plus more for dusting
1½ cups powdered sugar	1 tablespoon baking powder
2 teaspoons vanilla extract	2 ¼ teaspoons salt
1 teaspoon freshly grated lemon zest	½ cup white chocolate chunks
2 cups finely ground cornmeal	

1. Beat the butter and powdered sugar together in the bowl of a standing mixer fitted with the paddle attachment set on medium-high speed until light and fluffy. Reduce the speed to low and mix in the vanilla extract and lemon zest.

2. Stir together the cornmeal, 2 cups flour, baking powder, and salt in another bowl, then gradually mix into the butter mixture, beating on medium-low speed until just combined. Stir in the chocolate chunks. Shape the dough into a 2–3-inch-wide cylinder on a floured surface. Cover the dough and refrigerate for at least 2 hours.

3. Preheat the oven to 325°. Cut the dough crosswise into ¼-inch-thick cookies. Set the cookies on baking sheets about ½ inch apart and bake them until pale golden, about 12 minutes. Transfer the biscotti to a wire rack to let cool.

BUTTERMILK PANNA COTTA WITH STEWED BERRIES

Serves 6

This panna cotta is as easy as Jell-O; the only potential danger is scorching the gelatin. An easy way around that is to remove the pan from the heat before you add the gelatin. Stir it in well, make sure it's dissolved, then add the buttermilk. Buttermilk doesn't like too much heat either.

FOR THE PANNA COTTA

2 cups heavy cream	1 teaspoon freshly grated lemon zest
½ cup sugar	1 cup halved strawberries
2 packets unflavored gelatin	1 cup blueberries
3 ½ cups buttermilk	1 cup blackberries
	Leaves from 3 sprigs fresh mint, cut into thin strips

FOR THE BERRIES

½ cup light corn syrup	12 Cornmeal White Chocolate Biscotti (recipe, left)
1 vanilla bean, split lengthwise	

1. For the panna cotta, combine the cream and sugar in a medium heavy-bottomed saucepan. Heat over moderate heat, stirring often, until the sugar dissolves. Meanwhile, sprinkle the gelatin into ¼ cup of cool water in a small bowl and allow to swell and soften. Remove pot from heat and stir in the gelatin. Let the mixture cool for 15–20 minutes. Stir in the buttermilk. Divide the panna cotta mixture evenly between six 8-ounce ramekins or whatever mold you like. Refrigerate the panna cotta, uncovered, until set, 3–4 hours.

2. For the berries, put the corn syrup, vanilla bean, and lemon zest into a medium saucepan and bring to a boil over moderate heat. Remove the pan from the heat and let the syrup cool for 2–3 minutes. Add the berries and set them aside to macerate in the syrup.

3. Serve the panna cotta topped with a spoonful of the stewed berries and the mint strips and the Cornmeal Biscotti on the side.

LEMON VERBENA SORBET

Makes about 3 cups

This simple, refreshing sorbet is wonderful by itself but especially good with a berry pie. Instead of lemon verbena, try the same amount of mint, basil, or lemongrass.

2 cups sugar	¼ cup fresh lemon juice
½ cup fresh lemon verbena leaves, crushed	

1. Put the sugar, lemon verbena leaves, lemon juice, and 2 cups cold water into a large heavy-bottomed saucepan. Boil over medium-high heat, stirring often, until the sugar has dissolved, about 5 minutes.

2. Remove the pan from the heat and let the syrup cool completely. Strain the syrup through a fine sieve into a medium bowl.

3. Pour the syrup into the canister of an ice cream maker and process the sorbet according to the manufacturer's instructions.

DEWBERRY STREUSEL PIE

Serves 6–8

The dewberry is a large, sweet blackberry variety that grows close to the ground and often ripens earlier than the smaller and tarter wild blackberry. Any berry will work well with this recipe. The German streusel is a crumbly topping much like a crisp or a crumble.

1 recipe Basic Pie Dough (page 16)	**FOR THE STREUSEL**
	6 tablespoons butter, softened
FOR THE BERRIES	6 tablespoons brown sugar
3 ½ cups dewberries or blackberries	6 tablespoons flour
2 tablespoons butter, softened	6 tablespoons ground pecans
½ cup granulated sugar	1 pinch ground cinnamon
1 egg, beaten	1 pinch salt
2 teaspoons cornstarch	

1. Preheat the oven to 350°. Roll the pie dough out to a thickness of ¼-inch. Fit one 9-inch pie pan with the pie dough, making sure to trim the excess dough from the edges. Set the crust aside.

2. For the berries, mix together the dewberries, butter, granulated sugar, egg, and cornstarch in a mixing bowl and set aside.

3. For the streusel, in another bowl mix together the butter, brown sugar, flour, pecans, cinnamon, and salt.

4. Pour the berry mixture into the prepared pie pan and top with the streusel. Bake until the pie is golden brown, about 45 minutes. Transfer the pie to a wire rack to let cool completely.

Berry good: Ripe blueberries, opposite, soon to become hot pies. Ashley Hansen, left, took over her grandparents' renowned Sno-Bliz, a New Orleans institution, where she concocts luscious syrups to pour over shaved ice.

JEN'S WILD BERRY CREAM PIE

Serves 6–8

Jenifer uses whatever berries we can find for this pie; Jack and Luke are forever scouring the woods and fields nearby for blueberries and blackberries. For the Creole cream cheese, you may substitute crème fraîche, yogurt, or sour cream. Taste the filling and add a bit more sugar, if you like.

---

1 recipe Basic Pie Dough (page 16)	4 cups berries; any variety or combination will do
3 tablespoons flour, plus more for dusting	¼ cup graham cracker crumbs
1 cup Creole cream cheese (page 362) or fromage blanc	3 tablespoons brown sugar
1 cup granulated sugar	2 tablespoons butter, softened
1 teaspoon salt	

1. Preheat the oven to 375°. Roll the pie dough out on a lightly floured surface to a thickness of ¼ inch. Fit the dough into a 9-inch pie pan and trim off any excess dough from the edges. Set the crust aside.

2. Put the Creole cream cheese, granulated sugar, 3 tablespoons flour, and salt into a large mixing bowl and stir until well combined. Gently fold in the berries, being careful not to crush all of them. Pour the filling into the pie crust and bake the pie for 30 minutes.

3. Meanwhile, combine the graham cracker crumbs, brown sugar, and softened butter in a small mixing bowl and set aside.

4. Crumble the graham cracker topping all over the surface of the pie and continue baking the pie for 15 minutes more. Transfer the pie to a wire rack to let cool completely.

HOT BLUEBERRY PIE

Serves 6

This recipe works for all sorts of berries; use whatever's local. I love blueberry pie hot, just out of the oven, or removed from the pan and reheated in a warm oven just before serving. Top with your favorite ice cream (at my house it's homemade vanilla) or Lemon Verbena Sorbet (page 231).

---

4 tablespoons butter, softened	1 egg
3 tablespoons flour	3 cups blueberries
1 recipe Basic Pie Dough (page 16)	1 teaspoon freshly grated lemon zest
½ cup granulated sugar	¼ cup powdered sugar

1. Preheat the oven to 375°. Prepare one 9-inch tart pan or 6 individual 3–4-inch pans by greasing each with softened butter, using at most 2 tablespoons. Then dust the pans with 1 tablespoon of flour.

2. Roll the pie dough out on a lightly floured surface to a thickness of ¼ inch. Fit the large pan or 6 individual pans with the pie dough, making sure to trim the excess dough around the edges.

3. Beat together the remaining 2 tablespoons butter, the granulated sugar, and the egg in a mixing bowl until smooth and creamy.

4. Fold the blueberries, the remaining 2 tablespoons flour, and the lemon zest into the sugar mixture. Fill the large pie pan, or divide the berry filling between the 6 prepared tart pans, or fill one large pie pan. Arrange the pies on a baking sheet and bake until the crust is golden brown, about 20 minutes. Remove from the oven. Dust with the powdered sugar.

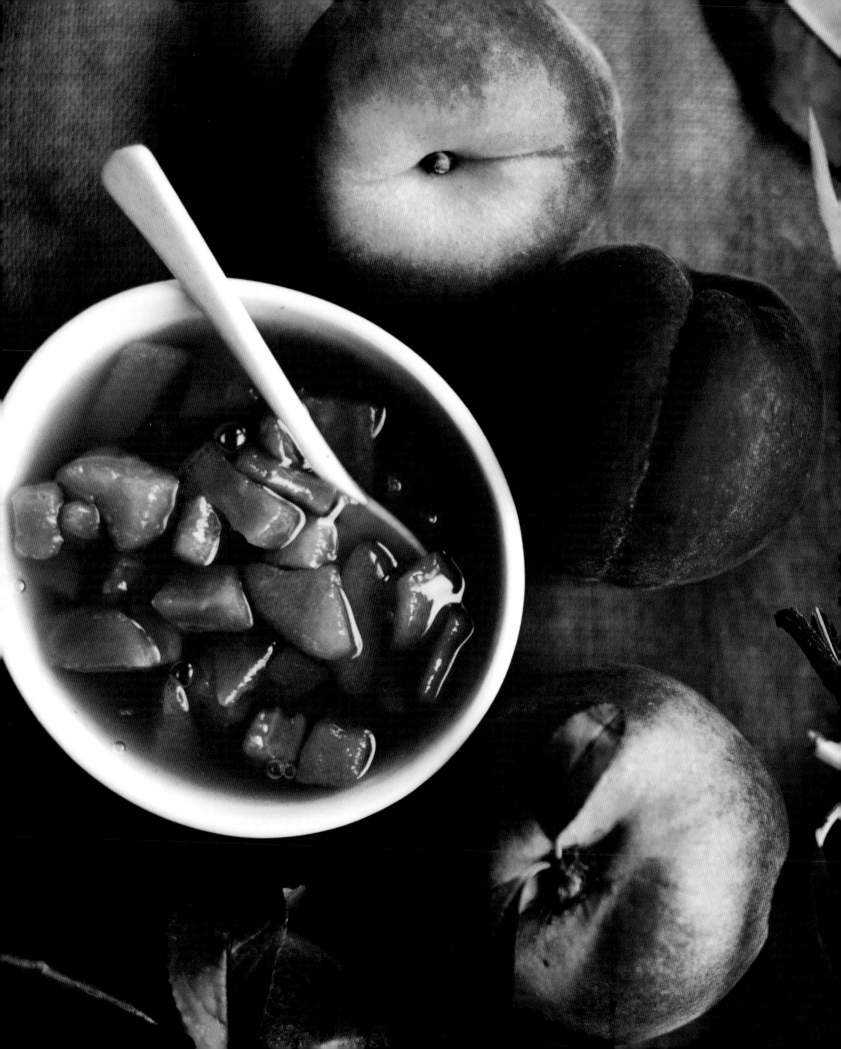

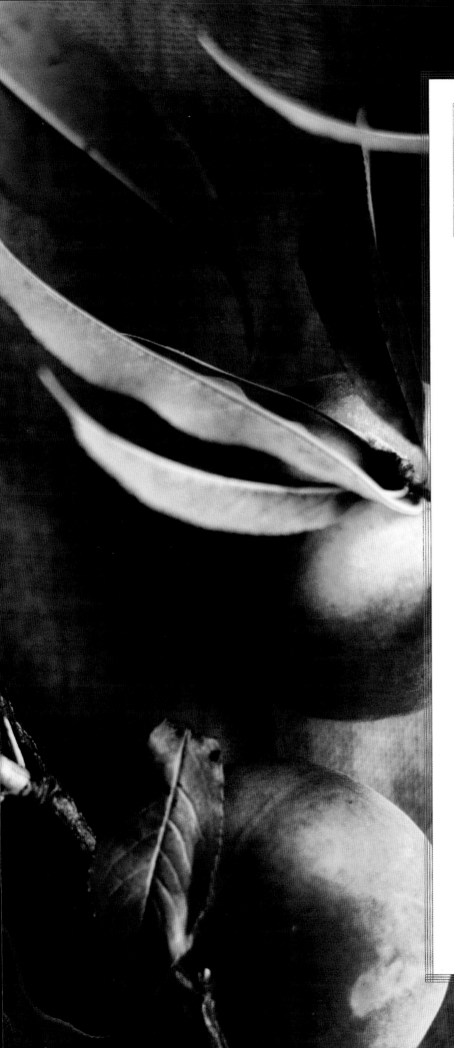

Grandaddy and the Fig

"Where I grew up, grown men did not eat grilled figs with baby greens and artisanal goats' milk cheese."

My maternal grandparents, Grace and Mitchell Walters, came from warm, happy-go-lucky Irish stock, and their house in Mississippi became my place of refuge, where I was treated to much love and affection, not to mention the best food I've ever eaten. The aromas of their joyous house will forever be imprinted in my brain: a mix of rendered bacon, fresh-baked biscuits, strong coffee, and tobacco. It's hard for me to walk down a street in New Orleans—or Paris, for that matter—without smelling similar aromas that instantly take me back to my childhood.

Their house looked like somebody's country place, with big porches front and back and rocking chairs.

It's all in the jar: From left, purple figs from Ben Becnel's farm; a table of preserves made in the kitchens of La Provence; just-picked sugar plums. Above, Sarah Albritton, of Ruston, Louisiana, filling jars, 1984; photo: Susan Roach-Lankford.

Pea season: Mary L. Gunn, above, shelling purple hull peas, 1984; photo: Susan Roach-Lankford.

A typical scene: sitting on the front porch shelling peas. They might have had air-conditioning, but they didn't use it. I was always drawn to their kitchen to be with my grandmother and Ruth, a woman who worked "with" her, never "for" her. And I'd be Ruth's helper.

A WHISTLE WOULD BLOW at noon at the sawmill in those timber-driven towns, which meant the entire population was off until 2:00 P.M. Lunch was the big meal, and they'd serve whatever was in season: lady peas, creamer peas, purple hull peas, or dried peas cooked with fatback or ham hocks. And, always, greens: mustard, collard, turnip. My grandfather made a vinegar sauce for greens with the little hot peppers he called "sport" peppers. There was corn bread and corn sticks that we'd bake in those black cast-iron pans. Bacon fat from breakfast would sit in a coffee can on the stove, and on special occasions we'd cook up a batch of cracklins bread to have with rutabagas or turnips, cooked with onions and salt pork. There'd be buttermilk and sweet milk and always long-grain Mahatma rice. There would be sliced tomatoes, heirlooms, like our Brandywines, picked just before they split. Later in the season, when blight set in, you'd pick those tomatoes green and cut and fry them.

There might be meat: venison, wild turkey, chicken, pork shoulder, or Boston butt picnic ham. It was always braised—they'd have called it "smothered"—with lots of onions, a little celery, and water, covered like a pot roast and cooked until the meat fell from the bone. Fridays had to be fish—bass or perch. Always there were pickles, put up every year—bread-and-butter, green tomato, onion, and quail egg; sweet and sour, with mustard seed and bay leaves. I became Granddaddy's apprentice in all things that required planting, harvesting, butchering, and bottling.

Not to get off the subject, but breakfast was an event, too: smoked pork sausage links, thick-sliced bacon cooked to medium, real grits—the slow-cooked, buttery kind. There were fresh eggs, of course, and cantaloupe, honeydew, watermelon, and berries. And, of course, fig preserves—not the syrup that I'd drizzle on biscuits but preserved figs taken from the jar and put into a bowl on the kitchen table. Those figs didn't die with breakfast; they'd reappear as a sweet glaze over a smoked ham or became part of a barbecue sauce, to be blended with vinegar, sliced hot pepper, and mustard and basted over slabs of smoked baby back ribs or beef brisket.

Granddaddy had fig trees, pear, plum, and quince trees, and scuppernong and muscadine vines. Peaches we would buy from a nearby farm, and we'd pick blackberries and huckleberries, which would make their way into a jar or two. Since we could not possibly eat it all, preserving was the best way to hold on to the essence of the fruit. In his heart of hearts, my grandfather believed cooking should be left to the women, but preserving was the man's job. He wouldn't let just anybody learn the process with him. If you committed to making preserves, it was not a 30-minute affair. You had to pick the fruit, clean it, cook it, and strain it and sterilize the jars, the lids. For me, even though it took way too long on the structured part to get to the eating part, preserving meant working with Granddaddy for the whole day, and that was the great thing.

F IGS HAVE LONG since had a special place in my heart and cupboard because Granddaddy was the connoisseur of preserved figs. Celeste figs were the king and the only variety he knew. If you were given a jar of his fig preserves, you knew you were somebody. The fig jar was always a topic of conversation in their house, especially after my grandfather took ill; as it turned out, he had jars of fig preserves stashed in various cabinets, armoires, and utility rooms. We didn't know how old some of those jars were, and we dared not ask; if you were offered a fig, you'd better eat it.

We ate those aged figs out of blind faith, as if to confirm our love and admiration for Granddaddy. Figs weren't eaten raw, nor were they grilled, fried, or baked. His figs met with only one certain fate: The Jar. To preserve the whole fig in syrup is an art form. Mishandle the figs, and they could crush, crack, rupture, or break. The perfect figs should be washed, trimmed, and softly poached in a simple syrup of sugar and water, gently packed into jars, covered with the reduced syrup, and sealed. No spices were added to Granddaddy's figs, which were unlike the preserved figs that Father Roux gives us every Christmas along with blue cheese. Father Roux's figs are perfumed with Meyer lemon peel and rosemary or bay leaves. Granddaddy would never hear of that; the ripe fig was all the spice he desired.

Putting things by: A variety of preserves—beet, pear, quince, and berry jams in the cabinet where they're sold at La Provence, below. The French country exterior of the restaurant, bottom, just across the lake from New Orleans.

OLD-FASHIONED FIG PRESERVES

Makes 5–7 pint jars

I love using my granddaddy's favorite Celeste figs, the most common in our neck of the woods, but just about any fig will work in these preserves. Larger figs should be quartered before the sugar is added.

5　pounds fresh figs
5　pounds sugar

1. Wash the figs, then trim off the stem ends. Put the figs into a large pot and cover with the sugar. Allow them to sit at room temperature for 3 hours or so.

2. Heat the figs and the sugar, stirring constantly, over moderate heat. Once the sugar has dissolved, increase the heat to high and bring to a hard boil.

3. Reduce the heat to medium-low and gently boil for 40 minutes, stirring frequently.

4. The preserves are done when the foam that has formed on the surface dissipates and the syrup coats the back of the spoon. Ladle the figs and syrup into hot, sterilized jars, leaving ¼ inch of headspace. Wipe the rims of the jars clean, then place sterilized lids on top and screw on the rings.

5. Put the filled jars into a canning pot and cover with water at least 2 inches over the jar tops. Bring to a boil and boil for 15 minutes. Use tongs to carefully remove the jars from the water; place on a kitchen towel. Allow the jars to cool completely before you move them.

NOTE

To sterilize the jars, bottles, and lids for all the preserves in this chapter, place them on a rack in a large canning pot, fill with water to the tops of the jars and bring the water to a boil for 5 minutes. Then, use tongs to carefully remove the jars and bottles. Drain them upside down on a clean kitchen towel until ready to fill.

FIG GLAZE FOR ROAST MEATS AND FOWL

Makes 2 cups

For this glaze, I like to use the fig syrup from my fig preserves, but any sweet preserve will work as a sauce base. I slather on the glaze before and during the roasting of hams, pork roast, ducks, and game. Sometimes, I'll add a tablespoon or two of hoisin sauce.

2　teaspoons canola oil
1　shallot, minced
1　clove garlic
1　teaspoon minced peeled fresh ginger
¾　cup rice wine vinegar
1¼　cups fig syrup from preserved figs
Salt
Freshly ground black pepper

1. Heat the canola oil in a saucepan over moderate heat. Add the shallots, garlic, and ginger and cook, stirring constantly, until the shallots are soft and translucent but not brown, about 5 minutes.

2. Increase the heat to high, add the vinegar and the fig syrup, and bring to a boil. Cook the glaze until it coats the back of a spoon, about 12 minutes. Season with salt and pepper. Spoon into jars and refrigerate for up to 6 months.

Canning: Processing canning jars, Ruston, Louisiana, 1984; photo: Susan Roach-Lankford, right. Opposite, old-fashioned fig preserves.

BROWN BUTTER FIG TART

Serves 6

Don't worry about browning the butter; even if you scorch it slightly so that you get a few specks, leave them in; they'll just add character. Since the butter will be hot when you add it to the egg-and-flour mixture, the tart may cook faster or slower by a few minutes, so check on it after a half hour or so.

8 tablespoons butter, plus more for greasing the pan	3 eggs, beaten
½ cup flour, plus more for flouring the pan	1 cup sugar
	1 teaspoon freshly grated orange zest
1 recipe Basic Pie Dough (page 16)	1 teaspoon vanilla extract
4 cups halved fresh Black Mission figs	1 pinch salt

1. Preheat the oven to 350°. Liberally grease a deep 8–9-inch false-bottomed tart pan with some butter and dust with a little flour. Roll the dough out on a lightly floured surface to a thickness of ¼ inch and fit it into the prepared pan. Trim off any excess dough.

2. Arrange the figs in the tart pan in a circular overlapping pattern.

3. Heat the 8 tablespoons butter in a small saucepan over medium-high heat until it has a nutty aroma and is a deep golden brown color. Remove from the heat.

4. Put the eggs and sugar into a mixing bowl and beat with an electric mixer on medium-high speed until light and fluffy, about 5 minutes. With a rubber spatula, fold the orange zest, ½ cup flour, vanilla, and salt into the eggs and butter.

5. Slowly add the brown butter to the batter, stirring constantly. Pour the mixture over the figs, smoothing the batter with a rubber spatula.

6. Bake until the crust is golden brown and the filling has nearly set in the center, about 40 minutes. Let cool on a wire rack for 20 minutes. Remove from the tart pan before serving.

Figs

There are few fruits more fascinating than the fig (*Ficus carica*), and in Louisiana we are spoiled, as they weigh down the trees in backyards all over the state, where they thrive on our abundant sunshine and temperate winters. Fresh figs are too perishable to be sold on a large scale commercially, so they're sold as an indulgent luxury item in specialty stores in big cities or, in our case, gorged on with abandon wherever they are grown. Our vast crop must be hastily stewed, canned, preserved, frozen, pickled, or dried.

Not surprisingly, the fig was one of the earliest fruit trees to be cultivated by the Egyptians and, later, the Romans; it migrated to our shores during the 16th century. Usually, nature knows best. But in the case of the fig, one has to wonder, because fertilization originally relied on a special wasp to enter the tiny opening at the tip of the fruit. The fig is, in fact, an inverted flower; what we think of as seeds are actually the remnants of those flowers, which give us fruit that tastes of resin. Nowadays, few varieties require pollination. The ones we grow the most in Louisiana are still the Celeste (which my granddaddy knew and loved), a small but resilient fruit with a purplish-brown skin and a reddish-pink flesh, and the larger and ruddier Southeastern Brown Turkey.

CANE SYRUP FIG CAKE

Serves 8–10

The success of this light and airy cake depends upon the care you give the egg whites. When you fold the whipped egg whites into the batter, make sure you add only a third of them at a time so that they won't deflate.

2	cups sugar	1	teaspoon vanilla extract
1	cup unsalted butter	3	cups all-purpose flour
1	cup milk	½	teaspoon salt
2	cups chopped fresh figs	2	tablespoons baking powder
	Grated zest from a quarter of a lemon	4	egg whites
½	teaspoon ground cinnamon		Cooking spray
3	tablespoons Steen's Cane Syrup (page 362)		

1. Preheat oven to 375°. Put the sugar and butter into a large mixing bowl and beat with an electric mixer on on medium-high speed until light and fluffy, about 7 minutes.

2. Add the milk, figs, lemon zest, cinnamon, cane syrup, and vanilla and beat on moderate speed until everything is mixed together.

3. Sift together the flour, salt, and baking powder into another large mixing bowl. Use a rubber spatula to fold the flour mixture into the sugar-and-butter mixture.

4. Beat the egg whites in another large mixing bowl with clean beaters on medium-high speed until stiff peaks form, about 5 minutes. Take care not to overbeat the whites, or they will curdle.

5. Carefully fold one-third of the whites into the batter. Repeat with the rest of the egg whites, a third at a time, taking care not to overmix and deflate the egg whites.

6. Spray a Bundt cake pan with a generous amount of cooking spray. Pour the batter into the pan and bake the cake until golden brown, 35–40 minutes.

GOLDEN FIGS BAKED IN BRIOCHE WITH COUNTRY HAM

Serves 10

In the kitchen at Restaurant August, we'll take this recipe a step further, stuffing each fig with a slice of duck foie gras. This simpler version makes a great starter with a salad of arugula or other sharp lettuces.

Back porch harvest: Mary L. Gunn with the bounty of her garden in her house in Ruston, Louisiana, 1984; photo: Susan Roach-Lankford.

⅓ cup warm milk (110°)

2 ½ teaspoons active dry yeast

⅓ cup sugar

3 ½ cups all-purpose flour

1 teaspoon salt

5 eggs, beaten

12 tablespoons butter, melted

10 very thin slices country ham or prosciutto

10 large fresh golden figs

1. Hand-mix the warm milk, dry yeast, sugar, and 1 cup of the flour in the bowl of a standing mixer until well combined. Set aside and allow the sponge to rise in the bowl for about 30 minutes.

2. Using the dough hook attachment, begin mixing the sponge on medium-low speed, adding the salt, eggs, remaining 2 ½ cups flour, and melted butter. Mix for 10 minutes. Cover the bowl with plastic wrap and set aside. Allow the dough to double in size, 30–45 minutes.

3. Preheat the oven to 400°. Punch the dough down. Working on a floured surface, cut the dough into 10 equal pieces. Roll each piece out to a thickness of ¼ inch.

4. Place a piece of ham on each piece of dough. Place a fig on each piece of ham and wrap the dough around the figs, conforming it to the shape of the fig. Crimp the dough around the stem of the fig and trim off all excess dough. (The extra dough can be formed into a roll or two and baked.)

5. Place the dough-wrapped figs on a cookie sheet and allow the dough to rest for 15 minutes. Bake until golden brown, 7–10 minutes. Serve while still warm.

SUGAR PLUMS IN SYRUP

Makes 8 pint jars

This is a very easy way to preserve sweet plums and then use them in many ways: I serve the tiny plums with everything from charcuterie to cheese and desserts, and I use the the syrup in a vinegar-based fruit reduction as a sauce for poultry.

4½ cups sugar

8–10 pounds sugar plums or other small plums

1. Put the sugar and 4½ cups water into a large heavy-bottomed pot over high heat. Bring to a boil and cook, stirring constantly, until all the sugar has dissolved. Remove from the heat and set aside.

2. Pack the sugar plums into hot, sterilized pint jars (page 240). Ladle the hot syrup over the plums, leaving ¼ inch of headspace. Wipe the rims of the jars clean, then place sterilized lids on top and screw on the rings.

3. Use tongs to put the filled jars into a canning pot; cover with water at least 2 inches over the jar tops. Bring to a boil and boil for 20 minutes. Use tongs to carefully remove the jars from the water; place on a kitchen towel. Allow the jars to cool completely before you move them.

BERRIES PRESERVED IN RED WINE

Makes 6–8 half-pint jars

In the Black Forest of Germany, this preserve is commonly made with cherries and red fruit and called *Rote Grütze*. I've made this idea work with our berries of South Louisiana. Wash but don't peel or core the apples; the apples are where the pectin is, and you'll need it to thicken this jam.

3 cups red wine

3 cups sugar

1 whole clove

1 bay leaf

1 cinnamon stick

6 cups chopped green apples

3 cups quartered strawberries

3 cups blueberries

3 cups blackberries

1. Mix together the red wine, sugar, clove, bay leaf, cinnamon, and green apples in a deep saucepan. Bring to a boil over high heat and cook until the wine has reduced by half, about 30 minutes.

2. Strain the reduced red wine into a larger pot. Add the strawberries, blueberries, and blackberries. Bring to a rapid boil over high heat until the juices thickly coat the back of a spoon, about 35 minutes. Skim off any foam from the surface.

3. Ladle the berries and juices into hot, sterilized jars (page 240), leaving ¼ inch of headspace. Wipe the rims of the jars clean, then place sterilized lids on top and screw on the rings.

4. Use tongs to put the filled jars into a canning pot; cover with water at least 2 inches over the jar tops. Bring to a boil and boil for 5 minutes. Use tongs to carefully remove the jars from the water; place on a kitchen towel. Allow the jars to cool completely before you move them.

Plenty of melons: The president's annual watermelon party at the University of Louisiana at Lafayette, 1940.

WATERMELON PICKLES

Makes 1 quart

Between the dark green skin of a watermelon and its pinky flesh lies an often discarded, pale green rind that's full of possibilities. Seasoned by aromatic spices in a quick boil, these pickles can be served the same way as other pickles, but they are especially fine with the pork recipes in Chapter 15, Boucherie.

1 whole medium watermelon	2 star anise
1 cup sugar	1 tablespoon fennel seed
1 cup white vinegar	1 tablespoon whole black peppercorns
1 tablespoon mustard seed	½ teaspoon salt

1. Cut the watermelon into manageable pieces. With a vegetable peeler, peel away the outer skin, trim away the pink flesh and save for granita or sorbet, and cube the white rind into 1-inch pieces.

2. Put 2 cups water, the sugar, vinegar, mustard seed, star anise, fennel seed, peppercorns, and salt into a medium saucepan and bring to a boil over medium-high heat. Add the watermelon rinds and gently boil until the rinds become tender, about 10 minutes, then remove the saucepan from heat.

3. Let the watermelon rinds and syrup cool to room temperature in the pot. Pack them into a sterilized jar or two (page 240), and refrigerate for up to 1 month.

MAYHAW JELLY

Makes 6–8 half-pint jars

Our Louisiana mayhaws don't have much juice, and so it takes an awful lot of them to make jelly. (Crabapples are a good substitute.) If you squeeze the fruit juices through the jelly bag or cheesecloth you'll have better yield, but the juice will be cloudy. Either way it'll taste great. Cooking pears are those hard varieties that are better cooked than raw.

12 **pounds mayhaws, halved (page 362)**	5–6 **cups sugar, approximately**
5 **pounds cooking pears, quartered**	

1. Put the mayhaws, pears, and enough water to cover the fruit halfway into a large heavy-bottomed pot. Cook over moderate heat until the fruit is very soft, at least 30 minutes.

2. Transfer the cooked fruit to a jelly bag or a cheesecloth-lined strainer suspended over a bowl. Allow the juice to drip through the cloth for a couple of hours (or overnight). Measure the juice and pour it back into the cleaned pot. For every cup of juice, add ½ cup sugar.

3. Bring the juice to a vigorous boil over high heat. Boil until the juice thickly coats the back of a spoon, 10–20 minutes.

4. Ladle the jelly into hot, sterilized jars (page 240), leaving ¼ inch of headspace. Wipe the rims of the jars clean, then place sterilized lids on top and screw on the rings.

5. Use tongs to put the filled jars into a canning pot of boiling water over high heat. Make sure the water covers the jars by at least 2 inches. Boil for 5 minutes. Use tongs to carefully remove the jars from the water; place on a kitchen towel. Allow the jars to cool completely before you move them.

GRANDDADDY'S QUINCE PRESERVES

Makes 6–8 pint jars

You really have to watch the pot to make sure the quince are boiling in the syrup before you start counting the hour's cooking time. Be sure to stir the fruit frequently while the quince boil so they'll become thicker.

5 **cups sugar**
5 **pounds quince, cored, peeled, and quartered**

1. Bring the sugar and 3 cups water to a boil in a large heavy-bottomed pot over high heat. Cook at a hard boil for 7 minutes, stirring frequently.

2. Reduce the heat to moderate, add the quince to the syrup, and cook for 1 hour at a gentle boil, stirring frequently. Be careful not to scorch the sugary syrup on the bottom of the pot.

3. After an hour's boiling, ladle the quince and syrup into hot, sterilized jars (page 240), leaving ¼ inch of headspace. Wipe the rims of the jars clean, then place sterilized lids on top and screw on the rings.

4. Use tongs to put the filled jars into a canning pot of boiling water over high heat. Make sure the water covers the jars by at least 2 inches. Boil for 5 minutes. Use tongs to carefully remove the jars from the water; place on a kitchen towel. Allow the jars to cool completely before you move them.

SPORT PEPPER SAUCE

Makes 1 ½ quarts

What my granddaddy and a lot of Southerners call sport peppers are little green and red and sometimes yellow hot peppers, *Capiscum annuum*, similar in taste to Tabasco and the Thai chiles found in many Asian markets. I store my pepper sauce in the refrigerator, not in the pantry, which means I hardly need to cook the peppers first. The sauce doesn't last as long, but the flavor is brighter. Use on slow-cooked greens when you want a jolt of flavor.

1 **quart white vinegar**	2 **teaspoons salt**
2 **cups mixed sport or Thai chile peppers**	

1. Put the vinegar, chiles, and salt into a medium pot and boil over medium-high heat for 2 minutes.

2. Working quickly and using a slotted spoon or tongs, divide the chiles evenly between several hot, sterilized jars and bottles (page 240). Using a sterilized funnel, fill the jars and bottles with the hot vinegar. Seal the jars and bottles with their sterilized lids and let them rest at room temperature until cool.

3. Store the bottles and jars in the refrigerator for at least 1 week to let the flavors develop before using. The sauce will last for 6 months in the refrigerator.

FRENCH TOAST

Serves 6

French toast is probably the first thing I ever cooked at home as a boy, and it's still one of my favorite breakfasts to make for my boys, who just love it. Milk, of course, may be used instead of half-and-half, and feel free to omit the Grand Marnier. Bread that's a couple of days old makes the best French toast, as it tends to absorb a bit more of the egg mixture.

5 eggs	¼ teaspoon vanilla extract
½ cup sugar	1 pinch salt
½ cup half-and-half	2 tablespoons Grand Marnier, optional
¼ cup fresh-squeezed orange juice	2 tablespoons canola oil
2 pinches ground nutmeg	12 slices day-old, 1-inch-thick French bread
2 pinches ground cinnamon	

1. Beat together the eggs and sugar in a large mixing bowl until they are well mixed. Add the half-and-half, orange juice, nutmeg, cinnamon, vanilla, salt, and Grand Marnier, if you like, and mix well.

2. Heat the oil in a large skillet over moderate heat. Working with 3–4 slices of bread at a time, dip the slices of bread into the egg mixture and submerge for a few moments. Remove the bread from the egg mixture and put into the skillet.

3. Fry the bread, turning once, until golden brown on both sides. Repeat with the remaining slices of bread. Serve the French Toast hot with homemade preserves like peach, quince, mayhaw, or fig.

PEACH JAM

Makes 8 half-pint jars

Louisiana peaches are a sweet treat. To enjoy them year-round, my boys and I make this jam and slather it on French toast or roll it up inside a warm crêpe. Using liquid or powdered pectin is an effective shortcut.

3 cups peeled, pitted, and chopped peaches	6 ounces liquid pectin, or 1.75 ounces powdered pectin
½ cup fresh lemon juice	
6 cups sugar	

1. Put the peaches, 1½ cups water, lemon juice, and 5¾ cups of the sugar into a large heavy-bottomed saucepan over high heat. Bring to a boil, stirring constantly. Mix the remaining ¼ cup sugar with the pectin and stir into the hot jam. Boil, stirring constantly for 1 minute. Remove the pan from heat.

2. Ladle the peaches and juices into hot, sterilized jars (page 240), leaving ¼ inch of headspace. Wipe the rims of the jars clean, then place sterilized lids on top and screw on the rings.

3. Use tongs to put the filled jars into a canning pot, and cover with water at least 1 inch over the jar tops. Bring to a boil and boil for 10 minutes. Use tongs to carefully remove the jars from the water, and place on a kitchen towel. Allow the jars to cool completely before you move them.

PEACH UPSIDE-DOWN CAKE

Serves 10

It's easy to peel the peaches by bringing a small pot of water to a boil, giving each peach a quick dip into the boiling water, then removing it quickly. Once you score it with a paring knife, the skins will fall right off.

¼ cup corn syrup	1½ cups all-purpose flour
1 cup brown sugar	½ cup almond flour
24 tablespoons unsalted butter, at room temperature	2 teaspoons baking powder
6 peaches, peeled, quartered, pits removed	1 teaspoon vanilla extract
2 cups granulated sugar	½ teaspoon almond extract
4 eggs, beaten	¾ cup sour cream

1. Preheat the oven to 350°. Put the corn syrup, brown sugar, and 8 tablespoons of the butter into a saucepan and bring to a boil over high heat. Reduce the heat to moderate and cook for 3 minutes. Pour into 10 individual 3-inch-diameter ramekins.

2. Place 4 peach quarters in each ramekin and set aside.

3. Put the remaining 16 tablespoons of butter, the granulated sugar, and beaten eggs into the bowl of a standing mixer and beat on medium-high speed until creamy and smooth, about 10 minutes.

4. Meanwhile, whisk the flour, almond flour, and baking powder together in a bowl. Then, using a rubber spatula, fold the vanilla and almond extracts into the egg batter. Fold in the flours and the sour cream. Pour some batter into each of the ramekins and bake until golden, about 35 minutes.

5. Unmold the cakes upside down, with the peaches on top, onto 10 dessert plates. Serve them warm with Blueberry Sorbet (recipe, right) or vanilla ice cream.

BLUEBERRY SORBET

Serves 10–12

Sorbets often contain too much sugar and too much water. I love using fresh berries at the peak of their ripeness to make very straightforward purées that can be frozen for sorbet. I use the egg method in step 2, below, to make sure the purées will freeze into a smooth sorbet with intense fruit flavor.

4 pints blueberries	
½ cup sugar, if needed	

1. Purée the blueberries in a blender for several minutes. Strain the purée through a fine sieve, pushing it through with a rubber spatula, into a medium bowl.

2. Test for the proper sugar content by floating a whole egg, shell and all, in the purée. If the egg floats so that only a nickel-size portion of the egg is exposed at the surface of the sorbet, there is enough natural sugar—no need to add more. If the egg sinks, remove the egg and add up to ½ cup sugar, blend, and retest with the egg. If it floats too high in the purée, then add water, a bit at a time, until the egg sinks to the correct height.

3. Pour the blueberry purée into the canister of an ice cream machine and freeze according to the manufacturer's directions.

Oysters and August: The dining room at Restaurant August bustles at lunch on Fridays, left and below. Oysters in competent hands at P&J Oyster, in the French Quarter. Opposite, New Orleans, 1947; photo: Henri Cartier-Bresson, Magnum Photos.

No More Oysters?

"After Katrina, we feared my beloved local oyster had disappeared, perhaps never to return again."

Tragedy! As if it weren't enough to have our city swept away by the floodwaters that followed Katrina when the levees failed us, it was rumored that we'd lost our entire oyster industry. Never could I have imagined life without a local oyster. What would become of my beloved oyster loaf? I can't picture home without Rockefellers, Bienville, pan roasts, dressings, or oysters on the half shell. Could we actually call this living, if we had to do without foot-long, overstuffed oyster po'boys? What would happen to the Sunseri family, of P&J Oyster in the French Quarter, or that superb oysterman Captain Pete? What would Drago's be without its grilled local oysters and garlicky butter? Seriously, all we basically have down here is great people and great food. It's not

Inside P&J: One of the oldest oyster houses in New Orleans, P&J is our major supplier. The current owners, the Sunseri brothers, are Italian; the oystermen, traditionally, are Croatian. Above, Willie Dove at work at P&J.

like folks come from around the world for much more than that. Would they still come if there were no more oysters? Oysters had long been the thing that I associated the most with the onset of fall; it used to be thought that oysters were the best when a month's name ended in the letter *r*. Well, October of 2005 certainly ended in *r*, and we were up the proverbial creek without a paddle. A sad day it was when we were forced to send out to Florida for Apalachicola oysters as we attempted to reopen Restaurant August just weeks after the storm displaced our entire city. Sad indeed, but to be perfectly honest we had no business being open in the first place, and in fact we wouldn't even be in business today if we hadn't ordered those oysters.

ON THE DAY before Katrina, we'd had a large staff—167 employees. We had valet parking, tasting menus, amuse-bouches, pretty hostesses and handsome captains, dish washers, pot washers, prep cooks, and office managers. No more. They apparently went the way of my beloved local oyster; they just disappeared, perhaps never to return again. At reopening, there were four of us. Steve McHugh, who, with his wife, Sylvia, had taken refuge in Chicago with my friend the chef Rick Tramonto, returned days after the storm in hopes of helping us and helping to rebuild his adopted city. Israel-born Alon Shaya, who was living like a caveman throughout the ordeal, fortunately never left. My partner, Octavio Mantilla, who went from wearing Brioni to bandanas and rubber boots, was about to be our one and only dining room attendant, and I was serving as poor cook and bottle washer.

You see, days after the storm, we (Octavio, Alon, Blake LeMaire, and I), along with the support of every sister, brother, in-law, former Marine, and friend that we could find, had begun feeding people. We fed anyone who was hungry, first from flatboats and eventually from mobile kitchens on trailers. We fed hospital workers and evacuees, National Guard troops and policemen. Eventually word spread, and people once again began to pay us for food. It was at that point we realized that we needed to cook something besides the red beans and rice that had sustained us for weeks after the storm. In early October, our first paid diners were the folks from CNN. I remember Soledad O'Brien especially, plus a long list of notables from our community who all apparently craved oysters as much as I did.

We did conjure up a nice plan for reopening day: we told both my wife and her old friend Margaret, who's also our accountant, that we needed them at the restaurant for a finance meeting. The truth was, we had no finances and we needed them there to help us make some. So, we reopened with Margaret as the bartender; Jenifer, my wife, mother of four and recovering attorney, as our only waitress; Octavio managed the door, took drink orders, bussed the tables, and sometimes served as spiritual director. I worked garde-manger, desserts, coffee, and food runner, while Steve and Alon worked the hot line, manning the ovens and stoves, cooking rabbits, steaks, and oysters.

FORTUNATELY, THIS ARRANGEMENT didn't have to last long. Slowly, one employee returned, then another. Each time one would come back to New Orleans to find that he'd lost everything, we'd put him up in the restaurant's penthouse or private dining room to stay until he got back on his feet. It didn't take long before we had enough people that we could actually behave like a proper restaurant. Never would the valet parking return, but our oysters would. Of course, Katrina decimated the oysters' habitat and necessitated a massively expensive and labor-intensive recovery operation. In fact, the storm did bring an influx of high-salinity water, which over time cleansed and renewed our marshes, swamps, sloughs, lakes, and bays. This had a beneficial effect on our seafood supply, and our oysters have never been happier. But with the storm damage and rising diesel prices, now it's the oystermen we need to worry about losing. Oysters, just like shrimp and crab, do have something like a cult status in New Orleans. Our oysters are big and meaty and splendid eaten on the half shell with cold beer and spicy cocktail sauce. They allow preparations that you just can't do with other oysters, like frying, roasting, and grilling. Those little briny ones from the other coastal states? They're fine, but they just don't work for us.

In my first childhood memory of oysters, I was just old enough to walk when my father took me to sit on the seawall on Lake Pontchartrain and split an oyster loaf. We ate it dressed with a touch of butter, lots of mayonnaise, dill pickles, shredded lettuce, thin-sliced sweet Creole tomatoes, and a few dashes of spicy Tabasco sauce and chased it down with a cold Barq's root beer. I was in ecstasy at first bite! And my life has never been the same.

Warm welcome: At August, we make sure our guests are greeted by a colorful floral arrangement, below. Oysters on the half shell; photo: WPA, 1940.

BAKED OYSTERS WITH WILD MUSHROOM RAGOUT AND AÏOLI

Serves 4

Making the aïoli—the garlic mayonnaise—is the hardest thing about this dish, and not very difficult at that. If the mixture looks too oily as you're blending it in the food processor, just add cold water, a little at a time. Make the aïoli in advance and refrigerate it until you're ready to use it. You can make the ragout ahead, too, and assemble the dish moments before you serve it. Allan Benton, near Madisonville, Tennessee (page 362), makes my favorite bacon, hickory-smoked on an old-fashioned wood stove.

FOR THE AÏOLI

- 2 cloves garlic, chopped
- 2 egg yolks
- 2 tablespoons fresh lemon juice
- 1 pinch salt
- 1 cup extra-virgin olive oil

FOR THE MUSHROOM RAGOUT

- 1 cup diced thick-sliced hickory-smoked bacon
- 1 or 2 shallots, minced
- 1 cup wild mushrooms, cleaned and sliced
- 2 cloves garlic, minced
- 2 tablespoons cold butter, cut into small pieces
- Leaves from 1 sprig fresh thyme
- Salt
- Freshly ground black pepper

FOR THE OYSTERS

- 2 dozen shucked oysters, on their half shells

1. For the aïoli, blend the garlic, egg yolks, lemon juice, and salt in a food processor. Continue processing while you slowly drizzle in the olive oil. Once all the oil has been incorporated and the aïoli has thickened, turn off the machine. Use a rubber spatula to transfer the aïoli from the work bowl to a small bowl, cover with plastic wrap, and chill.

2. For the mushroom ragout, cook the bacon in a skillet over moderate heat, stirring often, until crisp. Add the shallots and mushrooms and cook for 5 minutes, stirring frequently. Add the garlic and cook for 3 more minutes, then add butter and thyme. Season with salt and pepper. Remove from heat and set aside.

3. For the oysters, first preheat the broiler. To help steady the oysters, lay a slightly rumpled sheet of aluminum foil on a large baking sheet. Set the oysters, in their shells, on the foil. Top each oyster with a generous spoonful of the mushroom ragout. Then add a dollop of aïoli on top of the mushrooms. Place the baking sheet on the middle rack of the oven and broil until the aïoli turns golden brown. Serve right away.

Oystering: Boats used to seed oyster beds in the locks at Empire, Louisiana, 1938; photo: Fonville Winans.

OYSTER GRATIN WITH HORSERADISH AND PARMESAN

Serves 6–8

You can make this gratin in a single large baking dish, in several small casserole dishes, or even spoon the sauce and gratin topping onto each individual oyster on its half shell.

---

4 tablespoons butter	3 dozen shucked oysters, drained and patted dry
¼ cup flour	Freshly ground black pepper
½ medium onion, sliced	⅓ cup dry bread crumbs
1 clove garlic, crushed	⅓ cup extra-virgin olive oil
2 cups milk	⅓ cup freshly grated Parmesan cheese
1 clove	1 teaspoon crushed red pepper flakes
1 bay leaf	
½ cup prepared horseradish	
Salt	

1. Melt the butter in a large saucepan over moderate heat. Stir in the flour and cook the roux, stirring frequently, until it turns blond; this should take no longer than 5 minutes. Add the onions and garlic, reduce the heat to medium-low, and continue cooking, stirring often, until the onions are soft.

2. Slowly add milk, whisking constantly to prevent lumps. Increase heat to high, bring to a boil, then immediately reduce heat to low. Add the clove and bay leaf; let sauce simmer, stirring occasionally, until thick enough to coat the back of a spoon, about 30 minutes.

Old times: Martina's oysters being delivered by fancy truck to a New Orleans restaurant, 1970s, right.

3. Remove the pan from the heat and stir in the horseradish. Season with salt, then strain sauce through a fine sieve into a bowl. Lay a sheet of plastic wrap directly on the surface of the sauce to prevent a skin from forming. Set sauce aside and let it cool.

4. Preheat the oven to 450°. Season the oysters with salt and pepper and lay them in the bottom of a baking dish in a single layer; then pour the cooled sauce evenly over the oysters.

5. In another bowl, mix the bread crumbs, olive oil, Parmesan, and pepper flakes. Sprinkle over the oysters and sauce in the casserole. Bake for about 15 minutes or until the topping becomes golden brown.

OYSTER AND ARTICHOKE SOUP

Serves 8

This is a luscious two-step soup. It's best to prepare the soup base ahead, as soon as you prep the artichokes, so that the leaves won't discolor. Keep the hearts green in a solution of lemon juice and water. Then, cook the oysters and artichoke hearts close to serving time so they do not overcook.

FOR THE SOUP BASE

- 3 whole artichokes
- 1 onion, chopped
- 2 celery stalks, chopped
- 1 potato, peeled and chopped
- 1 leek, white part, cleaned and chopped
- 2 cloves garlic, minced
- 2 tablespoons olive oil
- 1 cup dry vermouth
- 3 cups oyster liquor or Basic Fish Stock (page 13)
- 1 cup heavy cream
  Leaves from 1 sprig fresh thyme
  Leaves from 1 sprig fresh tarragon
- 1 bay leaf
- 1 teaspoon Tabasco
- 2 teaspoons fresh lemon juice
  Salt
  Freshly ground black pepper

FOR THE OYSTERS

- 1 tablespoon olive oil
- 2 shallots, minced
- 1 small fennel bulb, minced
- 1 small tomato, peeled, seeded, and diced
- 32 oysters, shucked
- 1 tablespoon minced fresh chives

1. For the soup base, remove and discard the tough outer leaves of the artichokes, leaving only the pale green tender leaves. (If you like, you can scrape some of the meat from the bottom of the outer leaves before discarding.) Slice off and discard about 1 inch from the leaves' thorny tips, then pull the pale green leaves away from the artichoke heart. Use a spoon to scrape out and discard the fuzzy chokes. Cut the stems from the hearts and peel the stems. Chop the pale green leaves and peeled stems. Dice the hearts and reserve separately in a bowl of lemon juice and water.

2. Cook the artichoke leaves and stems, onions, celery, potatoes, leeks, and garlic in the olive oil in a large heavy-bottomed pot over moderate heat until the onions become translucent, about 15 minutes. Be careful not to brown the vegetables.

3. Add the vermouth, oyster liquor or Fish Stock, and cream to the vegetables. Increase the heat to high until the liquid comes to a boil, then lower the heat to moderate. Add the thyme, tarragon, and bay leaf and allow the liquid to reduce by a third. Season with Tabasco, lemon juice, salt, and pepper.

4. Remove and discard the bay leaf, then purée the soup in a food processor or a blender. Strain through a fine sieve back into the large heavy-bottomed pot. Season with salt and pepper. Keep warm over low heat.

5. For the oysters, just before you're ready to serve, heat the olive oil in a heavy skillet over moderate heat. Add the shallots, fennel, reserved diced artichoke hearts, and tomatoes and cook, stirring often, until the vegetables are soft, about 15 minutes. Add the oysters, then remove from heat. Ladle the hot soup into individual bowls, then divide the oysters and vegetables between the bowls and sprinkle minced chives over the top.

Oysters

Some folks call oysters Cajun Viagra because their high zinc content is said to increase potency. I don't know about that, but I do know that our Louisiana, or Gulf, oyster is the same species that's found the length of the East Coast, the *Crassostrea virginica*, or "cupped" oyster. Unlike the European flat oyster, *Ostrea edulis* (called the Belon in France), our oysters do not spawn inside the shell and therefore have no unpleasant grittiness; that's the chief reason, besides lack of refrigeration, for the old myth about eating them only in months with an *r* in their names. Our oysters release their eggs into the water and can therefore be eaten year-round, though they're plumper and sweeter in the winter months, turning milkier in the spring when they start spawning. By the summer, they've become skinnier and more watery but still taste delicious.

Most distributors do not specify their oysters' source, but each growing bay and bed along the lacy Gulf Coast bestows its particular flavor. About 65 percent of Louisiana oysters are farmed. The wild harvest runs from September to April on public grounds, and that's when oystermen skim the reefs for seed oysters. Louisiana produces around 13 million pounds of shucked oysters yearly, about a third of the American crop. Its millions of acres of marshland provide ideal growing conditions, blessedly far removed from urban and industrial pollution. Its rivers carry abundant freshwater into the Gulf, leavening the oysters' saltiness.

OYSTER STEW

Serves 6

The only trick to cooking oysters is to not overcook them. My advice is to make the soup first and keep it warm. Don't add the oysters until just before you're ready to serve the stew.

FOR THE BRUSCHETTA
- ½ cup olive oil
- Leaves from half a bunch Italian parsley
- 2 cloves garlic
- 1 pinch salt
- 1 loaf French bread, sliced

FOR THE SOUP
- 1 leek, white part, minced
- 1 shallot, minced
- 1 clove garlic, minced
- 1 tablespoon olive oil
- 1 large tomato, diced
- Leaves from 1 sprig fresh thyme
- 1 teaspoon minced fresh chives
- 3 cups Basic Oyster Pan Sauce (page 15)
- 36 oysters, shucked
- Tabasco
- A squeeze of lemon juice
- Salt
- Freshly ground black pepper

1. For the bruschetta, purée the olive oil, parsley, garlic, and salt in a blender or a food processor until smooth. Use a rubber spatula to transfer the purée to a small bowl and set aside. Just before you're ready to serve, preheat the broiler. Spread a generous amount of the parsley purée on each slice of bread. Grill the bread under the broiler just long enough to char it slightly.

2. For the soup, cook the leeks, shallots, and garlic in olive oil in a large saucepan over moderate heat until the vegetables soften, about 3 minutes. Add the tomatoes, thyme, chives, and Oyster Pan Sauce to the saucepan, increase the heat to high, and bring the soup to a boil, then reduce the heat to low. Add the oysters and cook just until they become firm and their edges begin to curl. Season the stew with Tabasco, lemon juice, salt, and pepper, stirring to combine the flavors.

3. Serve the stew garnished, if you like, with a few more chopped chives, along with the garlicky bruschetta.

CRISPY FRIED OYSTER SALAD WITH LOUISIANA CAVIAR

Serves 6

My friend John Burke's Louisiana Caviar Company, based in New Orleans, produces some incredible paddlefish caviar that has a lot less salt than other varieties. So, be sure to taste carefully what I call the caviar ranch dressing for this salad to determine exactly how much salt it needs.

FOR THE CAVIAR DRESSING

- ½ cup buttermilk
- ½ cup mayonnaise
- 2 tablespoons sour cream
- 1 clove garlic, minced
- 1 shallot, minced
- ½ teaspoon celery salt
- 2 teaspoons lemon juice
- 2 dashes Tabasco
- 1 pinch white pepper
- 2 tablespoons Louisiana paddlefish caviar (page 362)
- 2 tablespoons chopped fresh chives
  Salt
  Freshly ground black pepper

FOR THE FRIED OYSTERS

- 3 cups flour
- 1 cup cornmeal
- 1 cup dried bread crumbs
- 2 tablespoons Basic Creole Spices (page 13)
- 4 egg whites
- 3 dozen oysters, shucked and drained
- 1 quart canola oil
  Salt
- 4 cups frisée lettuce or curly endive
- ¼ cup Basic Walnut Oil Vinaigrette (page 19)

Bright greens: To set off our crispy fried oyster salad, above, we often use tiny, fresh greens like tatsoi and mizuna, left, or baby arugula.

1. For the caviar dressing, whisk together the buttermilk, mayonnaise, sour cream, garlic, shallots, celery salt, lemon juice, Tabasco, and white pepper in a medium bowl. Fold in the paddlefish caviar and chopped chives and season with salt and black pepper. You can make this dressing several hours ahead and refrigerate until you're ready.

2. For the fried oysters, use a big whisk to blend the flour, cornmeal, bread crumbs, and Creole Spices together in a large mixing bowl.

3. In another bowl, beat the whites with a balloon whisk or an electric mixer until stiff peaks form. Add the drained oysters to the egg whites.

4. Heat the oil in a large deep skillet over high heat until it reaches 350°. Use a candy thermometer to check temperature. Remove the oysters from the egg whites and toss them in the seasoned flour–cornmeal mixture. Fry the oysters in the oil, a few at a time, turning them with tongs, until golden brown, about 2 minutes. Drain the fried oysters on paper towels and season with a sprinkle of salt.

5. Toss the lettuce with the Walnut Oil Vinaigrette in a large bowl. Season with salt.

6. Spoon a pool of caviar dressing onto each of 6 plates, place 6 fried oysters on the dressing, and scatter the lettuce over the top of each plate.

BLACK PEPPER–SEARED OYSTERS WITH COUNTRY HAM AND TRUFFLED SPOON BREAD

Serves 6

My spoon bread is loose and cornmeal based, like polenta. Of course my grandmother would use bacon fat, not truffle oil, to perfume her spoon bread, but New Orleans cooking is known for adapting the best of the world's food ideas, so I say, "Why not?" This spoon bread is lightened with whipped egg whites. Be careful not to overwork the whites as you fold them in (it's fine if the mixture is a little streaky); otherwise, the spoon bread will quickly deflate. And remember to cook the oysters just until they plump up.

FOR THE SPOON BREAD

- 8 tablespoons butter, plus more for greasing the pan
- 1 cup cornmeal, preferably organic (page 362)
- 3 ounces very thinly sliced country ham, chopped into bite-size pieces (page 362)
- ½ cup mascarpone cheese
- 1 teaspoon white truffle oil

- Leaves from 1 sprig fresh thyme
- Salt
- 8 egg whites

FOR THE OYSTERS

- 30 shucked oysters, drained and patted dry
- Salt
- Freshly ground black pepper
- 2 tablespoons rendered bacon fat
- 6 tablespoons Basic Oyster Pan Sauce (page 15)

1. For the spoon bread, preheat the oven to 325°. Grease an 8-inch-square baking pan with some of the butter and set aside.

2. Bring a quart of water to a boil in a large heavy-bottomed saucepan. Briskly whisk in the cornmeal, reduce heat to low, and cook for 15 minutes, whisking occasionally. When the cornmeal begins to bubble, turn off the heat. Add the ham, mascarpone, 8 table-spoons butter, truffle oil, thyme, and 1 teaspoon salt to the cornmeal in the saucepan, stirring well to combine.

3. Whisk the egg whites in a medium mixing bowl until soft peaks form. With a rubber spatula, fold the egg whites into the cornmeal mixture in the saucepan, a third at a time, taking care not to overmix and deflate the batter.

4. Pour the batter into the prepared baking pan and bake for 18–20 minutes. The spoon bread should be slightly loose in the center and golden brown on top. Let it rest for a few minutes while you cook the oysters.

5. For the oysters, put them into a bowl and coat them with 1 teaspoon each of the salt and pepper. Heat a large cast-iron skillet over medium-high heat until hot, then add just enough bacon fat to coat the bottom of the skillet and keep the oysters from sticking. When the bacon fat is sizzling, quickly sear the oysters, turning them once with kitchen tongs, until they plump up and their edges begin to curl.

6. Warm the Oyster Pan Sauce in a small saucepan and, if you like, do as we do in the restaurant: froth it with a handheld immersion blender.

7. With a large spoon, scoop a portion of spoon bread onto each of 6 plates. Place 5 oysters on top of each serving. Top with a spoonful of Oyster Pan Sauce.

GRILLED OYSTERS WITH SPICY GARLIC BUTTER

Makes 2 dozen

This butter works the best when it's prepared ahead. Let it soften at room temperature, then season it, place it in plastic wrap, and roll it into a tight cylinder. Then chill it until it's hard. When it's chilled, it's easy to cut the spicy butter into disks to top each oyster just before grilling. I like to use this seasoned butter on just about everything, from pasta to sautéed shrimp.

1 pound butter, at room temperature

1 clove garlic, minced

1 teaspoon crushed red pepper flakes

1 teaspoon chopped fresh chives

Leaves from 1 sprig fresh thyme

1 teaspoon fresh lemon juice

2 dozen oysters, shucked and left on the half shell

1. Beat the butter with the garlic, pepper flakes, chives, thyme, and lemon juice in a mixing bowl with a wooden spoon or in the bowl of a food processor until well combined.

2. Using a rubber spatula, mound butter onto a wide sheet of plastic wrap. Drape one of the wide ends of the plastic wrap over the butter, then roll butter into a cylinder about 1 inch in diameter and twist ends tightly. Refrigerate butter until hard.

3. Prepare a charcoal or gas grill. Unwrap the spicy butter and slice it into disks about ½ inch thick. Put a disk of butter on each oyster, then put the oysters, butter side up, directly over the hot coals on the grill. Grill the oysters only until they start to curl and bubble around the edges and the butter melts. Serve them hot!

Raw bars: It has long been a tradition at New Orleans restaurants to present a lush oyster bar, so when we opened Lüke, I continued that tradition with an opulent raw bar, right.

Hunting season: Duck hunters Randy Farris, Drew Mire, Patrick Berrigan, and my son Jack, left. Sunrise over the Honey Island Swamp, when the ducks start flying, above. Okra pods await gumbo, left. Top right, hunter with his prey, 1969.

Duck Blind Talk

"Blake LeMaire swears his teal gumbo with Larry's chicken sausage beats Drew Mire's duck gumbo with andouille."

Down here, cooking that soupy stew called gumbo— or, for that matter, any wild game—requires bravado. Cooking what you hunt is considered a man's sport, and it's taken really seriously. My friends are fanatics; each displays a different style, rooted in where they come from. Because Drew, my brother-in-law Patrick, and I are from the New Orleans area, we make a dark roux, as befits the city's culinary complexity. It's always made with okra and sausage that yields (we think) a deeper flavor, whereas Blake and his people, from frugal Southwest Louisiana, prefer a real light roux, just a bit thicker than a rich chicken soup and served with both rice and potato salad. That's right: the potato salad is served on the side and at the last

Rituals: Jack and friends arrive at the duck blind early so there's time to brush and refresh the reeds and grasses.

minute scooped right into the bowl of gumbo. Today I hunt with the same group of guys that I've hunted with for the past 20 years. As young men, we were taught to identify ducks in flight so that we'd know our target before we shot. Since we were kids, we'd argue about how to cook each kind of duck we'd identify; we have the same arguments today. Drew Mire will fuss and fight anyone who disagrees with his style of making gumbo, as will my hunting buddy and fellow Marine Blake LeMaire. The two of them in a duck blind will send up any number of expletives, each convinced he makes the better gumbo. Patrick loves to get in the kitchen and experiment with me on all sorts of recipes, so he's the designated sous-chef. We cook, we sing, we play zydeco. We lie about how well we shoot, and we lie about how good our gumbos are. Each of us basically shoots as well as the next and cooks a great roux, but none of us can call a duck like Blake. Son of a zydeco musician and duck-call maker, Blake plays his duck call like a musical instrument. Both styles of gumbo are equally good, and every gumbo tells a story.

TO US, GUMBO is our Jesse Tree, the footprint of who we are and where we come from—a cultural stew. Africans gave us their word for okra, *kingombo*; Native Americans dried and powdered their sassafras leaves to make the thickener called filé; the French brought us their fat and flour base called roux; the Spanish, their sofrito, comprising what we call the holy trinity: onion, celery, and bell peppers. Croatians added oysters and shrimp; the Italians, a little tomato. Germans brought their andouille sausage, and the Caribbeans, their bright spices. And still today newcomers will leave their imprint on our beloved gumbo, and we'll all be better for it. Creole gumbo pays tribute to this rich variety of cultures and ingredients, whereas Cajun gumbo evolved as the essence of peasant food, a way to feed a large number of people making the very best of whatever meager ingredients were at hand—a chicken, usually a hen, and a little ham or sausage.

I don't remember a time in my life when I didn't hunt or fish. Other than a brief period after combat in the first gulf war, when I did shy away from deer hunting, I still had no qualms about hunting and killing ducks. Perhaps I was dropped on my head as a young child. But I love the camaraderie of going to the hunting camp, I love training my dog Schatzi to hunt and retrieve, I love strategically setting out the decoys, and I love rebrushing the duck blinds. But mostly it's about the gumbo.

ONE OF THE BEST parts of our duck hunt is getting there: rambling on country roads from town to town in pursuit of gumbo "mise en place"—plain ol' hunting-camp provisions. This is a task of such importance that it positively cannot be delegated; instead, it requires that I leave early so that there's plenty of time to shop and still arrive at the camp at Lac Arthur, deep in Acadiana, four hours west of here, with enough time to get a gumbo started.

Taking the interstate is a travesty; it's the small towns off the beaten path that have the finest foodways. I'll jump onto U.S. Highway 90, then make a number of tasty deviations, like dropping by Jacob's in LaPlace for the finest andouille sausage in the state. (Bailey's does a great job, but it's not the same. I'm a Jacob's man.) Without a good andouille, your chicken or duck gumbo will lack that faint smoky essence that I love. Deviation number two comes at Thibodaux, where I'll turn off on Louisiana Highway 24 for Bourgeois Meat Market. There I'll find some goodies to munch on while we're making gumbo and maybe get to watch them make my favorite versions of blood boudin and spicy *fromage de tête* (hog's head cheese).

It wouldn't be much of a gumbo without a little crusty baguette to sop it up with, so the next stop is off Highway 90 at Jeanerette at LeJeune's Bakery (said to be the oldest bakery in Louisiana) to pick up some of the best artisanal bread in these parts, plus a few pains d'épice—

Stirring the pot: I add stock slowly to the roux in my gumbo saucepan, above. Duck, sausage, and other game find their way into a massive cast-iron cook pot, 1970s.

Scenes from a gumbo: Sliced okra ready for the pot, above. Duck hunters in the marsh south of Lafayette, Louisiana, 1920s, top. Opposite, daybreak in the beautiful Manchac Swamp, just northwest of New Orleans, on our way to hunt ducks in the timber.

those gingerbread cookies that are so perfect with morning coffee. I'm only about an hour into my journey, but I'm always hungry, so I head to Black's Oyster Bar, in Abbeville, for some salty, fresh-shucked oysters. There, I usually eat a dozen raw, then some grilled and fried oysters, plus a little crab bisque to top it off. Just down the street from Black's, I'll of course have to stop by Steen's for some cane syrup before driving only another 15 or 20 minutes down the road to Kaplan, because I absolutely have to shop at Larry's. That is the local grocery store that makes any number of sausages and charcuterie products that LeMaire swears by, in particular the chicken jalapeño sausage and the smoked and spicy pork sausage links.

BACK ON THE ROAD for only a few more miles, I'll turn off to Elliott's Slaughterhouse, in Morse, Louisiana, where I'll pick up a few odds and ends, like smoked fatback and ingredients for dirty rice, and especially those pork-stuffed pigs' stomachs called chaudin, which, when cooked down in a brown gravy with onions and garlic, will make us a wonderful lunch.

One last deviation before I arrive at the camp is at Lagnon's, in Gueydan, where, if you see the red light flashing, you must stop. That light means hot lardons of cracklins are fresh from the fryer. You eat them tossed in salt and red pepper, from brown paper bags to blot up the extra grease. They make an incredible pistolette there, too, a treat involving a small roll, opened on one end, that is hollowed out and stuffed with spicy slow-cooked pork shoulder and rice, then fried and served hot like a meat pie. We usually save pistolettes for an after-hunt snack, but sometimes we can't wait.

I've got to expose my four boys to this madness—the glory of road food, the duck blind camaraderie, the thrill of the hunt, and the deep satisfaction of cooking gumbo. These experiences will shape their palates and teach them to appreciate what comes from the land: how to care for it, how to harvest it, how to cook it, and how to love it.

DREW'S CHICKEN AND SMOKED SAUSAGE GUMBO

Serves 10–12

Throughout this book, I've had a great deal to say about making the roux that's the base of our gumbo—and the other steps as well—but I'll recap it here so that it can be useful every time you start to make our signature dish. Yes, there are other thickeners besides flour that folks use for making their roux, but to my palate, only a flour-based roux yields that traditional flavor. As for the fats in a roux, just about anything works. I love rendered duck fat, chicken fat, or lard, but canola oil works nearly as well.

I always heat the oil first and whisk the flour into the hot oil. Not only does this speed up the process; it yields that deep, dark chocolate-colored gumbo I love. I always add the onions first to the dark roux, holding back the rest of the vegetables until the onion caramelizes. Otherwise, the water in the vegetables will keep the onion from browning and releasing its sweet juices. I like to add filé powder to the gumbo, then pass it at the table, too. Serve the gumbo hot with Louisiana rice; serve potato salad on the side, if you like.

---

1 cup rendered chicken fat or canola oil

1 cup flour

2 large onions, diced

1 large chicken, cut into 12 pieces

2 tablespoons Basic Creole Spices (page 13)

2 pounds spicy smoked sausage, sliced ½ inch thick

2 stalks celery, diced

2 green bell peppers, seeded and diced

1 tomato, seeded and chopped

2 cloves garlic, minced

Leaves from 2 sprigs fresh thyme

3 quarts Basic Chicken Stock (page 13)

2 bay leaves

6 ounces andouille sausage, chopped

2 cups sliced fresh okra

1 tablespoon Worcestershire

Salt

Freshly ground black pepper

Filé powder (page 282)

Tabasco

4–6 cups cooked Basic Louisiana White Rice (page 15)

1. Make a roux by heating the chicken fat or oil in a large cast-iron or heavy-bottomed pot over high heat. Whisk the flour into the hot oil. It will immediately begin to sizzle. Reduce the heat to moderate and continue whisking until the roux takes on a deep brown color, about 15 minutes. Add the onions, stirring them into the roux with a wooden spoon. Reduce the heat to medium-low and continue stirring until the roux is a glossy dark brown, about 10 minutes.

2. Season the chicken with Creole Spices. Add the chicken to the pot, raise heat to moderate, and cook, turning the pieces until browned, about 10 minutes.

3. Add the smoked sausage and stir for a minute before adding the celery, bell peppers, tomatoes, and garlic. Cook, stirring, for about 3 minutes. Add the thyme, Chicken Stock, and bay leaves. Bring the gumbo to a boil, stirring occasionally. Reduce the heat to medium-low and simmer for 45 minutes. Stir occasionally and skim off the fat from the surface of the gumbo every so often.

4. Add the andouille, okra, and Worcestershire and season with salt and pepper, several dashes of filé powder, and Tabasco. Simmer for another 45 minutes, continuing to skim the fat off the surface of the gumbo. Remove the bay leaves and serve in bowls over rice. Pass more filé at the table.

BLAKE'S DUCK, GREEN ONION, AND CHICKEN SAUSAGE GUMBO

Serves 10–12

The LeMaires come from the Acadian prairie, so Blake favors a lighter, brothier gumbo over our thicker and richer New Orleans–style gumbo. This recipe is designed for a mallard or a black duck, but any duck, or a goose for that matter, will work well, too.

1 cup canola oil	4 quarts Basic Chicken Stock (page 13)
1 cup flour	2 bay leaves
3 large onions, diced	1 pound smoked pork sausage links, chopped
1 large duck, cut into 12 pieces	1 tablespoon Worcestershire
2 tablespoons Basic Creole Spices (page 13)	Salt
2 pounds spicy chicken sausage links, sliced into ½-inch-thick rounds	Freshly ground black pepper
	Tabasco
2 green bell peppers, seeded and diced	4–6 cups cooked Basic Louisiana White Rice (page 15)
2 cloves garlic, minced	
6–8 green onions, chopped	

1. Make a roux by heating the oil in a large cast-iron or heavy-bottomed pot over high heat. Whisk the flour into the hot oil. It will immediately begin to sizzle. Reduce the heat to moderate and continue whisking until the roux takes on a nice brown color, about 15 minutes. Add the onions, stirring them into the roux with a wooden spoon. Reduce the heat to medium-low and continue stirring until the roux is a light brown color, about 10 minutes.

2. Season the duck with Creole Spices. Add the duck to the pot, increase heat to moderate, and cook, turning the pieces until browned, about 10 minutes.

3. Add the chicken sausage and stir for a minute, then add the bell peppers and garlic. Increase the heat to moderate and cook, stirring, for about 3 minutes. Add the green onions, Chicken Stock, and bay leaves. Bring the gumbo to a boil, stirring occasionally. Reduce the heat to medium-low and simmer for 45 minutes. Stir occasionally and skim off the fat from the surface of the gumbo every so often.

4. Add the smoked pork sausage to the pot, then the Worcestershire. Season with salt, pepper and Tabasco. Simmer for another 45 minutes, continuing to skim the fat off the gumbo. Serve in bowls over rice.

PATRICK'S THANKSGIVING POULE D'EAU GUMBO

Serves 10–12

Some of my fancier friends might turn up their noses at the American coot that we affectionately call poule d'eau or marsh bird, but they have never refused to eat the gumbo it makes. Make sure you simmer this gumbo long enough to fully cook the birds before you add the andouille, so that you don't overcook the sausages and lose their smoky essence. If you're not about to bag a poule d'eau, as Patrick Berrigan (right) does, make this gumbo with game hens or other small fowl.

1 cup rendered duck fat	2 cloves garlic, minced
1 cup flour	Leaves from 1 sprig fresh thyme
2 large onions, diced	3 quarts Basic Chicken Stock (page 13)
4 poules d'eau, each cut into 4 pieces	2 bay leaves
2 tablespoons Basic Creole Spices (page 13)	½ pound andouille sausage, chopped
1 pound spicy smoked sausage links, sliced into ½-inch thick rounds	2 cups sliced fresh okra
	Salt
1 cup poule d'eau gizzards or chicken gizzards, chopped	Freshly ground black pepper
1 stalk celery, diced	Worcestershire
1 green bell pepper, seeded and diced	Tabasco
	4–6 cups cooked Basic Louisiana White Rice (page 15)

1. Make a roux by heating the duck fat in a large cast-iron or heavy-bottomed pot over high heat. Whisk the flour into the hot oil. It will immediately begin to sizzle. Reduce the heat to moderate and continue whisking until the roux takes on a deep brown color, about 15 minutes. Add the onions, stirring them into the roux with a wooden spoon. Reduce the heat to medium-low and continue stirring until the roux is a rich dark brown, about 10 minutes.

2. Season the poule d'eau with Creole Spices and add it to the pot. Increase heat to moderate and cook, turning the pieces until browned, about 10 minutes.

3. Add the smoked sausage and gizzards and cook, stirring, for a minute before adding the celery, bell peppers, and garlic. Increase the heat to moderate and cook, stirring, for about 3 minutes. Add the thyme, Chicken Stock, and bay leaves. Bring the gumbo to a boil, stirring occasionally. Reduce the heat to medium-low and simmer for 45 minutes. Stir occasionally and skim off the fat from the surface of the gumbo every so often.

4. Add the andouille and okra to the pot. Season with salt, pepper, Worcestershire, and Tabasco. Simmer for another 45 minutes, continuing to skim the fat off the surface of the gumbo. Serve in bowls over rice.

SEAFOOD GUMBO

Serves 10

I'm a seafood gumbo snob! I look for two things: first is a deep shellfish flavor, which I accomplish by allowing quartered crabs to cook for at least 45 minutes before I even think of adding any other seafood. Second, I'm looking for the seafood—shrimp, crabmeat, and oysters—to be perfectly tender (not overcooked) precisely as the gumbo is served. So, plan ahead and add the seafood accordingly.

1 cup canola oil	2 bay leaves
1 cup flour	1 pound medium Louisiana or wild American shrimp
2 large onions, diced	
6 jumbo blue crabs, each cut into 4 pieces	1 cup shucked oysters
	1 cup lump crabmeat
1 pound spicy smoked sausage links, sliced ½ inch thick	1 cup minced green onions
	Salt
1 stalk celery, diced	Freshly ground black pepper
1 green bell pepper, seeded and diced	
	Basic Creole Spices (page 13)
2 cloves garlic, minced	
1 cup sliced fresh okra	Worcestershire
Leaves from 1 sprig fresh thyme	Tabasco
	4–6 cups cooked Basic Louisiana White Rice (page 15)
3 quarts Basic Shellfish Stock (page 13)	

1. Make a roux by heating the oil in a large cast-iron or heavy-bottomed pot over high heat. Whisk the flour into the hot oil. It will immediately begin to sizzle. Reduce the heat to moderate and continue whisking until the roux takes on a deep brown color, about 15 minutes. Add the onions, stirring them into the roux with a wooden spoon. Reduce the heat to medium-low and continue stirring until the roux is a rich dark brown, about 10 minutes.

2. Add the blue crabs and smoked sausage and stir for a minute before adding the celery, bell peppers, garlic, and okra. Increase the heat to moderate and cook, stirring, for about 3 minutes. Add the thyme, Shellfish Stock, and bay leaves. Bring the gumbo to a boil, stirring occasionally. Reduce the heat to medium-low and simmer for 45 minutes. Stir occasionally and skim off any fat from the surface of the gumbo.

3. Add the shrimp, oysters, crabmeat, and green onions to the pot and cook for 15 minutes. Season with salt and pepper, Creole Spices, Worcestershire, and Tabasco. Serve in bowls over rice.

BUTTERMILK FRIED QUAIL WITH ARTISANAL HONEY

Serves 6 as an appetizer

Here's a secret to frying quail: as you grab each bird with tongs, lower it into the oil only halfway for a moment before letting it go. This will keep the quail halves from curling up, which not only makes a for better presentation but ensures more uniform cooking, too.

6 semi-boneless quail, split in half through the breast	3 dashes Tabasco
	2 cups flour
Salt	¼ teaspoon onion powder
Freshly ground black pepper	¼ teaspoon garlic powder
	1 quart canola oil
2 cups buttermilk	1 cup honey

1. Season the quail with salt and pepper. Pour the buttermilk into a large bowl and add a few dashes Tabasco. Add the quail, making sure they are submerged in the buttermilk. Cover the bowl and let the quail marinate in the refrigerator for at least an hour.

2. Put the flour, ¼ teaspoon salt, ¼ teaspoon black pepper, the onion powder, and the garlic powder into a large bowl and mix together with a whisk.

3. Transfer the marinated quail from the buttermilk to a plate. Dredge the quail in the seasoned flour, then dip in the buttermilk, then dredge in the flour again, double-coating all the quail pieces.

4. Heat the oil in a large heavy skillet over medium-high heat until it reaches 350° on a candy thermometer. Using long-handled tongs, hold each piece of quail halfway into the hot oil for a moment, then release and fry for about 2 minutes. Turn the quail over with the tongs and continue frying until golden brown. Drain on paper towels. Serve with your best honey drizzled over the quail or in a small bowl for dipping.

Wild Ducks

Duck hunting in Louisiana is probably the best in the country, as some 10 million promising candidates swoop in to rest or winter with us after a long migration, predominantly from the Dakotas and the Canadian prairie. Ducks gravitate to Louisiana because our endless coastal marshes provide an ideal habitat. Many stay for the winter, while others continue on south to Mexico. Don't think it's easy hunting, though. They have smartened up by the time they get to us, as the season in Canada opens in September.

The blue-winged teal, a small duck but one of the finest eating birds around, is the first to arrive, for a special early season in September. The main duck season, however, kicks off early to mid-November and lasts about 60 days, when about a million birds are bagged by up to 80,000 licensed Louisiana hunters. Among the species we encounter are the gadwall, mallard, green-winged teal, pintail, wigeon, mottled duck, shoveler, resident wood duck, and lesser scaup. The scaup is not good to roast; it feeds on mollusks, which turn its skin oily and its flesh fishy. But pull off the skin and the fat, and it's fine in gumbos. The best ducks for roasting are the pintail, which is plump from eating grains throughout the heartlands of North America; the blue-winged teal, which stuffs itself on rice; and the wood duck.

SEARED BREAST OF WILD DUCK WITH RED WINE AND FIGS

Serves 4–6

As a hunter, I'm frequently invited to cook game, such as duck or venison, at the hunting camps and in the home kitchens of various friends. Since I never know what I'll find in those kitchens, this is one recipe that I can depend on. It works with almost any fruit preserves and nearly every kind of wild game I might be called on to roast or grill.

8 whole boneless wild duck breasts (any variety will do)	1 clove garlic, minced
	2 cups red wine
Salt	2 tablespoons red wine vinegar
Freshly ground black pepper	½ cup fig or other fruit preserves
2 pinches sugar	1 sprig fresh thyme, rosemary, or sage
1 medium onion, chopped	

1. Preheat the oven to 450°. Season the duck breasts with salt, pepper, and sugar.

2. Heat a large cast-iron skillet over medium-high heat until hot. Sear the duck breasts, skin side down, until the skin is golden and crisp, about 3 minutes. Turn the breasts over, then transfer the skillet to the oven and cook the breasts for 5 more minutes for medium rare. Turn off the oven.

3. Transfer the duck breasts to a cutting board and return the hot skillet to moderate heat on the stovetop. Add the onions to the skillet and cook, stirring occasionally, until golden, about 10 minutes. Add the garlic and cook for 1 minute. Stir in the wine, vinegar, fig preserves, and herb sprig and cook until the pan sauce has reduced by half, about 15 minutes. Strain the sauce into a small saucepan, discarding solids.

4. Return duck breasts to the turned-off but still-hot oven to just warm through. Slice the breasts crosswise into ½-inch-thick slices and set each breast on a warm plate. Spoon some of the sauce over each breast.

After the hunt: Two limits of bagged bobwhite quail hang at Covey Rise Lodge on the North Shore of New Orleans, above. A happy duck hunter in the 1930s, inset.

BONELESS ROAST WOOD DUCK PORCHETTA

Serves 4

I prepare these ducks in the manner of porchetta, that delectable boned, stuffed, and crisply roasted young pig that's served all over Italy. It's imperative to cook these birds in a hot oven for a short time to sear the bird on the outside. Then I quickly lower the oven temperature to ensure that the stuffing cooks adequately in the middle without overcooking the duck. Wood ducks and green or blue-winged teal will cook the same way, but if wild duck isn't available, this preparation works well with squab. The ultrasimple quince sauce that accompanies the duck is excellent with just about any roasted game bird, venison, or pork.

FOR THE DUCKS

- ¼ cup coarsely chopped bacon
- 1 medium onion, minced
- 2 cloves garlic, minced
- 1 cup fresh wild mushrooms, sliced
- ½ cup fresh bread crumbs
- 1 tablespoon dried porcini mushrooms, rinsed and chopped
- 1 teaspoon crushed red pepper flakes
- Leaves from 1 sprig fresh thyme
- 1 teaspoon minced fresh sage leaves
- Salt
- Freshly ground black pepper

- 4 dressed wood ducks or squab; head, neck, and backbone removed; birds deboned; wings and drumsticks left intact
- 4 pieces very thinly sliced country ham (page 362)
- 1 tablespoon extra-virgin olive oil

FOR THE SAUCE

- ½ cup quince preserves
- ¼ cup rice wine vinegar
- ¼ cup Basic Chicken Stock (page 13)
- 1 shallot, minced
- 1 clove garlic, minced
- 1 small piece fresh ginger, peeled and minced

1. For the ducks, preheat the oven to 500°. Fry the bacon in a 3–4-quart saucepan over medium-high heat, stirring frequently, for 3 minutes. Add the onions, reduce the heat to moderate, and cook, stirring occasionally, until the onions become translucent, about 5 minutes.

2. Add the garlic and fresh wild mushrooms to the pan and increase the heat to high. You'll notice the juices accumulating in the saucepan, which you'll want to cook down until nearly evaporated, about 5 minutes.

3. Remove the saucepan from the heat. Add the bread crumbs, dried porcini, pepper flakes, thyme, sage, salt, and pepper. Stir well to combine, then set aside to let cool. This mixture will be the stuffing for the birds, so taste it and make sure it is well seasoned.

4. Lay the ducks flat, skin side down, on a cutting board and season the breast and leg meat with a touch of salt and pepper. Lay a slice of country ham over each bird. Put one-quarter of the wild mushroom stuffing on top of each slice of country ham.

5. Carefully wrap the breasts of each duck around the stuffing, so that the stuffing is completely enveloped. Tie a couple of pieces of butcher's string around the body so that the duck will retain its shape while it cooks. Gather the tips of the drumsticks together and secure them with butcher's string. Rub ducks with a touch of olive oil and season with salt and pepper.

6. Place the birds breast side up in a shallow roasting pan and transfer them to the oven. Immediately reduce the oven temperature to 200°. Roast the birds for 15 minutes. I recommend cooking the ducks until they're warm in the center, which yields a duckling that's medium roasted.

7. For the sauce, put the preserves, vinegar, Chicken Stock, shallots, garlic, and ginger into a medium saucepan and cook over moderate heat, stirring occasionally, until it is thick enough to coat the back of a spoon, about 30 minutes. Strain the sauce through a sieve into a serving bowl, discarding solids.

8. Remove and discard the string from each duck. Serve the duck and the sauce together.

SUGAR AND SPICED DUCKLING WITH DUCK FOIE GRAS

Serves 6

This restaurant-style duck preparation may seem complicated, but it's actually rather basic: roast duck breast (pekin, not wild), seared duck foie gras, grits, and mayhaw sauce. It's as simple as grinding the spices ahead to season the duck, making a small pot of grits, and, while that's cooking, preparing the sauce with whichever fruit jelly you prefer. Our native mayhaws, the little red fruit of the hawthorn tree, make a distinctively tart jelly that's wonderful with duck.

Birds of a feather: Opposite, two mallards and a duck hen destined for dinner. Right, sugar and spiced duckling.

FOR THE SAUCE

- 1 tablespoon butter
- 1 onion, diced
- ¼ cup mayhaw or apple jelly
- ¼ cup rice wine vinegar
- 3 cups Basic Veal Stock (page 14)
- 2 cups Basic Chicken Stock (page 13)
- 1 teaspoon whole black peppercorns
- 1 sprig fresh thyme
- 1 bay leaf
- Salt

FOR THE GRITS

- ½ cup white corn grits, preferably organic (page 362)
- 3 tablespoons butter
- 2 tablespoons mascarpone cheese
- Salt

FOR THE DUCKLING

- 6 boneless pekin duck breast halves
- Salt
- 2 teaspoons ground star anise
- 2 teaspoons sugar
- Freshly ground black pepper
- 1 teaspoon ground cardamom
- 1 teaspoon ground cinnamon
- 6 2-ounce slices foie gras
- 1 shallot, minced
- 2 cloves garlic, minced
- ½ pound Tuscan kale or spinach, blanched

1. For the mayhaw sauce, melt the butter in a large saucepan over medium-low heat. Add the onions and cook, stirring occasionally, until soft and mahogany in color, about 20 minutes. Add the jelly and rice wine vinegar and simmer for several minutes. Add the Veal Stock, Chicken Stock, peppercorns, thyme, and bay leaf, then increase the heat to medium-high. Cook the sauce until it has reduced by half, about 30 minutes. Season sauce with salt, then strain into a small saucepan and set aside.

2. For the grits, bring 2 cups water to a boil in a medium pot over high heat. Gradually add the grits, stirring constantly. Reduce the heat to medium-low, cover the pot, and cook the grits for 20 minutes, stirring occasionally. Remove the pot from the heat, fold both the butter and the mascarpone into the grits, and season them with salt. Cover the pot to keep the grits warm.

3. For the duckling, preheat the oven to 350°. Using a sharp knife, score the skin of each breast, taking care not to cut through to the flesh, by making 3 evenly spaced cuts on the diagonal in one direction, then making 3 more cuts in the other direction to make a diamond pattern. Lightly season the duck breasts with salt.

4. Combine the star anise, sugar, 1 teaspoon ground pepper, cardamom, and cinnamon in a small bowl. Coat each breast with some of the spice mixture.

5. Heat a large ovenproof skillet over moderate heat, then sauté the duck breasts, skin side down, until golden, about 7 minutes. Turn breasts over and cook for 2 minutes more. Transfer the skillet to the oven and cook the breasts for an additional 5 minutes. Put the duck breasts on a cutting board to let rest for 10 minutes and return the hot skillet to the top of the stove over moderate heat.

MALLARD DUCK BREAST WITH PEPPERS AND BACON

Serves 4–6

We use this recipe with many meats, such as squab or venison. Be sure not to cook the duck beyond medium rare; it tends to be dry. Don't cook the duck skewers in advance; have them ready for the grill, and cook when you're about to serve.

¼ cup sugarcane vinegar (page 362) or balsamic vinegar

2 teaspoons sugar

2 shallots, minced

¾ cup canola oil

3 tablespoons pecan oil

Salt

Freshly ground black pepper

2 whole boneless, skinless mallard or pekin duck breasts, sliced across the breast into strips about ½ inch thick

6–9 strips Allan Benton's country-smoked bacon (page 362) or other thick-cut bacon, cut in half crosswise

3 pickled jalapeños, thinly sliced lengthwise

12 6-inch wooden skewers, soaked in water

1. Whisk the vinegar, sugar, and shallots together in a large bowl; gradually add the oils, whisking constantly. Season the marinade with salt and pepper. Add the strips of duck to the bowl and marinate for 30 minutes.

2. Lay a piece of bacon out on a work surface. Place a strip of duck on top of (and perpendicular to) the bacon and a piece of jalapeño on top of the duck. Season with salt and pepper. Wrap the bacon around the duck and jalapeño and slide a wooden skewer through to secure the roll. Repeat the process with the remaining bacon, duck, and jalapeños, seasoning each with salt and pepper. Discard the marinade.

3. Prepare a charcoal or gas grill. Meanwhile, wrap the ends of the skewers with aluminum foil to protect them from burning while on the grill.

4. Grill the duck skewers until the bacon crisps and has rendered its fat and the duck is medium, 5–7 minutes.

6. Lightly season the foie gras with salt. Sauté the foie gras in the hot skillet on one side only until it is browned and caramelized and warmed all the way through, about 3 minutes. Using a slotted spatula, transfer the foie gras to the cutting board with the duck and set aside.

7. Return the skillet to medium-low heat, add the shallots, garlic, and blanched kale, and cook, turning the kale in the pan fat, until heated through. Season with salt and pepper.

8. For each serving, thickly slice each duck breast and arrange the slices on a plate. Place a piece of foie gras next to the duck, browned side up. Put a spoonful of the grits and a spoonful of the kale on each plate and spoon some warm mayhaw sauce over all.

GRANDMOTHER'S RABBIT

Serves 6

This braised rabbit is actually quite easy to make in advance and serve with either pasta, polenta, or gnocchi. Be sure to pay close attention and don't overcook the rabbit. Once the meat is fork tender, remove it from the pot, or it can become stringy.

3 fresh rabbits	1 teaspoon crushed red pepper flakes
Salt	¼ teaspoon fennel seed
Freshly ground black pepper	1 bay leaf
¼ cup olive oil	5 large tomatoes, blanched, peeled, cored, and diced
1 onion, diced	
1 head garlic, halved crosswise	1 cup white wine
1 tablespoon tomato paste	2 quarts Basic Chicken Stock (page 13)
1 cup sliced fresh wild mushrooms	1 quart Basic Veal Stock (page 14)
1 stalk celery, diced	12 small carrots, peeled
Leaves from 1 sprig fresh thyme	3 tablespoons butter
Leaves from 1 sprig fresh sage, minced	

1. Using a cleaver or a large sharp knife, quarter the rabbits. Season them with salt and pepper. Heat the olive oil in a large, wide heavy-bottomed pot over medium-high heat and, working in batches, sear the rabbit until golden brown on all sides. When it's browned, transfer the rabbit to a bowl.

2. Add the onions and garlic to the pan and cook until golden brown, 5–10 minutes. Reduce the heat to moderate and stir in the tomato paste. Cook for 5 minutes, then add the mushrooms, celery, thyme, sage, pepper flakes, fennel seed, and bay leaf. Cook the vegetables for 5 minutes, stirring occasionally.

3. Add the tomatoes, wine, Chicken Stock, Veal Stock, and carrots to the pan. Increase the heat to high and bring to a boil. Reduce the heat to medium-low and return the rabbit and any accumulated juices to the pan. Cover the pan and cook the rabbit until it is fork tender and the meat nearly falls from the bone, 45 minutes to 1 hour.

4. Using a slotted spoon, carefully transfer the rabbit, carrots, and garlic to a bowl and set aside. Increase the heat to high and let the liquid in the pan boil off until it has reduced by half, 15–20 minutes.

5. Reduce the heat to medium-low. Stir the butter into the pan and season the sauce with salt and pepper. Return the rabbit, carrots, and garlic to the pan and let them warm through before serving.

Thanksgiving and the Berrigans

"In New Orleans, folks live to eat; they don't just eat to live. And the day after matters just as much as Turkey Day."

In my hometown, you don't celebrate Thanksgiving just by sitting down to Stove Top stuffing and a pop-up turkey. Preparing for Thanksgiving is an event in itself. We take our feasts quite seriously here, striving to serve as many people as possible as many dishes as possible, while staying very close to tradition, never straying from the recipes that have been passed down from generation to generation. In the Berrigan family it is no different. My in-laws, Patrick and Barbara Berrigan, may be the finest people I know. They are truly passionate cooks and ardent preservationists of the New Orleans Creole culinary tradition. That is why, incidentally, I took the approach I did to win their approval when I started to court their daughter, Jenifer.

At Molly Reily's: I look forward to the generosity and refinement of Molly's Thanksgiving table, above, in her glowing red dining room. A quiet corner in the Quarter, top left, and top right, a blue-shuttered stuccoed façade nearby. A Louisiana turkey farm, 1940, right. Far right, a calabaza squash will soon become soup.

Basically, I tried to charm my way to their hearts through their stomachs. Often, in the early mornings before going in to work as a poor line cook, I'd make them herb-roasted capons, smoky and succulent *cochon de lait* (suckling pig), and spicy crawfish étouffée. The more I cooked and the better I cooked it, the higher Patrick Berrigan would raise the bar. Eventually I wore them down with enough good food that they conceded and allowed me to marry Jen.

As an outsider at Thanksgiving—that is, a boy from down the road who married into and was not born into the family—I've learned to be thick-skinned, expect ridicule at the mere suggestion of a menu modification, be ready to whip up a flawless gravy on a moment's notice, or produce a turkey gumbo the day after Thanksgiving that is at least equal to or better than the patriarch's—as judged by said patriarch, his wife, his daughters, Jenifer, Mary Beth, Erin, and Kim, and the prince of the family, Patrick.

I WAS RAISED with more of a country upbringing, whereas Jen's family was from the big city across the lake, with an entirely different set of traditions. Over the years, I've come to learn and love many white-tablecloth rituals. My friend Molly Reily in her beautiful house in the Quarter celebrates Thanksgiving in many of the same ways that have been passed down through generations of New Orleanians. Thanksgiving is the time when many of those customs culminate in an extravagant feast. I came to realize that the dinner itself is only a fraction of the Berrigans' Thanksgiving traditions.

Anyhow, no matter how liberal the dining practices around the Berrigan household may be the rest of the year, come turkey time, as I learned the hard way, they are not open to the slightest suggestions or improvement. Every detail should be as it always has been. The turkey is to be roasted only by Barbara, who brines it beforehand in a solution of saltwater, stuffs it with French bread dressing, and roasts it—with butter and herbs under the skin— ever so slowly on a bed of onions, garlic, carrots, celery, thyme, and sage leaves. For the gravy, the drippings that have cooked on the bed of vegetables are thickened with a touch of blond roux and simmered for an hour before they're served. Barbara also does a dried cranberry compote just for good measure, so that folks'll know we're Americans.

My father-in-law will make the shrimp remoulade (whose seasoning is always adjusted by L'Oncle Cochon, aka Uncle Kurt), and a pâté made of game birds using whatever's been bagged on a recent hunt—quail, duck, or even woodcock.

In the Quarter: Courtyards, such as this romantic example, below, photographed in the 1930s, are, to me, the heart and soul of the French Quarter. Bottom, a Victorian house on Molly Reily's street. Opposite, mirlitons.

A Berrigan Thanksgiving: In 1985 the entire clan gathered at a cottage on Lake Toxaway, North Carolina. Molly Reily's abundant Thanksgiving plate, opposite.

Patrick Sr. also oversees (and only sometimes delegates) the oyster patties and dressing. Only in recent years has he allowed me to participate in the meal's preparation. Under his strict supervision, I'll cook shrimp and mirliton dressing, dirty rice dressing, and pecan-sautéed green beans. Jenifer always makes the same spinach Madeleine that her great-grandmother did, as well as a crawfish corn bread dressing from her father's recipe. My mother, Imelda, is an accomplished baker, and her apprentice, my little sister, Angela, are invited to bake desserts and several sweet potato dishes. A specialty is Mom's ambrosia of local citrus picked from the trees of Ben Becnel, down the river in Belle Chasse, and topped with fresh curls of coconut and three kinds of garden mint.

YOUNG PATRICK BERRIGAN is usually leaned upon for the day-after-Thanksgiving gumbo, made from the haul from a very recent duck hunt. If ducks aren't available, Pat's always good for a mess of poules d'eau, or marsh birds, that take no skill and little effort to bag but that do happen to produce the best gumbo and dirty rice around. On the rare occasion when Pat hasn't had a successful hunt, he'll make an oyster and artichoke soup instead. While little Miss Erin keeps everyone entertained, Patrick's sisters Mary Beth and Kim work on the fresh vegetables and Christmas potatoes—which aren't just for Christmas at the Berrigans'. They're puréed and whipped with butter, sour cream or Creole cream cheese, grated Mississippi Edam, lardons of Allan Benton's twice-smoked bacon, and chopped chives. The whole family has a role, and none of it is to be taken lightly. Colonel Newsome or Mr. Allan Benton usually provides the country ham that Mr. Berrigan will soak in water for three days (changing it each day). Then he'll glaze it with pepper jelly and vinegar and slow-roast it for about six hours. The result is worthy of the gods, a sweet, spicy, and salty country ham that's especially good the next day, paired with fresh-baked biscuits and red-eye gravy.

Now that our family has grown enormously over the past few years, 40 or more of us will gather at our house on Thanksgiving. There will be an eclectic group of family and friends who vary in age, race, political affiliation, and occupation, which makes the feast—as well as the conversation—all the richer. With food as the common thread, all of us can come together at the table, grateful for the shared abundance.

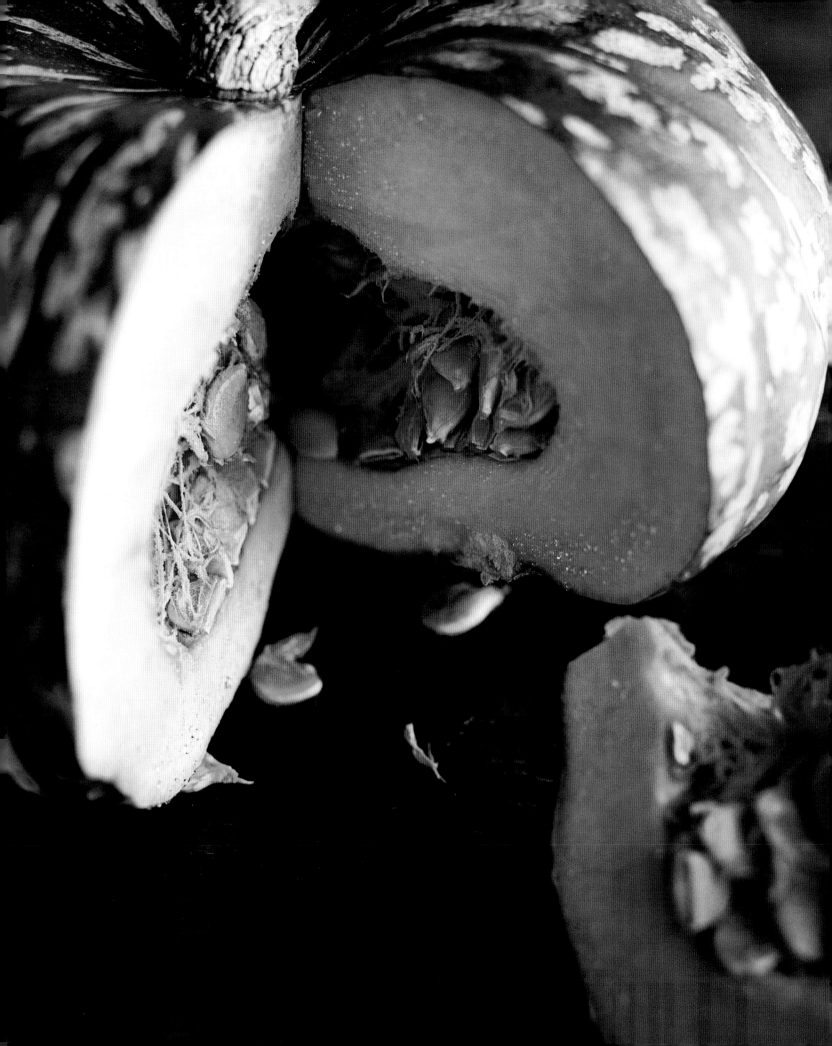

Pumpkin color:
Opposite, a calabaza squash reveals its golden interior. A favorite doorway at the Soniat House hotel, near right. Pumpkin soup with crabmeat, below.

PUMPKIN SOUP WITH CRABMEAT

Serves 6–8

Any variety of hearty fall squash or pumpkin can work well in this pumpkin soup. I like my puréed soups so refined that I strain them through a sieve just before serving.

3 tablespoons olive oil	1½ quarts Basic Chicken Stock (page 13)
3 cloves garlic, crushed	1 cup heavy cream
2 leeks, white parts, chopped	2 tablespoons butter
1 onion, chopped	2 cups jumbo lump crabmeat, picked over
1 stalk celery, chopped	2 tablespoons minced fresh chives
¼ teaspoon cayenne pepper	Salt
Leaves from 1 sprig fresh thyme	Freshly ground black pepper
1 pound pumpkin, peeled and cubed	
1 large Yukon Gold potato, peeled and cubed	

1. Heat the olive oil in a large heavy-bottomed pot over moderate heat. Add the garlic, leeks, onions, celery, cayenne pepper, and thyme and cook, stirring often, until the onions are soft, about 10 minutes. Add the pumpkin, potatoes, and Chicken Stock and simmer until the potatoes are soft, about 30 minutes.

2. Remove the soup from the stove; purée in a food processor or a blender until very smooth and velvety. Strain through a fine sieve back into the pot. Add the cream; cover and keep warm over very low heat or in a 200° oven.

3. Melt the butter in a small skillet over low heat. Add the crabmeat, and heat until it's completely warmed through (take care not to break up crabmeat too much). Remove the skillet from the heat. Scatter the chives over the crabmeat and season with salt and pepper.

4. Ladle the pumpkin soup into individual bowls, then put a large spoonful of warm crabmeat into each bowl.

WHOLE ROAST STUFFED TURKEY

Serves 12

We call stuffing what's cooked in the bird; dressing is what's served on the side. This stuffing is simple, based on the day-old French bread we always have around. But we like to make two other dressings as well—Shrimp and Mirliton and Crawfish Corn Bread—just to be safe! My mother-in-law, Barbara Berrigan, always brines the turkey, so of course I do here. You can do this a day ahead.

FOR THE TURKEY

- 2 cups sugar
- 2 cups plus ¼ teaspoon kosher salt
- 1 tablespoon crushed red pepper flakes
- 1 15-pound turkey, giblets and neck removed
- 2 carrots, peeled and chopped
- 1 large onion, coarsely chopped
- 1 stalk celery, chopped
- 2 cloves garlic, crushed
- 2–3 tablespoon canola oil
- 1 teaspoon minced fresh sage leaves
  Leaves from 1 sprig fresh thyme
  Flour, optional

FOR THE STUFFING

- 4 tablespoons butter
- 2 large onions, diced
- 1 stalk celery, diced
- 1 green bell pepper, seeded and diced
- 2 cloves garlic, minced
- 1 green onion, chopped
  Leaves from 1 sprig fresh thyme
  Leaves from 1 sprig fresh rosemary, minced
- 4 cups diced, day-old French bread
- 3 cups Basic Chicken Stock (page 13)

1. For the turkey, put 1 gallon of cold water into a large stockpot big enough to hold a whole turkey plus a total 2 gallons of liquid. Stir in the sugar, 2 cups of the salt, and the pepper flakes and bring to a boil over high heat. Reduce heat to moderate and simmer the brine for a minute, stirring until the sugar and salt have dissolved. Remove the pot from the heat, add 1 more gallon of cold water, and allow the brine to cool to room temperature. Submerge the turkey in the cooled brine and let it soak in the refrigerator or a very cool place for 12–24 hours. Discard brine

2. For the stuffing, melt the butter in a large skillet over moderate heat. Add the onions, celery, and bell peppers and cook, stirring often, until the vegetables are soft, about 10 minutes. Add the garlic, green onions, and fresh herbs and cook for an additional minute.

3. Transfer the cooked vegetables to a large mixing bowl. Add the French bread and gently toss to combine. Add the Chicken Stock, 1 cup at a time, gently mixing it in until the bread cubes are soft. Set the stuffing aside. (The stuffing may be made up to a day ahead and kept, covered, in the refrigerator. Bring it to room temperature before spooning it into the cavity of the turkey so that it will be thoroughly hot by the time the turkey has finished roasting.)

4. Preheat the oven to 325°. Scatter the chopped carrots, onions, celery, and garlic in the bottom of a large sturdy roasting pan and add 3 cups water. Set a roasting rack in the pan. Remove the turkey from the brine and pat it dry with paper towels inside and out. Slather the bird with canola oil and sprinkle it with the remaining ¼ teaspoon salt, and the sage and thyme.

Wild turkey: Granddaddy Walters, above left, with a hunting buddy in the 1970s, often shot a turkey like this one for our holiday table.

5. Spoon the stuffing into the cavity of the bird. Tie the legs together with kitchen string, if you like. Set the turkey on the rack above the vegetables. Roast the turkey in the oven, basting it every 30 minutes or so with the pan drippings until the thigh juices run clear when the thigh is pricked and the internal temperature of the stuffing reaches 165°, about 3½–4½ hours.

6. Transfer the turkey to a carving board or serving platter, loosely cover it with foil, and allow it to rest for 15 minutes before carving.

7. To make a simple gravy, just use the skimmed drippings. Or, make a gravy by straining the pan drippings into a bowl, discarding the vegetables. Skim and reserve the fat from the surface of the drippings.

8. Measure this fat, then heat it in a medium saucepan over moderate heat. Stir in an equal amount of flour (now you're making a blond roux) and let it cook, stirring frequently, until lightly colored, which shouldn't take longer than 5 minutes. Whisk in the pan drippings and cook the gravy, stirring often, until thickened, about 5 minutes longer. Serve the gravy with the roast turkey at the table.

OYSTER PAN ROAST WITH TURNIPS AND APPLES

Serves 6

This lovely first course is based on vol-au-vent, the classic French puff pastry shell that is indeed light as the wind. Fortunately, excellent frozen puff pastry shells are available to save time. To serve this dish flawlessly, bake the pastry shells ahead so that they're ready before you begin to make the filling. The pastry lids are a cook's treat to nibble. As soon as the turnip purée is done, fill each shell, and then, as the oysters cook, nestle them into the purée-filled shells. Top with the cooked turnip greens and a seared oyster.

FOR THE TURNIP PURÉE

- 2 tablespoons butter
- 4 medium turnips, peeled and diced
- 1 Granny Smith apple, peeled, cored, and diced
- ¼ cup heavy cream
- 1 pinch cayenne pepper
  Salt
  Freshly ground white pepper

FOR THE TURNIP GREENS

- ¼ cup chopped bacon
- 1 shallot, minced
- 1 clove garlic, sliced
- 2 tablespoons butter
- 2 tablespoons Herbsaint or Pernod

- ¼ cup Basic Fish Pan Sauce (page 15)
  Leaves fron 3 sprigs fresh tarragon, chopped
- ½ teaspoon crushed red pepper flakes
- 1 bunch turnip greens, coarsely chopped
  Salt
  Freshly ground black pepper

FOR THE OYSTERS

- 2 tablespoons olive oil
- 1 clove garlic, minced
- 30 shucked oysters, drained and patted dry
- 6 baked puff pastry shells

1. For the turnip purée, preheat the oven to 200°. Melt the butter in a medium ovenproof saucepan over moderate heat. Add the turnips and apples, and cook until they begin to soften, about 5 minutes. Add just enough water to barely cover the turnips and apples and cook, partially covered, until the turnips and apples are soft. Transfer the mixture to the bowl of a food processor. Add the cream, cayenne, and salt and white pepper and process until smooth. Using a rubber spatula, transfer the purée back into the saucepan, cover, and keep warm in the oven.

2. For the turnip greens, fry the bacon in a large skillet over moderate heat until crisp. Add the shallots and garlic and cook until soft, about 2 minutes. Add the butter, Herbsaint, Fish Pan Sauce, tarragon, pepper flakes, and turnip greens and cook, stirring often, until the greens are wilted. Season with salt and pepper. Set the skillet aside.

3. For the oysters, heat the oil and garlic together in another large skillet over moderate heat until garlic is fragrant. Increase the heat to medium-high and quickly sear the oysters, turning them once with kitchen tongs, until they plump up and their edges begin to curl.

4. Arrange the pastry shells on a serving platter or on individual plates. Fill each shell with some of the turnip purée, set 4 of the oysters in each, and top with the turnip greens and 1 seared oyster.

FALL GREENS SALAD WITH BLUE CHEESE AND PUMPKIN SEED BRITTLE

Serves 6

The happy surprise of this salad is the crunchy brittle made with pumpkin seeds. I like to bake it on those silicon mats; their nonstick surface works wonders with the sugars in the brittle. Be careful not to burn the pumpkin seeds. I'm a big fan of the blue cheese that's handmade at Clemson University in South Carolina.

FOR THE BRITTLE

- 1 cup sugar
- ½ teaspoon cayenne pepper
- 1 teaspoon salt
- 4 ounces pumpkin seeds
- 1 egg white

FOR THE VINAIGRETTE

- 1 teaspoon sugar
- ¼ cup sherry vinegar
- 1 shallot, minced
- Leaves from 1 sprig fresh thyme
- ¼ cup canola oil
- 2 tablespoons walnut oil

- 2 tablespoons pumpkin seed oil
- Salt
- Freshly ground black pepper

FOR THE SALAD

- 6 cups mixed baby fall greens such as tatsoi, mizuna, arugula, beet
- 1 cup Clemson Blue or other artisanal blue cheese (page 362)
- 1 tablespoon minced fresh chives
- Fresh chervil sprigs

1. For the brittle, preheat the oven to 375°. Mix together the sugar, cayenne, salt, and pumpkin seeds in a medium bowl. Whisk the egg white in a mixing bowl until foamy but not stiff. Fold the egg white into the pumpkin seeds.

2. Line a baking sheet with a silicon mat or parchment paper. Spread the brittle mixture thinly and evenly on the silicon mat and bake until the brittle turns completely golden brown, 20–30 minutes. Remove from oven and set aside to let cool. Break the brittle roughly into 2-inch shards.

3. For the vinaigrette, whisk the sugar and sherry vinegar together in a large mixing bowl or salad bowl until the sugar has dissolved. Add the shallots and thyme. Whisk in the canola, walnut, and pumpkin seed oils. Season with salt and pepper.

4. For the salad, put the greens into the bowl with the vinaigrette and toss well. Divide the greens between 6 individual plates and crumble blue cheese on top of each. Scatter shards of pumpkin seed brittle, chives, and chervil sprigs over the tops of the salads.

Ironwork galleries: Classic French Quarter buildings at the corner of Dauphine and Orleans streets, 1938; photo: Frances Benjamin Johnston.

MIRLITON AND SHRIMP DRESSING

Serves 10

Mirlitons, our local squash, are also know as chayote. Any variety of fall squash may be substituted. Diced day-old bread is the best to use for these kinds of dressings; bread crumbs will make the dressing too dry. Mirliton dressing is too loose for a stuffing, so it's always served as a side dish.

4 mirlitons, halved and seeded	1 pound medium Louisiana or wild American shrimp, peeled, deveined, and finely chopped
3 tablespoons olive oil	
8 tablespoons butter	
1 medium onion, diced	½ cup crabmeat, picked over
1 stalk celery, diced	
1 green bell pepper, seeded and diced	4 cups diced day-old French bread
2 cloves garlic, minced	2 cups Basic Chicken Stock (page 13)
Leaves from 1 sprig fresh thyme	½ teaspoon Basic Creole Spices (page 13)
Leaves from 1 sprig fresh rosemary, chopped	1–2 dashes Tabasco
	Salt
Leaves from 1 sprig fresh sage, chopped	Freshly ground black pepper

1. Preheat the oven to 350°. Rub the mirlitons with oil. Place them on a baking sheet cut side down and bake until they are fork tender and easily peeled, about 45 minutes. Set the mirlitons aside to let rest until they are cool enough to handle, then peel and cut them into 1-inch pieces.

2. Melt the butter in a large skillet over moderate heat. Add the onions, celery, and bell peppers and cook until the onions are translucent, about 5 minutes. Add the garlic and cook for another minute. Increase heat to medium-high, add the fresh herbs and shrimp, and stir frequently, until shrimp are just cooked , 3–5 minutes. Stir in the crabmeat. Transfer to a large mixing bowl. Add the diced mirlitons and the remaining ingredients and stir until well combined.

3. Spoon the dressing into a large buttered baking dish and bake until golden brown, 20–30 minutes.

Mirlitons

The mirliton is an inexpensive and versatile staple of Louisiana cooking; it's known in other cultures as chayote, custard marrow, or vegetable pear. This unusual gourd contains one large seed and is a member of the cucurbit family—think cucumbers and watermelon—similarly mild and fibrous and distinctive for the vinelike growth of its plants, many of which bear edible fruit. It is indigenous to the Americas. How you pronounce *mirliton* depends on where you live: some folks call it "mellaton"; others, "milly-ton"; I call it "mir-le ton."

These squash are typically pale green and pear shaped, with ridges along the skin. Their flavor is really delicate; once you start cooking mirlitons, they can almost melt away. Mirlitons work well with crabmeat and shrimp and are most often served roasted and stuffed with a mixture of seafood. Down here, mirlitons are not always available in supermarkets (but, as chayote, they are easily found in Hispanic markets). Mirlitons are so easy to grow that many of us cultivate them in our gardens and backyards. All you have to do is stick the end of the fruit in the ground at a 45-degree angle and give it lots of water, and a wild and vigorous vine will clamber over a fence or trellis, producing a crop in the early fall. Young mirliton leaves are delicious steamed or sautéed, so nothing goes to waste.

CRAWFISH CORN BREAD DRESSING

Serves 10

You can make the corn bread ahead or use leftover corn bread. In fact, the dressing may be prepared a day ahead and kept in the refrigerator until an hour before serving. This recipe makes 8–10 cups, more than enough to stuff a turkey, but at our Thanksgiving we stuff our bird with French bread and serve dressings like this alongside.

4 tablespoons rendered bacon fat	1 small jalapeño pepper, chopped
¼ pound andouille sausage, diced	1 teaspoon chopped fresh parsley
¼ pound hot pork sausage meat, removed from casing	Leaves from 1 sprig fresh thyme
1 medium onion, chopped	2 tablespoons Basic Creole Spices (page 13)
1 stalk celery, diced	6 cups crumbled Basic Corn Bread (page 15)
½ green bell pepper, diced	2 cups Basic Chicken Stock (page 13)
1 clove garlic, minced	½ cup heavy cream
2 cups peeled crawfish tails, chopped (page 362)	2 eggs, lightly beaten
2 green onions, chopped	Salt
	Freshly ground black pepper

1. Put the bacon fat, andouille, and pork sausage into a large skillet and cook over medium-high heat, breaking up the pork with the back of a wooden spoon. When the pork sausage meat has browned, add the onions, celery, bell peppers, and garlic and cook, stirring occasionally, until the onions are translucent, about 5 minutes. Add the crawfish and cook for 2 minutes. Transfer the mixture to a large mixing bowl.

2. Add the remaining ingredients to the bowl with the sausage and crawfish and stir together until well combined. Spoon the dressing into a large heatproof dish. At this point, the dressing may be covered and refrigerated (for up to 1 day) until you are ready to bake it. Bake the dressing in a preheated 350° oven until it is piping hot and golden brown, 15–30 minutes.

SPINACH MADELEINE

Serves 6

Creole cream cheese is a local farmer cheese whose flavor is tarter than that of cream cheese. Even though folks were using Creole cream cheese in Louisiana long before they'd ever heard of mascarpone, the tart Italian cheese is more widely available and is an acceptable substitute in the recipes in this book.

4 tablespoons butter	¾ teaspoon celery salt
2 shallots, minced	½ teaspoon cayenne pepper
1 clove garlic, minced	1 teaspoon Worcestershire
2 tablespoons flour	2 cups Creole cream cheese or mascarpone
2 pounds fresh spinach, well washed	Salt
½ cup heavy cream	
½ teaspoon freshly ground black pepper	

1. Preheat the oven to 375°. Melt the butter in a large nonreactive, heavy-bottomed pot over moderate heat. Add the shallots and garlic and cook for about 2 minutes. Add the flour and cook, stirring with a wooden spoon, for 2–3 minutes. Add the spinach to the pot and cook, stirring often, until the spinach is wilted, 3–5 minutes. Add the cream, black pepper, celery salt, cayenne, and Worcestershire and cook for 5 more minutes.

2. Add the Creole cream cheese or mascarpone, stirring it into the spinach as it melts. Season with salt. Spoon the spinach into an ovenproof dish and bake for 20 minutes.

CANE SYRUP–CREAMED SWEET POTATOES

Serves 6

Is the rendered bacon fat really necessary? I think its smoky flavor adds some complexity to the sweet potatoes. Roasting the potatoes first gives them a smoother texture, and a fluffier potato makes mashed potatoes velvety. Make sweet potatoes in advance and finish them in the oven with their topping just before serving.

FOR THE SWEET POTATOES

- 5 large sweet potatoes, unpeeled
- 2 tablespoons rendered bacon fat
- 2 sticks butter (16 tablespoons)
- 1 cup Steen's or other cane syrup (page 362)
- Salt

Freshly ground black pepper

FOR THE TOPPING

- ½ cup flour
- ¼ cup crushed pecans
- ¼ cup sugar
- 2 teaspoons ground cinnamon
- 1 pinch salt
- ½ cup melted butter

1. For the sweet potatoes, preheat the oven to 350°. Rub the potatoes with the rendered bacon fat and put them on a baking sheet. Bake for about 1 hour, until the potatoes are very soft when pierced with a paring knife. Remove them from the oven and set aside to let rest until they are cool enough to handle. Split the potatoes in half lengthwise and scoop out all the pulp into a bowl. Discard the skins.

2. Heat the butter and the cane syrup in a medium saucepan over low heat until the butter has melted. Add the sweet potatoes and mash with a potato masher until smooth. Season with salt and pepper. Using a rubber spatula, transfer the sweet potatoes to a heatproof baking dish.

3. For the topping, whisk together the flour, pecans, sugar, cinnamon, and salt in a medium bowl. Still whisking, slowly drizzle in the melted butter. Spread the topping over the sweet potatoes and bake in a 350° oven until heated through, about 15 minutes.

The fixin's: Crawfish corn bread dressing, top; cane syrup–creamed sweet potatoes, above; spinach Madeleine, left.

BOURBON PECAN PIE

Serves 8

My grandmother Grace used pure molasses in her pecan pie, and my mother, Imelda, uses only corn syrup. It may be good family politics, but I happen to like using both in my pecan pie. In fact, you may substitute either syrup for the other. The molasses doesn't have to come to room temperature exactly, but it should be cool enough that when you add the eggs, they won't be tempted to scramble.

¾ cup blackstrap molasses	1 teaspoon vanilla extract
¾ cup brown sugar	¼ cup bourbon
½ cup light corn syrup	1½ cups pecan halves
4 tablespoons unsalted butter	1 recipe Basic Pie Dough (page 16), fitted into a 9-inch pie pan
¼ teaspoon salt	
3 eggs, beaten	

1. Place a rack in the middle of the oven and preheat the oven to 350°.

2. Put the molasses, brown sugar, corn syrup, butter, and salt into a medium saucepan over moderate heat. Stir with a wooden spoon until the butter has melted and the sugar has dissolved.

3. Increase the heat to high and let the mixture boil for 1 minute. Remove from the heat, then pour into a mixing bowl and set aside to let cool to room temperature.

4. Whisk the eggs, vanilla, and bourbon into the molasses. Stir in the pecans, then pour into the prepared pie crust. Bake until the pie is set around the sides and nearly set in the middle (it shouldn't wobble when you give it a nudge), about 1 hour. The color should be mahogany and the crust golden. Allow to cool completely before serving.

Native nuts: Pecans are plentiful in Louisiana and are grown all over the south and central parts of the state, above. Opposite, bourbon pecan pie.

PEAR TART

Serves 6–8

Make this tart in a long pan with a removable bottom, or use a round one that's eight to nine inches in diameter. A store-bought pie shell will save time but sacrifice flakiness.

---

14 tablespoons unsalted butter, at room temperature

6 tablespoons all-purpose flour, plus more for dusting

1 recipe Basic Pie Dough (page 16)

¾ cup granulated sugar

3 eggs

¼ teaspoon vanilla extract

5–6 ripe pears, peeled, cored, and cut into ¼-inch-thick slices

½ cup almond flour

¼ cup brown sugar

¼ cup sliced almonds

¼ cup chopped pecans

½ teaspoon ground cinnamon

Powdered sugar for dusting

1. Grease a 4-by-14-inch long or a 9-inch round removable-bottom tart pan with 1 tablespoon of the butter, dust it with some of the all-purpose flour, and set aside.

2. Roll the dough out onto a lightly floured surface to a thickness of ¼ inch and fit it into the prepared pan, trimming off excess dough. Using a fork, prick bottom lightly, then refrigerate the pastry for 30 minutes.

3. Preheat the oven to 375°. Carefully fit a large sheet of parchment paper or aluminum foil into the pastry in the pan, allowing edges to hang over by at least 2 inches, then fill with pie weights or dried beans. Bake until the crust is set and begins to color slightly, about 8 minutes. Remove parchment and weights and set crust aside.

4. Melt 6 tablespoons of the butter and reserve. Using an electric mixer, beat the granulated sugar and eggs in a mixing bowl until fluffy. Beat in the vanilla, melted butter, and 2 tablespoons all-purpose flour. Pour the filling into the prepared crust; arrange the pears on top.

5. Combine the remaining 7 tablespoons butter, 4 tablespoons all-purpose flour, the almond flour, brown sugar, sliced almonds, chopped pecans, and cinnamon in a small mixing bowl. Mix well, then scatter over the top of the pears. Bake until topping has turned golden brown, about 15 minutes.

6. Let tart cool on a rack for at least 15–20 minutes before removing it from its pan and dusting it with powdered sugar.

Embellishments:
Decorative houses like these, below, are common sights on the charming streets of the Quarter.

CHAPTER 15

BOUCHERIE

High on the hog: The smokehouse at Red Bluff Farm in Folsom, Louisiana, our partners in hog production, where we finish our Berkshires, right. Butchers at the French Market in the French Quarter, 1888–1920; photo: George François Mugnier, top right.

A Smokehouse of My Own

"My granddaddy Mitchell Walters looked like the perfect Southern gentleman. He was tie and hat proper."

Yet he had this unpredictable, wild side. Once, finding himself on the wrong side of a river, he just chopped down some trees and built a bridge right there and then. Self-sufficiency was the message he'd pound home. And I loved his stories. My father was tough, like the Great Santini; Granddaddy was accessible, the male figure I was drawn to. From the ages of about nine to 12, when I was not in school, I'd hop on the train called the *City of New Orleans* and go all by myself to my grandparents' house near Meridian, Mississippi, sometimes carrying my shotgun in its case.

Granddaddy was in the furniture business, but like everybody around there, he came from a farm and never really left it. He was an avid horticulturist who loved growing fruits and vegetables in those red clay fields amid rolling hills, pine trees, and hardwood bottoms.

I'd ask as many questions as I could and listen to his spellbinding tales of what sounded to me like a wildly romantic pursuit of food. I'd ride around the country with him in his crazy vehicles, like a Land Rover or a Jeep (he always made sure my grandmother drove a Cadillac), and he'd tell me stories of his past—none of them easy. He grew up on a farm a few hours north of Slidell; hunting, harvesting, and a childhood of hunger and hardship were his frequent themes. His stories were filled with ways to carry on traditions, like how to manage the pecan trees and how to use lye to sweeten the soil and how chitterlings, or chitlins, the intestines of hogs, were sometimes the only things they had to eat; everything else had to be saved to last the rest of the year.

Pig tales: My favorite andouille sausage from Jacob's in LaPlace, Louisiana, below. We raise our Berkshire hogs under the live oaks behind La Provence, where they benefit from cool shade and tasty acorns, opposite. Boudin sausage vendors at the International Rice Festival, Crowley, Louisiana, 1970, far right.

GRANDDADDY would talk in glowing terms about "The Home Place" and about the boucherie—the hog slaughter—and how it epitomized self-reliance, family and community working together. He made a big effort to take me back to the smokehouse at "The Home Place" before he died. He told me that the boucherie took place once a year, often on the coldest day of winter, when families and neighbors would gather to butcher and process enough pork to sustain them for a year. These people showed a degree of mastery and frugality that Americans who did not experience the Depression in the rural South could never relate to. They would prepare and revere every part of the beast; nothing was taken for granted, and nothing was wasted.

After the slaughter, the hogs'

heads were cooked and picked clean for making *fromage de tête*, or hog's head cheese; tongues, ears, tails, and feet were pickled and put up in jars. Hams and bellies were cured and smoked; shoulders were cooked down into grillades or potted meat and packed into jars. Livers became liver cheese or pâté de foie. The stomach was stuffed, the intestines were cleaned, and those that weren't stuffed were cooked and jarred to be consumed as chitlins or made into andouillette sausage. The blood was used in boudin noir, or blood sausage, as was every little scrap of meat; the skin was cut and rendered into crisp cracklins. The hot fat that remained would seal every jar of conserved pork and was saved as lard.

All those jars were conserved in the smokehouse. Granddaddy would tell me how they'd get a vast block of ice and insulate it with wood chips and sawdust. The jars of potted preserved pig would be lowered into the pit in the smokehouse floor and stored right next to the ice. Folks would eat off those pigs until the next year's boucherie. Pigs weren't a cliché to my people (you'd never consider a pig tattoo!). The pig meant survival, and its life was met with only one certain destiny: the boucherie.

Curing pork: We age country hams, bacon slabs, and saucisson in our smokehouse at La Provence, top. The window of a meat market in New Iberia, Louisiana, 1938; photo: Russel Lee, above. Smoked pork shoulder with purple plum glaze, opposite (recipe, page 324).

GRANDDADDY'S LESSONS didn't totally click until I went to Germany in 1993. After two and a half years of culinary school, I knew I needed a European apprenticeship. After a couple of failed attempts to get papers for France, where I'd be able to work legally and get paid, I turned to Jenifer's family, who had been in the German-glass-importing business. Their suggestion was that I go to work in the Black Forest, the breadbasket of Germany and the most beautiful part of the country. The restaurant called Der Romantic Hotel Spielweg turned out to be the perfect place.

On my first day at work in the little hamlet of Obermünstertal, my assignment was to care for the hogs. Though this was a foreign country with a different culture and climate, what surprised me was that there was nothing I had not seen before. The pigs were kept in the *Keller*, or cellar, and each day we apprentices were told to feed them all the green scraps from the restaurant. The Spielweg's renowned chef, Karl-Josef Fuchs, was an avid hunter and dedicated to a sustainable food movement that had existed in Baden-Württemberg centuries before American chefs ever even thought about going green. Karl-Josef understood the importance of cooks' developing a rapport with the origins of all our food products. We quickly became friends. Imagine my surprise when Chef had us work with him on the pig slaughter, just as Granddaddy and generations of Southerners have done. From his pigs we'd make *Leberkäse, Sülze, Blutwurst, Speck,* and *Schinken,* products that, despite their German names, were fundamentals of our boucherie. We processed the pig just as we have done for generations.

Every spring we'd help Karl-Josef butcher 20 baby goats at a time; at summer's end, it was spring lamb; throughout hunting season our coolers were stocked with fresh-killed wild boar, venison, mountain goats, and hares. Working for Karl-Josef in his 300-year-old restaurant taught me much about many of our own food traditions, which I'd grown up considering the essence of down-home Louisiana. At last I appreciated the love of tradition that Granddaddy instilled in me a decade earlier. Today, I have a smokehouse of my own, and now it's up to me to make sure my children remember these stories.

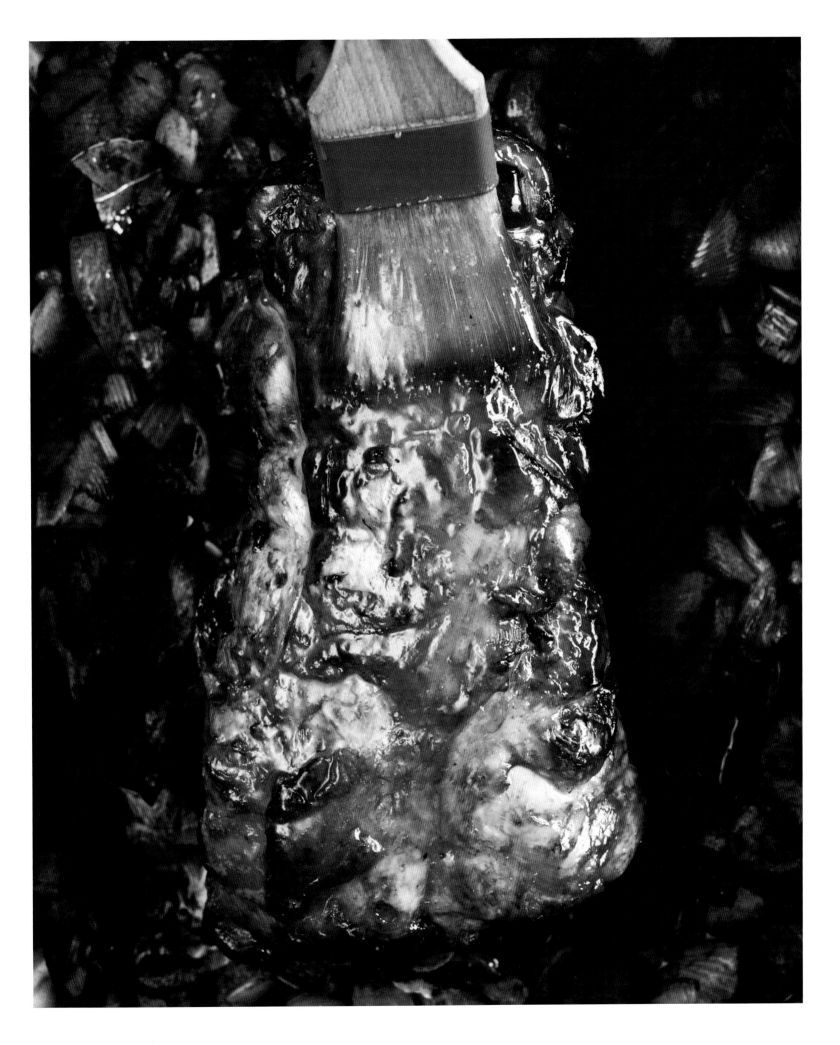

SMOKED PORK SHOULDER WITH PURPLE PLUM GLAZE

Serves 6–8

For the best results, rub the pork roast with the seasoning spices and refrigerate it for a good 12 to 24 hours before slow-cooking it with indirect heat. If you're using a charcoal grill, make a small fire on one side of the grill and let the pork cook on the other side. Make sure to turn the roast frequently to ensure that it cooks evenly. In the winter, when we don't have fresh plums for the glaze, I'll substitute half a cup of plum preserves and reduce the amount of sugar to half a cup. (See photograph, page 323.)

FOR THE PORK

2	teaspoons brown sugar
¼	teaspoon ground cumin
¼	teaspoon dried lemon zest
¼	teaspoon cayenne pepper
¼	teaspoon onion powder
¼	teaspoon garlic powder
	Salt
1	4-pound boneless pork shoulder roast

FOR THE PLUM GLAZE

2	tablespoons rendered bacon fat
1	onion, chopped
6	large purple plums, pitted and chopped
2	cloves garlic, minced
1	tablespoon minced peeled fresh ginger
½	cup granulated sugar
¼	cup white vinegar
½	cup Basic Chicken Stock (page 13)
1	bay leaf
1	pickled jalapeño pepper, diced
	Salt

1. For the pork, combine the brown sugar, cumin, lemon zest, cayenne, onion and garlic powders, and 1 tablespoon salt in a large wide bowl. Put the pork shoulder into the bowl and rub it all over with the seasonings. Cover the bowl with plastic wrap and let the pork marinate in the refrigerator for at least a day and as long as overnight.

2. Preheat a smoker or a grill set up for indirect heat, with the charcoal moved to one half of the grill. Add soaked hickory or pecan chips often to the fire to flavor the pork during the smoking process. Remove the pork shoulder from the refrigerator and transfer it to a smoker or to the cooler half of the grill, opposite the hot coals. Cover and maintain a smoking temperature of 250°–300° for 3 hours, turning the roast occasionally so that the meat cooks evenly.

3. For the plum glaze, heat the rendered bacon fat in a medium saucepan over moderate heat. Add the onions and cook, stirring occasionally, until browned, 10–15 minutes. Add the plums, garlic, ginger, granulated sugar, and vinegar and cook, stirring frequently, until the sugar dissolves.

4. Add the Chicken Stock, bay leaf, jalapeños, and a pinch of salt to the pan. Increase the heat to high, bring to a boil, then reduce the heat to medium-low and simmer for 30 minutes. Season the plum glaze with a touch of salt. Set glaze aside.

5. After the pork roast has smoked for 3 hours, begin basting it with the plum glaze every 15 minutes or so and continue to smoke the pork at 300° for 1 hour more. After 4 hours, the roast should have a dark, lacquered finish. If you are not ready to serve the roast right away, wrap it in aluminum foil and keep it warm in a 200° smoker, grill, or oven until you're ready to serve it.

Before and after: Pork shoulder rillettes (in jar above) on toast. Pigs at Farley's Farm, 1943; photo: Charles L. Franck Photographers, The Historic New Orleans Collection, left.

PORK SHOULDER RILLETTES

Makes 10–15 small jars

Rillettes are meats cooked in lard, shredded, packed into jars, and then chilled and spread like pâté on toast. It is certainly an ambitious recipe, which is precisely why I love to put up jars of rillettes and give them to friends around the holiday season. Cooked duck legs and their fat, the skin and bones removed, can easily be substituted for the pork shoulder and pork fat.

1 pound lard	1 stalk celery, halved
3 onions, chopped	1 quart Basic Chicken
1 4–5-pound boneless Boston butt pork roast	Stock (page 13)
Salt	1 cup white wine
Freshly ground black pepper	2 sprigs fresh thyme
	2 bay leaves
5 cloves garlic, chopped	1 teaspoon crushed red pepper flakes

1. Melt the lard in a large enameled cast-iron pot with a lid over moderate heat. Add the onions and cook, stirring occasionally, until they are soft and translucent, about 10 minutes. While the onions are cooking, cut the pork into large pieces and season with salt and pepper.

2. Add the pork to the pot along with the garlic, celery, Chicken Stock, wine, thyme, bay leaves, and pepper flakes. Increase the heat to medium-high and bring to a gentle boil. Reduce the heat to low, cover, and slowly simmer for 3 hours.

3. Remove the pork from the pot and place in the bowl of a standing mixer fitted with a paddle attachment, and mix on low speed.

4. Remove and discard the celery, thyme sprigs, and bay leaves from the pot. Slowly add the remaining broth from the pot to the meat in the mixer bowl, continuing to mix at low speed until all the broth has been incorporated back into the meat. Season with salt and pepper. Pack the cooled pork in a terrine or in small sterilized jars. Cover well and refrigerate. Jarred rillettes will keep for 6 months.

LÜKE HOMEMADE BRATWURST

Serves 6–8

Making sausage is not as daunting as it may seem. I like to use the sausage attachment of our standing mixer for making small amounts of sausage like bratwurst. Every mixer comes with such attachments and stuffing directions; good butchers carry sausage casings.

1 pound pork shoulder, cubed	¼ teaspoon ground marjoram
¼ pound pork fat, cubed	½ teaspoon onion powder
1 pinch allspice	½ teaspoon white pepper
1 pinch ground caraway seeds	1 teaspoon salt
¼ teaspoon ground mace	½ cup crushed ice
	½ pound pork sausage casings, rinsed

1. Mix together the pork, pork fat, allspice, ground caraway seed, mace, marjoram, onion powder, white pepper, and salt along with the crushed ice in a large mixing bowl.

2. Using the food grinder attachment of a standing mixer, grind the meat mixture twice into the mixer's bowl. Then, using the paddle attachment with the mixer set on low speed, blend all the ground meat together along with ¼ cup cold water.

3. Remove a small amount of meat from the bowl and shape into a little patty. Fry the patty in a small pan over high heat and then taste it for seasonings. If it needs a bit more, add more salt to the ground meat.

4. Using the sausage stuffer attachment on the standing mixer, fill the casings with the sausage meat and twist into 4- to 6-inch sausages. These bratwurst are delicious pan-fried, grilled, or added to a choucroute. Store them in resealable plastic bags in the refrigerator or freezer until ready to use.

LÜKE CHOUCROUTE

Serves 6

The secret to an authentic choucroute is slow cooking. Steam the pork belly with the natural juices from the sauerkraut, the wine, and stock until it's tender. You may need to add a cup or so of water after the first hour if the choucroute appears dry. Make sure there is at least an inch or so of liquid at the bottom of the pot to prevent scorching. If you wait until the pork belly is nearly cooked to add the sausages, you will have perfectly cooked sausages and potatoes.

1 cup diced thick-sliced bacon ends and pieces	2 smoked pork jowls, quartered and cut into chunks
4 onions, thinly sliced	1 apple or pear, peeled, cored, and diced
1 pound pork belly, sliced crosswise into 6 pieces	2 bay leaves
Salt	2 bottles Riesling
Freshly ground black pepper	¼ cup honey
3 pounds refrigerated sauerkraut	1 cup Basic Ham Hock Stock (page 13)
2 cloves garlic, minced	1 pound whole fresh pork bratwurst
1 tablespoon caraway seed	1 pound smoked pork sausage, like kielbasa
	12 fingerling potatoes

1. Brown the bacon pieces in a large heavy-bottomed pot over medium-high heat. Add the onions, reduce the heat to moderate, and cook, stirring often, until the onions are soft and translucent, about 10 minutes.

2. Season the pork belly with salt and pepper, add to the pot along with the sauerkraut, garlic, caraway seed, pork jowls, apples or pears, and bay leaves, evenly distributing everything in the pot. Add the Riesling, honey, and Ham Hock Stock. Cover and bring to a simmer. Reduce heat to low and cook for about 1½ hours, adding up to a cup of water, if needed.

3. Add the bratwurst, pork sausages, and potatoes; cover and cook until the potatoes are fork tender and the sausages are cooked through, 15–30 minutes. Arrange on a platter and serve with sharp hot mustard.

Lüke at lunch: Our restaurant celebrates an old New Orleans brasserie tradition. Here, dishes feature every inch of the the hog, from head to toe, plus a raw bar, right.

Berkshire Hogs

Since childhood, I've dreamed of raising my own pigs. At last, a few years ago our executive chef, Steve McHugh, and I embarked on a project to breed our own Berkshires, the black-bodied, white-hoofed purebred brought here from Great Britain in the 1820s. Steve and his six brothers grew up on a dairy farm in Wisconsin, so he was the man for the job. As Steve tells it: "We went to the Berkshire Breeders Association and discovered that the closest breeder was in Oklahoma, so we borrowed a trailer and returned with two large sows for breeding, one male, and four feeder hogs. From that stock we've bred all our pigs. We feed them organic scraps saved in the kitchens of our restaurants. Each cook takes turns carting them out to our little pig farm under the live oaks behind La Provence. We supplement the feed with barley (a by-product of our own beer making) and whey from a nearby cheese maker.

"If a chef is just opening up a package of pork chops, he's far too removed from the animal to learn to respect it, but if he's saving fava bean peels and feeding the animals himself, he truly connects with them. For breeding, we let nature take its course; then we send the piglets over to Bryant Laird at Red Bluff Farm, where he raises and finishes the pigs the same way he does our goats and sheep."

PORK CHEEK DUMPLINGS, HAM HOCK POT LIQUOR, AND MUSTARD GREENS

Serves 6

In preparation for making the dumplings, have all the ingredients at your fingertips so that the wonton wrappers won't dry out and make it more difficult to form the proper little square-shaped ravioli. The dumplings can rest briefly on a wax paper–lined cookie sheet or be stored frozen until you're ready to cook them.

- 1 tablespoon rendered bacon fat
- 1 pound pork cheeks or other good braising cut of pork
- Salt
- Freshly ground black pepper
- 1 onion, diced
- 1 carrot, peeled and diced
- 1 clove garlic, thinly sliced
- ½ cup canned tomatoes
- 1 bay leaf
- Leaves from 1 sprig fresh thyme
- ½ teaspoon crushed red pepper flakes
- ½ cup red wine
- 1 cup Basic Veal Stock (page 14)
- 1 tablespoon cornstarch
- 36 fresh wonton wrappers
- 8 cups Basic Ham Hock Stock (page 13)
- 4 ounces mustard greens, coarsely chopped

1. Heat the rendered bacon fat in a medium heavy-bottomed pot over medium-high heat. Season the pork with salt and pepper. Working in batches, add the pork to the pot and brown all over, transferring it to a bowl as it's browned.

2. Add the onions, carrots, and garlic to the pot and cook, stirring frequently, until browned, 5–10 minutes. Add the tomatoes, bay leaf, thyme, pepper flakes, wine, and Veal Stock to the pot and bring to a boil. Reduce the heat to medium-low. Return the pork and any accumulated juices to the pot, cover, and gently simmer for 1 hour.

3. Transfer the pork with a slotted spoon to a cutting board to cool. Reduce the braising liquid in the pot by at least half over medium-high heat, about 15 minutes.

4. Coarsely chop the pork and transfer it to the bowl of a food processor. Discard the bay leaf from the braising liquid, then add the liquid and vegetables to the pork. Pulse the mixture several times so that it is just well combined and the texture is still chunky. Transfer the pork filling to a mixing bowl and season with salt and pepper. Cover and refrigerate until cold.

5. Stir cornstarch and ¼ cup water together in a small bowl to make a slurry. Lay out 6 of the wonton wrappers on a work surface. Put a small spoonful of the pork mixture in the center of each wrapper. Using a pastry brush or your finger, brush along the edges of the wrapper with the cornstarch slurry. Cover filling and wrapper with another wonton wrapper and gently press edges together to seal. Trim edges of the dumplings with a crimped-edge pastry wheel, if you like.

Transfer dumplings to a wax paper–lined sheet pan. Repeat process, filling and sealing the wonton wrappers, making 18 dumplings in all. (The dumplings at this point may be stored in the freezer and cooked at a later time. They don't need to be defrosted; just put them into the simmering broth straight from the freezer.)

6. Bring the Ham Hock Stock to a simmer in a medium pot over moderate heat. Add the mustard greens and cook for 1 minute, then add the dumplings and cook them for 2 minutes. Taste the pot liquor and season it with salt and pepper.

7. To serve, ladle the dumplings, greens, and pot liquor into soup bowls.

Head cheese: The most delectable meat on the hog is in the head, left, here submerged in brine. A terrine of *fromage de tête*, above.

FROMAGE DE TÊTE (HOG'S HEAD CHEESE)

Serves 10–15

Like many natives of South Louisiana, I was brought up on a terrine of hog's head cheese, or *fromage de tête*, a pâté that's still sold in small shops and often made at home. Of course, it takes time and attention to detail to prepare, but the result is well worth it. If you can, cook the pig's head in a large pot over an outdoor propane burner. The first step is to brine the pig's head; if you just don't have the space in your refrigerator, then skip this step, but be sure to add crushed red pepper flakes and a little mustard seed to the cooking water. Once it's brined and cooked, you can easily finish the preparation for the terrine on an indoor burner.

½ cup salt, plus more for seasoning	1 red or green bell pepper, seeded and diced
¼ cup sugar	1 stalk celery, diced
½ teaspoon black peppercorns	3 medium red onions, quartered
1 teaspoon crushed red pepper flakes	3 small carrots
½ teaspoon mustard seed	4 cloves garlic, minced
1 pig's head, halved (ask your butcher to do this)	2 jalapeño peppers, seeded and diced
2 tablespoons rendered bacon fat	1 bay leaf
	1 sprig fresh thyme
4 medium yellow onions, chopped	2 green onions, chopped
	Freshly ground black pepper

1. Mix the ½ cup of salt, the sugar, black peppercorns, pepper flakes, and mustard seed into 1 gallon of lukewarm water in a large stockpot or plastic pail. Add the pig's head halves and let soak in the brine in the refrigerator for 1–2 days. Drain the head in a large colander and discard the brine.

2. Heat the rendered bacon fat in a large stockpot over moderate heat. Add the yellow onions, bell peppers, and celery and cook, stirring occasionally, until soft, about 15 minutes. Add the red onions, carrots, garlic, jalapeños, bay leaf, thyme, and pig's head halves to the pot.

3. Cover the pig's head with cold water by 2 inches and bring to a boil over high heat. Reduce the heat to low, cover the pot, and simmer slowly for 8 hours. Transfer the pig's head to a large colander and set aside to let rest until cool enough to handle.

4. Meanwhile, increase the heat to moderate and let the broth in the pot gently boil, uncovered, until it has reduced by about half, or to 3–4 cups of broth, about 30 minutes.

5. Pick all the tender meat from the pig's head, putting it into a large bowl as you work. Discard the skin, bones, and any cartilage. Mince the meat with a sharp knife on a cutting board and return the minced meat to the bowl. Add the green onions and season with salt and pepper.

6. Lift the carrots and red onions out of the reduced broth, finely chop them, and add them to the bowl with the minced meat. Discard the bay leaf and thyme sprig, then pour the broth from the pot into the bowl. Stir to combine. Taste the meat mixture and add more salt and pepper if needed.

7. Line an 8-cup mold or terrine as smoothly as possible with a large sheet of plastic wrap, allowing it to hang over the edges by at least 2 inches. Pour the meat and broth mixture into the mold and cover it completely with another sheet of plastic wrap. Chill the terrine completely before serving. It will keep in the refrigerator for up to 7 days.

8. To serve, tip the terrine out of the mold, unwrap, and slice into ½- to 1-inch-thick slices. Serve the hog's head cheese with Watermelon Pickles (page 248) and Creole mustard, if you like.

BOUDIN NOIR WITH POMMES SAUTÉES (BLOOD SAUSAGE WITH SAUTÉED APPLES AND POTATOES)

Serves 6–8

Making blood sausage is not for the faint of heart, but this gutsy dish is a valuable connection to our boucherie tradition. This recipe does require a well-thought-out plan, and it's important to follow these steps exactly. First, make sure the sausage casing is well rinsed, and check that the funnel's mouth is large enough in diameter to accommodate the diced bacon. Ask your butcher for bacon ends and pieces; he'll have an abundance left from slicing bacon slabs. Pork blood is available at some Asian and ethnic markets. I use more eggs so that the sausages will be heartier. I always serve boudin with chunky sautéed apples and potatoes, onion sprouts, and plenty of Dijon mustard.

FOR THE BOUDIN NOIR
- 1 3-foot-long section salted, cleaned pork sausage casing
- 6 tablespoons rendered bacon fat
- 1 onion, chopped
- 1 cup diced bacon fat, ends and pieces
- ⅓ cup heavy cream
- 3 eggs, beaten
- Leaves from 1 sprig fresh thyme
- ½ teaspoon freshly ground black pepper
- 3 dashes smoked paprika
- 1 dash ground nutmeg
- 1 dash ground mace
- 1 dash ground cloves
- 2 cups fresh pork blood
- Salt

FOR THE POMMES SAUTÉES
- 2 tablespoons rendered bacon fat
- 2 medium Yukon Gold potatoes, peeled and cubed
- 2 Granny Smith apples, peeled, cored, and cubed
- 1 pound cipolline onions, quartered
- Salt
- Freshly ground black pepper
- Dijon mustard

1. For the boudin noir, soak the sausage casing in a large bowl of cold water for 1 hour, changing the water every 10 minutes or so. Run cold water through the casing to thoroughly rinse it of any remaining salt. Drain the casing and set aside.

2. Heat 4 tablespoons of the rendered bacon fat in a medium skillet over moderate heat. Add the onions and cook, stirring occasionally, until soft and translucent, about 10 minutes. Transfer the onions to a large mixing bowl and set aside to let cool completely.

3. Add the diced bacon fat, cream, and eggs to the onions and mix well. Season the mixture with the thyme, black pepper, smoked paprika, nutmeg, mace, and cloves. Stir in the pork blood and 1 teaspoon salt.

4. Fit the entire casing onto the nozzle end of a large funnel, bunching it up as you fit it on. Pull enough of the casing end down to be able to tie it off, then tie it securely. Ladle the filling into the mouth of the funnel and push it through until the casing is filled. Tie off the open end of the casing. The sausage should be about 2 inches in diameter and 12–16 inches long.

5. Bring a gallon of lightly salted water to a gentle simmer (a temperature of 200° is ideal) in a large wide pot. Add the sausage and poach it for 20 minutes. Drain the sausage and set it aside to let cool completely. The boudin noir will keep, covered and refrigerated, for up to 5 days.

6. For the pommes sautées, heat the rendered bacon fat in a medium skillet over moderate heat. Add the potatoes and cook, stirring occasionally, until lightly browned and beginning to soften, 15–20 minutes.

7. Add the apples and onions to the potatoes and cook, stirring occasionally, until the onions are lightly browned and soft, about 10 minutes. Season with salt and pepper. Cover to keep warm.

8. To serve the boudin noir, slice the sausage into 1½-inch-thick rounds. Heat the remaining 2 tablespoons rendered bacon fat in a large nonstick skillet over medium-high heat. Sauté the boudin noir until the pieces are seared and somewhat crisp, about 5 minutes. Serve the sausage immediately with the warm pommes sautées and mustard.

Boudin noir: Ingredients for homemade blood sausage, above, from top, pig's blood; eggs; cubed smoked bacon; a spice mix of black pepper, caraway, star anise, and coriander; and salt. Left, blood sausage with sautéed apples and potatoes.

FOR THE PIGS' FEET

- 4 pigs' feet, whole or split lengthwise
- 1 onion, coarsely chopped
- 1 stalk celery, coarsely chopped
- 1 leek, cleaned and coarsely chopped
- 2 bay leaves
- 1 bottle white wine

   Leaves from 1 sprig fresh thyme
- 1 shallot, minced
- 1 clove garlic, minced
- ½ teaspoon crushed red pepper flakes

   Leaves from 1 sprig fresh tarragon, chopped

   Salt

   Freshly ground black pepper
- 2 cups flour
- 2 cups buttermilk
- 2 cups finely ground dried bread crumbs
- 1 quart canola oil

FOR THE SAUCE GRIBICHE

- 1 cup Basic Sauce Ravigote (page 19)
- 1 hard-cooked egg, peeled and minced
- 1 tablespoon chopped chives
- 1 teaspoon capers, chopped
- 1 cornichon, chopped
- ½ shallot, minced

   Leaves from 2 sprigs fresh tarragon, chopped
- 2 cups baby lettuces and the leaves from a mixture of fresh herbs
- 2 tablespoons Basic Walnut Oil Vinaigrette (page 19)

CRISPY PIEDS DE COCHON (PIGS' FEET)

Serves 6

Pigs' feet are a special treat. They're on the menu at Lüke, and our guests can't get enough of them. At home, they're easy to prepare in several stages before a dinner. You can make the roulade of pigs' feet a couple of days in advance and store it in the refrigerator. The Sauce Ravigote may be made a day ahead, too. Then, all you have to do is bread the individual rolls and fry them. Fry only two at a time, though, or the oil will cool, the breading will fall apart, and the pigs' feet will just melt away. They're far too good for such a fate!

1. For the pigs' feet, put feet, onions, celery, leeks, bay leaves, and wine into a large pot and cover with cold water. Bring to a boil over high heat. Reduce the heat to medium-low, cover, and gently simmer for 2 hours.

2. Remove one of the pigs' feet from the pot with tongs and test to see whether it's done by pulling the flesh from the bone. If it pulls free easily, it is done cooking; if it does not, then return it to the pot and continue simmering, covered, for another 30 minutes or so or until the flesh pulls easily away from the bone.

3. Carefully transfer the feet to a pan and discard the cooking liquid. To pick the meat from the bones easily, let the feet cool just enough that you can handle them without burning your fingers. Once the feet are cool enough, remove the skin and every bone and hard piece of cartilage. Put the picked meat into a bowl and season it with the thyme, shallots, garlic, pepper flakes, tarragon, salt, and pepper.

4. Lay a large sheet of plastic wrap on a work surface. Spoon the seasoned pigs' feet mixture onto the plastic wrap, then wrap the plastic around the mixture and shape it into a 12-inch-long cylinder about 2 inches in diameter. Twist each end of the plastic wrap and tie closed with butcher's string. Refrigerate the cylinder until completely cool, about 1 hour; or you may keep it in the refrigerator for up to 2 days.

5. For the sauce gribiche, mix together the Sauce Ravigote, hard-cooked eggs, chives, capers, cornichons, shallots, and tarragon in a small bowl. Cover and refrigerate until just ready to serve.

6. To finish the pigs' feet, put the flour, buttermilk, and bread crumbs into 3 separate bowls. Slice the cylinder of pigs' feet through the plastic wrap into 2-inch-long rounds. Peel off the plastic wrap and dredge the rounds in the flour, then the buttermilk, then back into the flour, then back into the buttermilk, and finally into the bread crumbs.

7. Heat the canola oil in a wide deep pot over medium-high heat until the temperature reaches 350° on a candy thermometer. Working in batches, deep-fry two of the pigs' feet at a time until golden brown, 3–5 minutes. Drain the pigs' feet on paper towels and season with a touch of salt.

8. Toss the lettuces and herbs with the Walnut Oil Vinaigrette in a bowl.

9. Spoon a generous portion of sauce gribiche onto each of 6 plates. Set a fried roll of pigs' feet on each plate and garnish each with the greens.

Andouille Sausage

There's a lot of baloney out there that is not andouille. For the real thing you have to go to LaPlace, Louisiana, to Jacob's or Bailey's (page 362), whose andouille is so good that even though we now make many of our own dry-cured sausages, we do not make andouille.

Andouille may bear a French name—a reference to the renowned smoked tripe sausages of Brittany and Normandy—but the Cajun version most likely originated on our German coast, the Côte d'Allemands, on the Mississippi, about 30 miles upriver from New Orleans, and does not contain tripe. By the mid-19th century several thousand Germans were arriving every year, bringing with them an expertise in brewing, baking, and sausage making. Cross-cultural variations of the sausages they had known in coastal France, Alsace, and Baden-Württemberg emerged from the communal boucherie they shared with their Acadian French neighbors. Unlike the European andouille, which consists of the small intestines and stomach lining of the pig, Cajun andouille (pronounced ahn-DOO-ee) is made from a diced, lean cut of pork—the shoulder, butt, or shank—mixed with a little pork fat and generously seasoned with garlic, salt, and black and often red pepper. The pork mixture is usually stuffed into beef casings and smoked for several hours over fragrant pecan, hickory, or oak wood. Andouille sausages are then dry-cured, which gives them their signature deep pink color.

REVEILLON

Holidays: Jack Besh, left, hovers over our Père Roux cake. The good father himself, Father Randy Roux, with his famed pound cake, below left. St. Louis Cathedral, below, as seen from the balcony of the Pontalba building in Jackson Square, 1940. Opposite, my mother-in-law, Barbara, as a little girl in 1951.

Awake and Eat

"Reveillon—Awakening— was originally an elaborate Creole feast served on Christmas Eve."

Midnight mass is celebrated at churches across the city but most famously at St. Louis Cathedral, in the heart of the French Quarter. Traditionally, after mass, a lavish meal, called Reveillon, would be served. People would fast in the days leading up to the splurge, even as they prepared a lush parade of food that carried on throughout the night, often until sunrise on Christmas morning: slow-cooked daubes, roasts, braises, egg dishes, étouffées, and elaborate pastries. That Reveillon feast could have been the precursor to our New Orleans jazz brunch.

Today, our city of parties has figured out how to make the traditional Reveillon celebration last for an

Kids at Christmas: The Besh children in 1968, left to right, Elaine, John, Kathleen, Steven, and Laura, top. (Angela wasn't born yet.) Christmas tree structures of wood are traditionally built all along the Mississippi River to be lit on Christmas Eve, 1969.

entire month. Many of New Orleans's best kitchens offer fine dishes in the French Creole tradition, and an air of celebration fills our streets from early December through New Year's Day. It's a time when we chefs like to return to our roots and display our best versions of a Creole holiday menu. Our cooks, who come from around the globe, are particularly thrilled to prepare what folks have cooked here for centuries.

MANY OF THE very things that I cook during Reveillon season are the old, traditional dishes of my childhood: such Creole classics as turtle soup laced with sherry, oyster dressing, a standing roast of our famed Charolais beef, and, of course, Mom's many wonderful cookies, dried fruit and rum cake, pecan sweet potatoes, and black-bottom pie. Those long gatherings of yesteryear shape my menus today in a way that no culinary school could do. In this way, Christmastime connects us to our South Louisiana roots. Every year, I do versions of these favorite Creole foods, and every year I search for ways to be innovative without losing the very soul of the dish. It's one of the things I love the most about cooking here: not just that food matters so much but that it matters the most to locals, who have always held chefs and cuisine in high esteem.

To clarify points about the foodways of old New Orleans, I always turn to my friend the priest and accomplished baker Father Randy Roux, who never fails to enlighten me with an insightful tidbit of local culinary trivia—or is only too happy to make one up on the spot. Though Saint Nicholas may be long gone, his spirit lives on in Père Roux. Over the years he has entranced our entire staff with tales of our city's culinary traditions. In sharing his passion for baking with us all, he has influenced the way we eat and cook, not just for our guests but for our families, too.

Father Roux, who started cooking from Julia Child's books when he was nine, comes from Harahan, Louisiana, west of New Orleans, and, like many of us, has French–German roots, in Alsace Lorraine. While he was in training at St. Joseph Seminary, run by Benedictine monks, across the lake in Covington, Louisiana, he worked in the kitchen as a baker. My family is the direct beneficiary of his baking skills. Every Christmas Eve we look forward to the two large cakes he'll drop by the restaurant for us to take home for Christmas Day.

"Pound cake is the cornerstone of Southern baking," he says, "the kind of thing you always have on the table. You bake it, toast it, grill it, slather it with butter and fig preserves." We're addicted to his famed kugelhopf, actually a buttery, vanilla-scented pound cake baked in a heavy ceramic Bundt-style pan, unfrosted except for a blushing camellia plunked in its center. The recipe, he says, came from a group of French Carmelite nuns at a New Orleans convent. Father Roux was able to finagle the recipe from the niece of one of them, Sister Alberta of the Angels, who agreed to give it to him as long as he'd take it to his grave without telling another soul. As far as I know he's told no one and certainly not me, though I've had no qualms about trying to suss it out for myself.

THEN THERE'S FATHER Roux's version of the birthday cake his mother baked for him when he was a child. It's six layers, soaked in fine rum, smeared with bananas cooked in brown sugar and butter, frosted with butter-cream, and decorated with flowering herbs and roses from his parish garden. He'll often make it for my birthday and leave it at our front door with a note: "Bon Anniversaire, Père Roux." We've developed our own version of his recipe, which we call Père Roux cake. It was the first dessert we put on the menu after reopening August, just two weeks after Hurricane Katrina sank our city, and it's a specialty at Christmas.

The good father bakes a particularly mean hummingbird cake, too, a three-layer confection with pineapple and banana, a favorite of many a Southern grandmother in the old days. Edible flowers decorate the Creole cream cheese and pecan buttercream frosting. Just the other day, I lost a pastry chef after I had her taste Father Roux's hummingbird cake. This pastry chef, it seems, was insulted by my insistence that she take some inspiration from a cake baked by a priest. Needless to say she wasn't from New Orleans and left soon thereafter. The point she missed, of course, is how we cooks constantly draw on memory and nostalgia to create the kind of great recipes that keep tradition alive.

Gingerbread man: Our youngest son, Andrew, has no compunctions about biting off the head of his Christmas cookie.

La Provence was made for the holidays: Roaring fires, glowing tile floors, and my son Brendan showing off a prize Charolais standing rib roast.

CHRISTMAS DINNER

HORSERADISH-RUBBED STANDING CHAROLAIS RIB ROAST

Serves 12

If you're unable to find a butcher who carries perfect Charolais beef, any fine standing rib roast of beef will do. Two things to remember about preparing such a roast: season it well and cook it long and slow. I like beef to reach an internal temperature of 130 degrees. This leaves the midsection medium rare, the end cuts well done, and most of the rest of the meat close to medium, which satisfies the tastes of a wide variety of folks.

16 tablespoons (2 sticks) butter, softened	3 sprigs fresh sage, coarsely chopped
Cloves from 1 head garlic	1 16-pound rib roast of Charolais beef, tied with butcher's string
1 cup prepared horseradish	Salt
Leaves from 1 bunch fresh thyme	Freshly ground black pepper
Leaves from 3 sprigs fresh rosemary, coarsely chopped	

1. Preheat the oven to 325°. Put the butter, garlic, horseradish, thyme, rosemary, and sage into the bowl of a food processor and process to a paste.

2. Stand the rib roast fatty side up in a very large, sturdy roasting pan. Season generously all over with salt and pepper. Spread the horseradish–herb butter all over the top of the roast. Roast the beef until it is medium rare or until the internal temperature of the meat registers 130° on a meat thermometer, about 3½ hours.

3. Transfer the roast to a carving board to let rest for at least 20 minutes or up to 1 hour before carving. Reserve 3 tablespoons of the beef fat from the roasting pan if you're making Popovers (page 349).

Charolais Beef

There was a time when Louisiana had a thriving cattle business on the North Shore of New Orleans, and it included breeders of the famed French Charolais cattle. I became quite attached to the heavily marbled meat of this excellent breed while I was living in Europe, so a few years ago I joined forces with my friend Chris Meredith, aka Chicken Man (it's a long story, and it did involve raising chickens), in an attempt to develop a breed that would thrive here and, in the process, to supply ourselves with sustainably raised, grass-fed beef. It began as a veal operation so that we could have heads for tête de veau, for which there is a stipulation that the calf be purchased live.

We started out buying young male calves from dairy farmers, but before long we began cross-breeding heifers carrying Brahman blood with Charolais bulls to ensure that the mothers produced strong calves with solid bone and mass (from the father) and the ability to withstand our humid conditions and resist parasites (from the mother). On average we now produce one sire a month, which is a cow that weighs up to 1,000 pounds and is approximately one year old. Once the calves are weaned, they graze freely in pastures, and their feed is topped off with a tasty supplement of spent barley from the Heiner Brau microbrewery in Covington.

MASTER RECIPE

BEEF DAUBE GLACÉE
(TERRINE OF BEEF SHORT RIBS)

Serves 8–10

Our classic cuisine has many examples of making a chilled terrine from a rich game or beef stew, a process that lets us experience the same dish in two distinct versions. The key to making this great stew and its jelled second act is to brown and sear the meat carefully on all sides before proceeding with the onions and other ingredients. Once the meat is perfectly seared, remove it from the pot, then add the onions and other vegetables and caramelize them. Summon the patience to stir and wait until the vegetables turn a deep mahogany color. Such is the way to a great daube. Serve it as a stew and/or refrigerate it overnight as a terrine.

---

4 pounds boneless beef short ribs, cut into 2-inch cubes

¼ cup sugar

Salt

Freshly ground black pepper

¼ cup canola oil

2 large onions, diced

1 stalk celery, diced

3 cloves garlic, minced

1 carrot, peeled and diced

2 cups red wine

2 bay leaves

1 cup canned chopped tomatoes

2 cups Basic Veal Stock (page 14)

2 ounces dried mushrooms, softened in warm water and minced

Leaves from 3 sprigs fresh thyme

1 envelope gelatin

Pickles

1. Season the short ribs with the sugar, salt, and pepper. Heat the canola oil in a large heavy pot over high heat. Add the meat, several pieces at a time, taking care not to crowd the pot, as crowding will prevent the meat from browning. Turn the meat often, carefully allowing each piece to brown before transferring it from the pot to a platter.

2. When all the beef has browned and has been removed from the pot, add the onions, celery, garlic, and carrots. Stirring constantly, allow the vegetables to cook until the onions become mahogany in color, about 20 minutes.

3. Return the beef to the pot. Then add the wine, bay leaves, tomatoes, Veal Stock, mushrooms, and thyme.

Bring to a boil, then reduce the heat to low, cover, and cook until the beef is fork tender, about 2 hours.

4. Once the beef is cooked, remove from the stove, discard the bay leaves, and skim off any fat floating on the surface. Season the daube with salt and pepper. If serving the daube hot, serve it over rice, pasta, or potatoes.

5. To serve the daube as a cold terrine, soften the unflavored gelatin in 2 tablespoons cold water in a small bowl, then stir into the hot daube. Let cool to room temperature, then refrigerate in the pot, as it is traditionally done, or transfer the stew to a terrine and refrigerate overnight or until cold and set.

Hearty, healthy beef: Chicken man (don't ask) Chris Meredith, who breeds and raises our Charolais–Brahman cattle, far left. Daube of beef short ribs, left, and the jellied terrine it becomes, above.

HOT SPICED WINE

Serves 12

Red wine and kirsch (a brandy made from cherries) make the base for this delicious holiday drink, laced with citrus and warming spices like cinnamon, cardamom, and black pepper. The spiced wine will keep overnight at room temperature. Reheat before serving.

2 bottles light-bodied red wine, such as pinot noir, gamay, or cabernet franc	3 black peppercorns, crushed
1¼ cups sugar	2 cardamom pods, crushed
Strips of zest from 1 orange	1 3-inch cinnamon stick, crushed
Strips of zest from 1 lemon	1 clove, crushed
	½ cup kirsch

1. Put the red wine, sugar, and orange and lemon zests into a large saucepan. Put the crushed spices into a tea ball and add it to the saucepan.

2. Bring the wine to a very gentle simmer over moderate heat, stirring until the sugar dissolves. Remove the pan from the heat, remove the tea ball from the pan, and stir the kirsch into the spiced wine.

3. Ladle the spiced wine into heatproof glasses and serve at once.

MY NOT-SO-CLASSIC TURTLE SOUP

Serves 10–12

This is quintessential, one-pot Creole cooking, where each ingredient should be handled just so. The soup's rich brown color will develop when the turtle meat is properly seared and the onions and carrots properly caramelized. Once you add flour, the soup will become quite thick and likely to burn, so be mindful and keep stirring the pot. After you've added the liquid, there's not much to worry about.

2½ pounds turtle meat, minced (page 362)	2 bay leaves
Salt	½ cup flour
Freshly ground black pepper	2 cups dry sherry
¼ cup olive oil	1 cup crushed canned tomatoes
2 yellow onions, diced	3 cups orange juice
1 carrot, diced	6 cups Basic Veal Stock (page 14)
1 tablespoon tomato paste	Leaves from 1 sprig fresh thyme
2 stalks celery, diced	Leaves from 1 sprig fresh oregano
1 red bell pepper, seeded and diced	Leaves from 1 sprig fresh rosemary, chopped
1 jalapeño, minced	
4 cloves garlic, minced	2 teaspoons Worcestershire
2 teaspoons smoked paprika or pimentón	Several dashes Tabasco
½ teaspoon crushed red pepper flakes	3 hard-cooked eggs, minced
¼ teaspoon ground cumin	2 green onions, finely chopped
1 teaspoon ground allspice	

1. Season the turtle meat with salt and black pepper. Heat the olive oil in a large heavy pot and sear the turtle meat over high heat. Keep stirring until the turtle meat has browned. Add the onions and carrots, reduce the heat to moderate, and cook slowly until browned, 10–15 minutes. Add the tomato paste, stirring well so nothing burns on the bottom of the pot.

2. Add the celery, bell peppers, jalapeños, and garlic to the pot and cook, stirring often, until soft, about 5 minutes. Add the smoked paprika, crushed pepper flakes, cumin, allspice, and bay leaves. Add the flour, stirring constantly for about 3 minutes, then increase the heat to medium-high. Add the sherry drop by drop, and continue stirring, until you have a smooth base.

3. Add the crushed tomatoes, orange juice, Veal Stock, thyme, oregano, and rosemary, bring to a boil, then reduce the heat to low. Cover and simmer for 1 hour.

4. Add the Worcestershire and Tabasco; taste a spoonful to check for seasoning. Season with salt and pepper if needed. Serve each bowl with minced hard-cooked egg and green onions sprinkled over the top.

SHRIMP REMOULADE

Serves 12

I like to boil the shrimp ahead, even a day or two, so that I'm not peeling shrimp just before my guests arrive. Then, an hour or two before serving, I'll peel and marinate them with the remoulade sauce.

FOR THE BOILED SHRIMP
- ½ cup kosher salt
- ¼ cup sweet paprika
- 1 teaspoon cayenne pepper
- 1 teaspoon garlic powder
- ¼ cup fresh lemon juice
- 4 bay leaves
- 1 onion, sliced
- 1 head garlic, halved crosswise
- 1 sprig fresh thyme
- 1 tablespoon whole black peppercorns
- 1 tablespoon ground coriander
- 24 jumbo shrimp, unpeeled

FOR THE REMOULADE SAUCE
- 1 cup mayonnaise
- ¼ cup Dijon mustard
- 2 tablespoons prepared horseradish
- 2 tablespoons chopped fresh parsley
- 1 shallot, minced
- 1 clove garlic, minced
- 1 tablespoon white wine vinegar
- 1 teaspoon fresh lemon juice
- 1 teaspoon hot sauce
- ½ teaspoon sweet paprika
- ¼ teaspoon cayenne pepper
- ¼ teaspoon garlic powder
- Salt
- 6 cups baby arugula, mâche, or other greens

1. For the boiled shrimp, put the salt, sweet paprika, cayenne, garlic powder, lemon juice, bay leaves, onions, garlic, thyme, peppercorns, and coriander into a large pot. Add 1 gallon cold water and boil over high heat for 10 minutes. Add the shrimp, reduce the heat to moderate, and simmer for 5 minutes. Remove the pot from the heat and let the shrimp finish cooking off the heat, until they are just cooked through, 5–7 minutes more.

2. Drain the shrimp and plunge them into a large bowl of ice water to stop them from cooking. Drain the shrimp once they are cool. Reserve for up to a day or two in the refrigerator. About 2 hours before serving, peel the shrimp and devein them.

3. For the remoulade sauce, combine the mayonnaise, mustard, horseradish, parsley, shallots, garlic, vinegar, lemon juice, hot sauce, sweet paprika, cayenne, garlic powder, and salt in a large bowl and stir well. Set aside.

4. Toss the shrimp in the remoulade sauce. Cover the bowl and let the shrimp marinate in the refrigerator for 1–2 hours. Serve the shrimp with the greens.

POPOVERS

Serves 12

Preheating the popover pans with beef drippings in each cup is the first key to a successful popover. The second is: *Do not disturb*. Once you begin the baking process, reduce the heat and allow the popovers to finish baking at 350° until they're fully cooked. Touching them could cause collapse!

1½ cups milk
1½ cups all-purpose flour
  4 eggs
1½ teaspoons salt
  3 tablespoons rendered beef fat (from your roast, page 343) or vegetable oil

1. Preheat the oven to 425°. Put a large 12-cup popover or muffin pan into the oven to heat. Mix together the milk, flour, eggs, salt, and 1 tablespoon of the beef fat in a medium bowl. Beat the batter with an electric mixer until very smooth.

2. Remove the hot popover pan from the oven and add ½ teaspoon of the beef fat to each cup. Return the popover pan to the oven and heat until the fat is very hot, about 5 minutes. Remove the pan from the oven and carefully and quickly pour the batter into the popover cups. Bake for 20 minutes; and don't open the oven door!

3. Reduce the heat to 350° and bake until the popovers are golden brown and puffed, about 20 minutes. Serve immediately.

RAGOUT OF ROOT VEGETABLES, PEAR, AND CHESTNUTS

Serves 12

The best way to prepare this ragout is to have the celery root, turnips, pears, and beets prepped but kept separately until you are ready for them. They will look and taste much better if you wait to combine them and finish the cooking just minutes before serving.

Salt	3 cloves garlic, minced
1½ pounds celery root, peeled and cut into 1-inch dice	1 large shallot, minced
	1 tablespoon chopped fresh thyme
1¼ pounds turnips, peeled and cut into 1-inch dice	1½ cups Basic Chicken Stock (page 13)
4 Bosc pears, peeled, cored, and cut into 1-inch dice	1 cup jarred roasted peeled chestnuts
1¼ pounds baby golden beets, stems trimmed	Freshly ground black pepper
2 tablespoons extra-virgin olive oil	3 tablespoons butter, at room temperature

1. Bring a large pot of salted water to a boil over high heat. Add the celery root and boil until tender, about 6 minutes. Use a slotted spoon to transfer the celery root to a large pan or platter. Add the turnips to the pot and cook until tender, about 5 minutes. Transfer to the pan. Repeat with the pears, cooking them for 2 minutes, then transferring them to the pan. Add the beets to the pot and boil for 15 minutes. Drain the water from the pot and transfer the beets to a large plate. When they're cool enough to handle, peel and quarter the beets.

2. Return the same pot to the stove over moderate heat. Add the olive oil and, when it's hot, add the garlic, shallots, and thyme and cook until softened, about 3 minutes. Add the stock and boil over high heat until reduced to 1 cup, about 5 minutes.

3. Add the celery root, turnips, and pears, cover, and cook over medium-high heat, folding the vegetables gently a few times with a rubber spatula, until heated through. Add the beets and chestnuts. Season with salt and pepper. Cover and cook until heated through, about 3 minutes more. Gently stir in the butter and transfer the ragout to a serving bowl.

CHRISTMAS POTATOES

Serves 12

You can make these potatoes with any good cheese, such as cheddar, baking them a couple of hours ahead and keeping them warm in a low oven until you're ready to serve them.

5 pounds Yukon Gold potatoes, peeled and cut into 3-inch chunks	1 cup heavy cream, warm
	½ cup sour cream
Salt	½ cup grated Edam or other sharp cheese
1 pound thick-sliced bacon	½ cup minced chives
16 tablespoons (2 sticks) butter, softened	Freshly ground black pepper

1. Put the potatoes into a large pot, cover with cold water, and add 2 large pinches salt. Gently boil the potatoes over medium-high heat until tender, about 20 minutes.

2. Meanwhile, fry the bacon in a large skillet over moderate heat until crisp on both sides, 8–10 minutes. Drain on paper towels. Coarsely chop the bacon and set aside.

3. Drain the potatoes and return them to the pot. Shake the pot over medium-high heat for about 20 seconds to dry or cook out some of the moisture from the potatoes.

4. Pass the potatoes through a potato ricer into a large pot. Add the butter, heavy cream, sour cream, cheese, chives, and bacon and stir well. Season with salt and pepper and transfer to a serving bowl.

OYSTER DRESSING GRANDMÈRE

Serves 12

Prepare this dish a day or so ahead, but don't bake it until just moments before serving. After you've combined the ingredients, evaluate the consistency. If the French bread seems too dry, add a cup or two of chicken stock.

8 tablespoons butter, cubed	2 large baguettes, cubed (to yield about 12 cups)
2 ounces slab or thick-cut bacon, diced	4 dozen shucked oysters
1 stalk celery, diced	1 cup oyster liquor
½ green bell pepper, seeded and diced	2 green onions, minced
½ onion, finely diced	2 tablespoons chopped fresh parsley
2 cloves garlic, minced	4 eggs
2 tablespoons sweet paprika	1 teaspoon hot sauce
½ teaspoon garlic powder	1 teaspoon salt
½ teaspoon cayenne pepper	

1. Preheat the oven to 350°. Grease a 10-by-14-inch or other similar-size shallow baking dish with 1 tablespoon of the butter and set aside.

2. Cook the bacon in a large skillet over moderate heat until crisp, about 5 minutes. Add the remaining 7 tablespoons butter and let it melt, then add the celery, bell peppers, onions, and garlic and cook until the vegetables are soft, about 10 minutes. Add the paprika, garlic powder, and cayenne and cook, stirring occasionally, for 2–3 minutes.

3. Put the baguette cubes into a large bowl. Spoon the bacon and vegetable mixture on top. Add the oysters and their liquor, along with the green onions and parsley.

4. Beat the eggs with the hot sauce and salt in a small bowl. Pour the eggs into the bowl with the bread cubes and gently stir until the dressing is well combined. Spoon the dressing into the prepared baking dish and bake in the upper third of the oven until heated through and crisp on top, about 45 minutes. Serve hot.

Christmas cooking:
My son Luke, top, sets out our Nativity scene, a Besh family heirloom. Left, a ragout of root vegetables, pear and chestnuts. Above, Christmas potatoes.

PÈRE ROUX CAKE

Serves 12

This is the four-layer cake we make that's inspired by Father Randy Roux. To simplify it, okay, go ahead and use a cake mix: make two standard white cakes, slice each in half, slather each layer with the banana filling (it's the filling that makes the cake), and frost with the Creole cream cheese.

FOR THE CAKE

- 2 tablespoons unsalted butter, softened
- 2¾ cups all-purpose flour, plus more for dusting
- 3 tablespoons baking powder
- ½ teaspoon salt
- 1 cup vegetable shortening
- 2¼ cups granulated sugar
- 1½ cups skim milk
- 7 egg whites, at room temperature
- 1 teaspoon vanilla extract
- ½ teaspoon almond extract

FOR THE FILLING

- 16 tablespoons (2 sticks) unsalted butter
- 1¾ cups lightly packed light brown sugar
- ½ teaspoon ground cinnamon
- 6 overripe bananas, coarsely mashed
- ½ cup plus 2 tablespoons Myers's dark rum

FOR THE FROSTING

- 16 tablespoons (2 sticks) unsalted butter, softened
- 1½ cups powdered sugar
- 1½ teaspoons vanilla extract
- ¼ teaspoon almond extract
- 4 ounces softened Creole cream cheese (page 362) or fromage blanc
- 1 4-ounce block room-temperature white chocolate for chocolate curls, optional

1. For the cake, preheat the oven to 350°. Grease two 9-inch round cake pans with 1 tablespoon butter. Line the bottoms with waxed paper and grease the paper with the remaining 1 tablespoon butter. Dust the pans with some of the flour, tapping out the excess.

2. Put the flour, baking powder, and salt into the bowl of a standing mixer fitted with the paddle and mix on low speed to combine. Beat in the shortening, add the granulated sugar, and mix on moderate speed until the batter masses around the paddle. Reduce the speed to low and gradually add ¾ cup of the milk, beating until smooth and scraping down the sides of the bowl with a rubber spatula as necessary.

3. Whisk the egg whites together with the remaining ¾ cup milk and the vanilla and almond extracts in a medium bowl. Gradually beat the egg white mixture into the batter on moderate speed until the batter is silky smooth, about 5 minutes. Scrape the batter into the prepared cake pans and bake the cakes until they are golden, 30–35 minutes. Transfer the cakes to a wire rack to cool for 15 minutes in the pans, then invert them onto the rack to let cool completely. Peel off the waxed paper and make 4 layers by slicing each of the 2 cakes in half horizontally.

4. For the filling, put the butter, brown sugar, and cinnamon into a large saucepan and cook over medium-high heat until the butter and sugar have melted. Remove the pan from the heat and stir in the bananas and ½ cup of the rum. Return the pan to moderate heat and cook the filling, stirring, until it is very thick and the butter just begins to separate, about 25 minutes.

5. Transfer the filling to the bowl of a food processor. Add the remaining 2 tablespoons rum and purée until smooth. Let the filling cool to room temperature, about 30 minutes.

6. For the frosting, beat the butter in the bowl of a standing mixer fitted with the whisk on moderate speed until creamy and pale yellow, about 3 minutes. Add the powdered sugar and beat on low speed until well combined. Add the vanilla and almond extracts and beat on medium-high speed until fluffy, about 3 minutes. Add the cream cheese and beat on medium-high speed until light and fluffy, about 3 minutes.

7. To assemble the cake, place 1 cake layer on a plate, cut side up. Spread one-third of the filling over the cake. Set another layer on top, pressing gently, and spread half the remaining filling on top. Set another cake layer on top, pressing gently, and spread with the remaining filling. Top the cake with the last layer, cut side down. Frost the top and sides of the cake.

8. Decorate the cake with white chocolate curls, using a vegetable peeler to shave the block of chocolate into curls and scattering the curls all over the cake as you work. Refrigerate the cake until it has set, about 2 hours. Let the cake come to room temperature before serving.

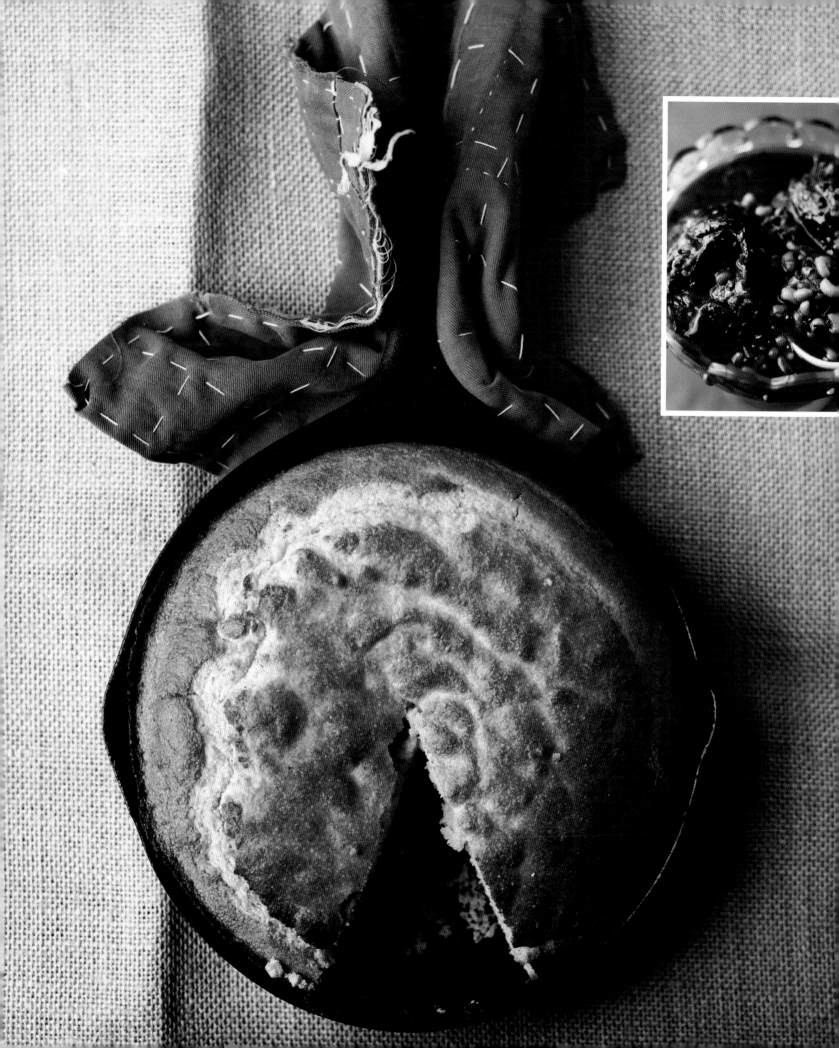

SAZERAC COCKTAIL

Makes 1

It may or may not be America's first cocktail, but it is one of my favorite drinks. Famously made in the Sazerac Bar at the Roosevelt Hotel (which is now home to our new Italian restaurant, Domenica), my version has Herbsaint, the anise-flavored liqueur invented in New Orleans when absinthe was banned in the 1930s.

Herbsaint or absinthe

Twist of lemon peel

2 shots rye whiskey

1 shy shot simple syrup

4 dashes Peychaud's or Angostura bitters

1. Rim the glass with Herbsaint or absinthe. Twist the lemon peel to releases oils, then drop it into the glass.

2. Pour the rye, simple syrup, and bitters into a cocktail shaker filled with crushed ice and shake well. Strain into the prepared glass.

CRACKLINS CORN BREAD

Makes one 9-inch round loaf

When the oven, the pan, and the fat are so hot that the fat actually fries the bread as you pour the batter into the skillet, you'll have the most wonderful crust in the world.

3 tablespoons rendered bacon fat

1 cup organic white cornmeal (page 362)

1 cup all-purpose flour

2 tablespoons sugar

1 teaspoon salt

1 dash cayenne pepper

2 tablespoons baking powder

2 eggs

1¼ cups milk

2 tablespoons butter, melted

½ cup pork cracklins (fried bits of skin and meat)

1. Put the bacon fat into a 9-inch cast-iron skillet. Preheat the oven to 425° and slide the skillet in to heat.

2. Combine the cornmeal, flour, sugar, salt, cayenne, and baking powder in a large mixing bowl.

3. Put the eggs, milk, and melted butter into another bowl and mix well.

4. Stir the egg and milk mixture into the cornmeal mixture and gently fold in the cracklins.

5. Carefully remove the hot skillet from the oven and pour in the batter. Return the skillet to the oven and bake until the corn bread is golden brown, 15–20 minutes. Serve immediately.

BLACK-EYED PEAS WITH LOUISIANA POPCORN RICE

Serves 8

This is such a simple dish, but too often it's not well executed. The key is to let the peas cook slowly and to give them some love. If they need more water, let them have it. We don't want the peas to overcook so they explode in the pot; we want them soft enough to burst in your mouth.

¼ cup rendered bacon fat

2 onions, diced

1 stalk celery, diced

1 pound dried black-eyed peas

1 pound smoked pork jowls or smoked ham hocks

2 bay leaves

Salt

Freshly ground black pepper

Tabasco

4 cups hot cooked Basic Louisiana Popcorn Rice (page 15)

1. Melt the bacon fat in a large heavy-bottomed pot over moderate heat. Add the onions and celery and cook, stirring often, until the onions are translucent.

2. Add the black-eyed peas and the pork jowls to the pot, cover with 2 inches cold water, and add the bay leaves. Bring to a boil, reduce the heat, and cover the pot.

3. Gently simmer the peas, adding more water as necessary to keep the peas covered by 2 inches, until the peas are soft, about 2 hours. Discard bay leaf. Season with salt, pepper, and Tabasco. Serve over Louisiana Popcorn Rice.

ANDOUILLE-SMOTHERED CABBAGE

Serves 6–8

There's lots of great cabbage out there to choose from, and it's one of our truly local vegetables that's everywhere in this country. Be sure to cook it long and slow, adding a bit more water as needed. I like to serve it with a dash or two of my homemade Sport Pepper Sauce (page 250).

2 tablespoons rendered bacon fat	1 stalk celery, chopped
2 heads cabbage, sliced	2 cloves garlic, minced
2 onions, diced	1 bay leaf
1 pound pickled pork or salt pork	Salt
1 pound andouille sausage, chopped	Freshly ground black pepper

1. Heat the bacon fat in a large heavy pot over medium-high heat. Add the cabbage and onions and cook, stirring often, until soft, 5–10 minutes.

2. Add the pickled pork, andouille sausage, celery, garlic, and bay leaf and cook, stirring constantly, for 5 minutes.

3. Add enough water to cover the cabbage, then bring to a boil. Reduce the heat to medium-low, cover, and slowly simmer the cabbage until it's tender, about 1½ hours. Season with salt and pepper.

SLOW-COOKED BEEF BRISKET

Serves 8

Make sure the meat is nearly covered by the broth while it's cooking. If your pot is too large, this might not happen, but all you have to do is add a bit more stock or water and continue cooking with the pot slightly uncovered so that the liquid will reduce at a faster pace.

1 4–5-pound beef brisket	1 sprig fresh thyme
Salt	1½ quarts Basic Chicken Stock (page 13)
Freshly ground black pepper	1 pound small red bliss or new potatoes, peeled
2 tablespoons olive oil	
2 cups pearl onions peeled	1 pound baby turnips, peeled
1 stalk celery, diced	
1 large carrot, diced	½ pound fresh wild mushrooms or ½ cup dried
3 cloves garlic, minced	
1 branch fresh rosemary	

1. Season the beef brisket on both sides with salt and pepper. Heat the olive oil in a large cast-iron or enameled iron pot with a lid over high heat and sear the brisket on both sides.

2. Add the onions, celery, carrots, garlic, rosemary, thyme, and Chicken Stock to the pot. Bring the stock to a boil, then reduce the heat to low, cover, and simmer for 1½ hours.

3. Remove the lid and turn the brisket over. Add the potatoes, turnips, and mushrooms to the pot, then cover and continue cooking the brisket until tender, about another hour. Remove the pot from the heat. Transfer the meat to a cutting board and slice it against the grain. Arrange the meat and vegetables on a platter.

4. Use a large spoon to skim the fat from the surface of the broth in the pot. Season the broth with salt and pepper. Spoon the broth over the meat and vegetables.

Lights and action:
The annual Christmas Festival in Natchitoches, Louisiana, 1969. To this day, the lights attract vistors from near and far.

BRENDAN'S BREAD PUDDING WITH BROWN BUTTER STICKY RUM SAUCE

Serves 10

My eldest son loves to make this bread pudding, so I named it for him. It's best straight from the oven, so mix the pudding ahead and cook it just before you serve it. Because all stale French breads aren't created equal, you might need to add more milk, as dry bread keeps absorbing liquid.

FOR THE BREAD PUDDING

4	cups whole milk
2	cups heavy cream
1½	cups sugar
1½	teaspoons ground cinnamon
1	teaspoon vanilla extract
	Grated zest of 1 orange
11	eggs, beaten
4	cups stale French bread, in small cubes
1	tablespoon unsalted butter

FOR THE SAUCE

8	tablespoons unsalted butter
½	cup light corn syrup
1	cup sugar
1	cup dark rum
1	cup heavy cream
1	pinch salt
1	teaspoon vanilla extract

FOR THE CANDIED ALMONDS

1	cup sliced almonds
1	egg white
½	cup sugar

1. For the bread pudding, preheat the oven to 350°. Whisk together the milk, cream, sugar, cinnamon, vanilla, orange zest, and eggs in a large bowl. Stir in the bread cubes and soak them for 30 minutes. Butter a 9-by-13-inch baking dish and pour the mixture into it. Bake until golden, about 45 minutes.

2. For the sauce, melt the butter in a medium saucepan over moderate heat, until it turns a light brown color, with a rich, hazelnut aroma, about 5 minutes. Add the corn syrup, sugar, rum, cream, salt, and vanilla. Reduce the sauce until it thickens enough to coat the back of a spoon, about 15 minutes. Remove from the heat.

3. For the candied almonds, mix the almonds, egg white, and sugar together in a bowl. Spread the almonds on a cookie sheet and bake in a 350° oven until golden brown, 15–18 minutes. Stir nuts every 4–5 minutes to ensure that they bake evenly.

4. To serve, scoop a large spoonful of warm bread pudding onto each of 10 plates. Pour the buttered rum sauce over the puddings and scatter candied almonds over the top.

My boys take the cake: Andrew, Brendan, Jack, and Luke devour their favorite Père Roux cake at La Provence.

ACKNOWLEDGMENTS

THE THOUGHT OF THANKING those responsible for the outcome of this book scares me because there are not thanks enough for all the generosity that has been bestowed on me, not just in creating *My New Orleans* but in the formation of my calling.

Being a chef here in New Orleans is more an act of stewardship than a job. Our city's rich culture has a way of incubating passionate cooks from every walk of life; to become a chef is an honor that is given, and much is expected in return.

In 1977, I took up cooking breakfast for my family while they tended to Dad after the tragic accident that paralyzed him for life. While enduring the pain of his long convalescence, my father, Ted Besh, had the foresight to encourage me to pursue my passion to cook. He has always urged his six children to follow their dreams. Those dreams and the drive that he instilled in me guide me well each day.

Were it not for three very powerful women in my life—my wife, Jenifer Ann Berrigan; my mother, Imelda Besh; and my friend and editor Dorothy Kalins—this book would never have gotten off the ground. Jenifer, whom I've known all my life, whom I fell in love with and married, has raised our four wonderful boys, Brendan, Jack, Luke, and Andrew, to be good people. Jen supported me through the hard times so that I could learn and grow, tolerating years of no weekends, no holidays, and no nights off. My mother, Imelda, held our big family together, nourishing us with great love, food, and faith, and taught me a sense of service to others. Hers are principles I let guide me every day. Dorothy Kalins gave me the confidence—and occasionally the kick in the rear— that I needed to tell my story in my own voice. Because she believed in the message and understood *My New Orleans*, Dorothy pulled together a team of the best in the business to help us make this book great.

Then there are the fellows in my life like Octavio Mantilla, Steve McHugh, Mike Gulotta, Erick Loos, Alon Shaya, and Todd Pulsinelli who have been with me every step of the way, cooking and building our restaurants and rebuilding them after the inevitable and awful storms. My beautiful late sister Kathleen, Marine comrade Blake LeMaire, brother-in-law, Patrick Berrigan, lifelong friend Drew Mire, and cousin Chris Gibson—all were there to help whenever times got really tough, especially after Katrina, helping to make a difference not only in our lives but in the lives of our neighbors, too. Without their support we surely would never have survived to tell this story.

My in-laws, Pat and Barbara Berrigan (besides allowing me to marry their daughter and employ my sisters-in-law Kim Bourgault and Mary Beth Berrigan), opened many doors for me, broadening my horizons, giving me an understanding of the culinary arts, and introducing me to my German "families," the Conzens and the Fuchses. Because of them, and through countless meals together, I grew in both girth and wisdom. My German chef, Karl-Josef, who took me back to the land, helped give my cooking not just technique but soul. Thanks to my late mentor, chef Chris Keragiorgiou, who connected me to my French "families," the Baurs and the Bérauds, and all the others along the way who gave me such a strong foundation.

I am so grateful to my friend Sasha—the painter Alexander Stolin—for setting aside his fine arts work to produce the charming illustrations of Louisiana produce that animate the map of *My New Orleans* on the endpapers and enliven the sidebars throughout the book. I thank both Timmy Reily and Molly Reily for their grace and goodwill and for turning their houses (and lives) upside down to help me tell this story; to Francis and Rodney Smith, for allowing us to photograph in their beautiful Soniat House hotel; and to Uncle Cochon, Kurt Sins, who was always so generous with his Pontalba apartment.

My heart goes out to the people of New Orleans, who have embraced me with much love, generosity, and support, for allowing me to realize my dreams and to tell their stories and mine.

—John Besh

FROM THE EDITOR

FIRST, PURE AND SIMPLE, I thank John Besh for the opportunity to dwell in the sunshine of his world. (He really is as good as he seems.) From the beginning, our ambitions were huge: I believed the book should tell a genuine story of a boy and a place; recipes, sure, but their roots, too, that John knows and loves so well. Not that there weren't times I'd look up from some agony or other and admit, "You know, it didn't have to be this complicated." Always, he'd respond, "But it wouldn't be as good!" What excellent fortune to connect with our fine publisher, Kirsty Melville at Andrews McMeel (thanks, Bruce Harris), who immediately matched our enthusiasm and our standards. We are indebted, too, to the wise counsel of Steve Sheppard.

It was both a thrill and a relief to turn to my colleague Don Morris to bring his uncommon design intelligence to this book. I thank him for welcoming me into his studio over many months, working with him and the delightful Tannaz Fassihi as her deft fingertips touched every page. Imagine explaining the arcane rituals of Mardi Gras to a photographer raised in Denmark. Whether shooting in a tippy pirogue in the predawn drizzle or facing down a sow with day-old piglets, Ditte Isager always delivered. So, too, did Allan Ng and Erin DeLaney of Digital Media, who happily met our exacting color demands.

In New Orleans, John is surrounded by a passionate team: executive chef Steve McHugh, who's in love with the origin of every living thing, or at least those you can eat; Kim Bourgault, queen of a thousand tiny details; Mary Beth Berrigan, loyal organizer and even better driver; and Jenifer and the Besh boys, who were either truly excited to have their lives overrun or too polite to let us think otherwise.

When we turned to valued friends and former *Saveur* colleagues Christopher Hirsheimer and Melissa Hamilton for wrangling the recipes into submission, they immediately interrupted the creative beehive of their business, Canal House; we are forever in their debt. Two other *Saveur*-ites were crucial: Megan Wetherall, who has never met a fact she didn't question, and Judith Sonntag, who, with her erudite copy sense, has never met a sentence she couldn't clarify. We could not have done it without them. Thanks, too, to the team at Andrews McMeel, especially Jean Lucas and Dave Shaw.

For help with archival photo research we thank: Gemma Hart Ingalls; Daniel Hammer and Sally Stassi, The Historic New Orleans Collection; Tanya Arant, Louisiana Tech University; Charlene Bonnette, State Library of Louisiana; Christopher Herter, Amistad Research Center; and, especially, the New Orleans photographers Mark J. Sindler, John Menszer, Josephine Sacabo, and Kerri McCaffety; to my sister, Marjorie Kalins, for her good eyes.

We thank these experts for their generosity: from Louisiana State University AgCenter, Dr. James E. Boudreaux and Dr. Daniel J. Gill, professors of horticulture, School of Plant, Environmental, and Soil Sciences; Dr. John Pyzner, associate professor, Pecan Research; James A. Vaughn, parish chair, Plaquemines Parish; Dr. John E. Supan, assistant professor, School of Renewable Natural Resources; Dr. Greg C. Lutz, professor of fisheries, Aquaculture Research Center. From Louisiana Department of Wildlife & Fisheries: *Marine Fisheries Division*, Patrick D. Banks and Harry Blanchet, biologist managers; Martin Bourgeois, biologist; Vincent Guillory, biologist manager. *Wildlife Division*, Larry Reynolds, biologist manager. And Ike Forester, Gulf States Mycological Society; Dr. Karen Leathem, Louisiana State Museum; Charles Smith, Louisiana regional director, Ducks Unlimited; Alfred Sunseri, P&J Oyster Company; Daniel H. Usner, professor, Vanderbilt University; James White, professor and chair, Plant Biology Department, Rutgers.

And to my beloved family, Roger, Lincoln, and Sandrine, serious thanks for spending a year in *My New Orleans*.   —Dorothy Kalins

RESOURCES

ALGIERS HONEY is a amalgam of the widest variety of Louisiana flower blossoms (blueberry, citrus, holly, tupelo) imaginable in one pot. Its creator, Adrian Jüttner, has hives that stretch from the mouth of the Mississippi to the North Shore and even into the city of New Orleans.

Adrian's Tree Service: 2031 Farragut Street, New Orleans, LA • 504-367-1160 • adriantree@aol.com

ANDOUILLE, boudin, hog's head cheese, filé powder, and other Cajun specialties.

Jacob's Andouille: 505 West Airline Highway, LaPlace, LA • 877-215-7589 • cajunsausage.com

Bailey's Andouille: 513 West Airline Highway, LaPlace, LA • 985-652-9090 • baileysandouille.com

CAVIAR from my friend John Burke's freshwater choupiquet roe (in season from December to February), as well as paddlefish caviar from the Mississippi River (in season from late November to April).

Louisiana Caviar Company • 504-813-3515 • johnecaviar@yahoo.com • cajuncaviar.com

CLEMSON BLUE CHEESE has been handcrafted since the 1940s, when it was aged in the Blue Mountains of South Carolina. Nowadays, although this mild blue is no longer made by the Clemson University professors who created it, it is still made on campus and cured for at least six months.

Clemson University • 800-599-0181 • campusdish.com/en-US/CSSE/Clemson/BlueCheese

CREOLE CREAM CHEESE is made with whole, slowly pasteurized milk from the family's own grass-fed cows by Warren Smith of Smith's Creamery. Smith's supplies our restaurants with milk, cream, and butter, too.

Smith's Creamery: 29184 Mt. Pisgah Road, Mount Hermon, LA • 985-877-4445 • smithcreamery.com • mhickman@rocketmail.com

CRAB, CRAWFISH, OYSTERS, SHRIMP, TURTLE MEAT, AND FISH, all from Louisiana waters, are available from our favorite places. My old friend Brian Cappy, at Kenney's, runs the best seafood shop and will ship what's in season.

Kenney Seafood • 400 Pontchartrain Drive, Slidell, LA • 985-643-2717

New Orleans Fish House stocks all manner of seafood and will ship your order via UPS overnight. 921 South Dupre Street, New Orleans, LA • 800-839-3474 • fax 504-821-9011

Bayou Land Seafood will ship live crawfish when they're in season, usually beginning in May. All other seafood is frozen. 1008 Vincent Bayard Road, Breaux Bridge, LA • 337-667-6118 • fax 337-667-6059

Louisiana Seafood has more information and sources, as many seafood companies are open only at the time of year when their specialty is in season. • louisianaseafood.com

COUNTRY HAM AND BACON, unsmoked and hickory-smoked by my friend Allan Benton.

Benton's Smoky Mountain Country Hams: 2603 Highway 411, Madisonville, TN • 423-442-5003 • bentonshams.com

CREOLE MUSTARD AND CRAB BOIL SPICES for crab, shrimp, and crawfish boils (available in both dry and liquid form) and seasonings. Although Zatarain's products are readily available in stores throughout the South, their distribution in the rest of the country is spotty, so the website is your best bet.

Zatarain's • 888-264-5460 • zatarains.com

GRITS, CORNMEAL, POLENTA, and other stone-ground, organic products from white, yellow, and blue corn made fresh by Frank McEwen in his stone burr gristmill to ensure that the all the goodness, flavor, and nutrients are retained.

Coosa Valley Milling: 30620 Highway 25 South, Wilsonville, AL • 205-669-6605 • fax 205-669-0113 • coosavalleymilling.com

KONRIKO RICE, from a historic Louisiana rice mill believed to be the oldest in the country, is available in medium- and long-grain white rice as well as brown rice and aromatic wild pecan rice. You might be lucky enough to find Konriko products at your supermarket; you can order the brown and wild pecan varieties by mail. Better still, stop by, tour the mill, and stock up on rice to take home.

Conrad Rice Mill: 307 Ann St, New Iberia, LA • 800-551-3245 • conradricemill.com

LOUISIANA CITRUS is rarely shipped out of state. However, if you are in New Orleans, it's worth the half-hour drive to the Becnel's Plaquemines Parish farm stand to sample what's in season: satsumas; navel, blood, or Louisiana Sweet oranges; Meyer lemons; and kumquats.

Ben and Ben Becnel's Produce Stand: 14977 Highway 23, Belle Chasse, LA • 504-656-2326

MAYHAW JELLY, homemade from Briarhill Farm's fruit trees.

Dobie Enterprises • 985-877-5946 • georgedobie@bellsouth.net

OYSTERS The Sunseri brothers at P&J in the French Quarter will send fresh shucked oysters (minimum order is a pint— between two and three dozen, depending on the size and season) or unshucked (minimum of 110) by the bagful. For an informal tour of the processing facility and to slurp down an oyster or two, stop by the oyster house.

P&J Oyster Company: 1039 Toulouse Street, New Orleans, LA • 888-522-2968 • fax 504- 529-7966 • oysterlover.com

TABASCO PEPPER SAUCES are available in a range of potencies, from the classic original to Sweet & Spicy, Chipotle, Habanero, and even Garlic Sauce. If you are visiting New Orleans, consider a side trip to Tabasco headquarters, on the lush Avery Island plantation, just over two hours by car. Tabasco sauces are available in most supermarkets, or use the product locator tool on the company's website to track down a favorite.

McIlhenny Company: Avery Island • 888-222-7261 • tabasco.com

Fresh direct: At the St. Roch Market, 1976; photo: Josephine Sacabo, The Historic New Orleans Collection.

POTTERY BOWLS AND SERVING PIECES We were delighted to discover the outstanding work of New Orleans master potter Charles Bohn in his shop, Shadyside Pottery, on Magazine Street. We used many of his pieces in the course of photographing this book. Bohn has studied in Japan and uses the *raku* process as well as the traditional stoneware method, experimenting with some 30 different glazes.

Shadyside Pottery: 3823 Magazine Street, New Orleans, LA • 504-897-1710

CULINARY ANTIQUES, from table linen to silver serving pieces, copper cookware, and furniture, are collected by proprietor Patrick Dunne and sold in his two shops.

Lucullus Culinary Antiques, Art, and Objects: 610 Chartres Street, New Orleans, LA • 504-528-9620 • 107 North Main Street, Breaux Bridge, LA • 337-332-2625 • lucullusantiques.com

JOHN BESH HANDCRAFTED PRODUCTS, such as seasoned butters, vinaigrettes, and sour mash steak sauce, are now available at selected retail outlets. For more information, please visit our website: chefjohnbesh.com.

PHOTO CREDITS

All photographs are by Ditte Isager/Edge Reps, except for family pictures and historical images from the archival sources listed below.

Page 22: Joe L. Herring, 1965, State Library of Louisiana; Alexander Stolin, 2008

Page 25: Unknown, 1972, State Library of Louisiana

Page 26: Alexander Stolin, 2008

Page 34: Unknown, 1970s, State Library of Louisiana

Page 39: Russell Lee, 1938, Library of Congress

Page 40: Russell Lee, 1938, Library of Congress

Pages 44–45: A. L. Barnett, 1910, Library of Congress

Page 46: Unknown, State Library of Louisiana

Page 47: From the documentary *Always for Pleasure*, 1978, Everett Collection

Page 48: John N. Teunisson, 1912, Louisiana State Museum

Pages 58–59: Charles L. Franck Photographers, 1935, The Historic New Orleans Collection

Page 62: Unknown, 1930s, State Library of Louisiana

Page 63: Louisiana Tourist Bureau, 1930s, State Library of Louisiana

Page 64: Unknown, 1960s, State Library of Louisiana

Page 66: *Iron Chef America*

Page 87: Covert, Louisiana State Museum

Page 88: Kerri McCaffety, *St. Joseph Altars*, 2003, Pelican Publishing Co.

Page 94: John Menszer, 1998

Page 114: Roby's Photo Studio, 1940s, The Historic New Orleans Collection

Page 117: Unknown, 1970s, State Library of Louisiana

Page 118: Unknown, 1970s, State Library of Louisiana

Page 128: G. E. Arnold, The Historic New Orleans Collection

Page 132: (and page 373) Josephine Sacabo, 1978, The Historic New Orleans Collection

Page 153: Unknown, The Historic New Orleans Collection

Page 155: Manuel C. DeLerno, 1960, The Historic New Orleans Collection

Page 156: W. Knighton Bloom Pictures, 1928, Amistad Research Center

Page 168: Kathy Bloodworth, 1980s

Page 178: Mark J. Sindler, 1978–1985, The Vietnamese Documentary Project

Page 180: Mark J. Sindler, 1978–1985, The Vietnamese Documentary Project

Page 181: Kim Bourgault, 2008

Page 182: Mark J. Sindler, 1978–1985, The Vietnamese Documentary Project

Page 186: L. J. Laughlin, 1955, The Historic New Orleans Collection

Page 198: Unknown, 1970s, State Library of Louisiana

Page 200: Charles L. Franck Photographers, 1941, The Historic New Orleans Collection

Page 216: Whitesell, 1934. State Library of Louisiana

Page 218: WPA photograph, 1940, State Library of Louisiana

Pages 237, 238, 240, 244: Susan Roach-Lankford, 1984, North Central Louisiana Folk Traditions, Louisiana Tech University

Page 248: Southwestern Louisiana Institute, 1940, University of Louisiana at Lafayette

Page 258: Henri Cartier-Bresson, 1947, Magnum Photos

Page 261: WPA photograph, 1940, State Library of Louisiana

Page 263: Fonville Winans, 1938, State Library of Louisiana

Page 264: Unknown, 1970s, State Library of Louisiana

Page 273: Unknown, 1969, State Library of Louisiana

Page 275: Unknown, 1970s, State Library of Louisiana

Page 276: Unknown, 1920s, State Library of Louisiana

Page 287: Unknown, 1930s, State Library of Louisiana

Page 297: Unknown, 1940s, State Library of Louisiana

Page 299: WPA photograph, 1930s, State Library of Louisiana

Page 308: Frances Benjamin Johnston, 1938, Everett Collection

Page 319: George François Mugnier, 1880–1920, Louisiana State Museum

Page 321: Unknown, 1970, State Library of Louisiana

Page 322: Russell Lee, 1938, Farm Security Administration, Library of Congress

Page 324: Charles L. Franck Photographers, 1943, The Historic New Orleans Collection

Page 328: WPA photograph, 1940, State Library of Louisiana

Page 340: Unknown, 1969, State Library of Louisiana

Page 357: Unknown, 1969, State Library of Louisiana

METRIC CONVERSIONS AND EQUIVALENTS

APPROXIMATE METRIC EQUIVALENTS

Volume	Metric
¼ teaspoon	1 milliliter
½ teaspoon	2.5 milliliters
¾ teaspoon	4 milliliters
1 teaspoon	5 milliliters
1¼ teaspoon	6 milliliters
1½ teaspoon	7.5 milliliters
1¾ teaspoon	8.5 milliliters
2 teaspoons	10 milliliters
1 tablespoon (½ fluid ounce)	15 milliliters
2 tablespoons (1 fluid ounce)	30 milliliters
¼ cup	60 milliliters
⅓ cup	80 milliliters
½ cup (4 fluid ounces)	120 milliliters
⅔ cup	160 milliliters
¾ cup	180 milliliters
1 cup (8 fluid ounces)	240 milliliters
1¼ cups	300 milliliters
1½ cups (12 fluid ounces)	360 milliliters
1⅔ cups	400 milliliters
2 cups (1 pint)	460 milliliters
3 cups	700 milliliters
4 cups (1 quart)	0.95 liter
1 quart plus ¼ cup	1 liter
4 quarts (1 gallon)	3.8 liters

Weight	Metric
¼ ounce	7 grams
½ ounce	14 grams
¾ ounce	21 grams
1 ounce	28 grams
1¼ ounces	35 grams
1½ ounces	42.5 grams
1⅔ ounces	45 grams
2 ounces	57 grams
3 ounces	85 grams
4 ounces (¼ pound)	113 grams
5 ounces	142 grams
6 ounces	170 grams
7 ounces	198 grams
8 ounces (½ pound)	227 grams
16 ounces (1 pound)	454 grams
35.25 ounces (2.2 pounds)	1 kilogram

Length	Metric
⅛ inch	3 millimeters
¼ inch	6 millimeters
½ inch	1¼ centimeters
1 inch	2½ centimeters
2 inches	5 centimeters
2½ inches	6 centimeters
4 inches	10 centimeters
5 inches	13 centimeters
6 inches	15¼ centimeters
12 inches (1 foot)	30 centimeters

METRIC CONVERSION FORMULAS

To Convert	Multiply
Ounces to grams	Ounces by 28.35
Pounds to kilograms	Pounds by .454
Teaspoons to milliliters	Teaspoons by 4.93
Tablespoons to milliliters	Tablespoons by 14.79
Fluid ounces to milliliters	Fluid ounces by 29.57
Cups to milliliters	Cups by 236.59
Cups to liters	Cups by .236
Pints to liters	Pints by .473
Quarts to liters	Quarts by .946
Gallons to liters	Gallons by 3.785
Inches to centimeters	Inches by 2.54

OVEN TEMPERATURES

To convert Fahrenheit to Celsius, subtract 32 from Fahrenheit, multiply the result by 5, then divide by 9.

Description	Fahrenheit	Celsius	British Gas Mark
Very cool	200°	95°	0
Very cool	225°	110°	¼
Very cool	250°	120°	½
Cool	275°	135°	1
Cool	300°	150°	2
Warm	325°	165°	3
Moderate	350°	175°	4
Moderately hot	375°	190°	5
Fairly hot	400°	200°	6
Hot	425°	220°	7
Very hot	450°	230°	8
Very hot	475°	245°	9

COMMON INGREDIENTS AND THEIR APPROXIMATE EQUIVALENTS

1 cup uncooked white rice = 185 grams
1 cup all-purpose flour = 140 grams
1 stick butter (4 ounces • ½ cup • 8 tablespoons) = 110 grams

1 cup butter (8 ounces • 2 sticks • 16 tablespoons) = 220 grams
1 cup brown sugar, firmly packed = 225 grams
1 cup granulated sugar = 200 grams

Information compiled from a variety of sources, including *Recipes into Type* by Joan Whitman and Dolores Simon (Newton, MA: Biscuit Books, 2000); *The New Food Lover's Companion* by Sharon Tyler Herbst (Hauppauge, NY: Barron's, 1995); and *Rosemary Brown's Big Kitchen Instruction Book* (Kansas City, MO: Andrews McMeel, 1998).

INDEX

Illustrated map by Alexander Stolin